THE FLETCHER JONES FOUNDATION
HUMANITIES IMPRINT

The Fletcher Jones Foundation has endowed this imprint to foster innovative and enduring scholarship in the humanities.

The publisher and the University of California Press Foundation gratefully acknowledge the generous support of the Fletcher Jones Foundation Imprint in Humanities.

The Global Edge

The Global Edge

MIAMI IN THE TWENTY-FIRST CENTURY

Alejandro Portes and
Ariel C. Armony

With the collaboration of Bryan Lagae

UNIVERSITY OF CALIFORNIA PRESS

University of California Press, one of the most distinguished university presses in the United States, enriches lives around the world by advancing scholarship in the humanities, social sciences, and natural sciences. Its activities are supported by the UC Press Foundation and by philanthropic contributions from individuals and institutions. For more information, visit www.ucpress.edu.

University of California Press
Oakland, California

Library of Congress Cataloging-in-Publication Data

Names: Portes, Alejandro, 1944– author. | Armony, Ariel C., author. | Lagae, Bryan, researcher.
Title: The global edge : Miami in the twenty-first century / Alejandro Portes and Ariel C. Armony with the collaboration of Bryan Lagae.
Description: Oakland, California : University of California Press, [2018] | Includes bibliographical references and index. |
Identifiers: LCCN 2018006263 (print) | LCCN 2018013432 (ebook) | ISBN 9780520969612 (epub and ePDF) | ISBN 9780520297104 (cloth : alk. paper) | ISBN 9780520297111 (pbk. : alk. paper)
Subjects: LCSH: Miami (Fla.)—Social conditions. | Miami (Fla.)—Economic conditions. | Sociology, Urban—Florida—Miami.
Classification: LCC HN80.M53 (ebook) | LCC HN80.M53 P67 2018 (print) | DDC 306.09759/38—dc23
LC record available at https://lccn.loc.gov/2018006263

Manufactured in the United States of America

26 25 24 23 22 21 20 19 18
10 9 8 7 6 5 4 3 2 1

Alejandro Portes—To PFK

Ariel C. Armony—To my family

Contents

Illustrations

Tables

Acknowledgments

The idea for this study came from several conversations we had at the University of Miami in 2012 and 2013. Portes's *City on the Edge* (with Alex Stepick, 1993), on Miami's recent history, was used extensively in university courses and received several awards. However, events in Miami picked up speed in the 1990s and the first years of the new century, rendering that work less applicable for understanding the contemporary scene. In addition, the city had gained increasing status globally as a strategic center for trade and finance, making an account of recent developments increasingly important.

This study could not have been carried out without several significant turns of events and the assistance and support of several key people and institutions. First, the affiliation of both authors with the University of Miami gave us a key vantage point and valuable base of operations. Even after the departure of Armony, the ties established during his many years at the university continued to prove a valuable asset. Portes is indebted to the university and, in particular, its Schools of Law and Arts and Sciences for the support they provided in the form of able and devoted assistants over the years. One of them, Bryan Lagae, involved himself so closely with the study that he deserves recognition as a supporting author.

The Knight Foundation, based in Miami, provided invaluable financial support during the key years of the project, 2016–17. We are indebted to its president, Alberto Ibargüen, both for his steady assistance and support and for his willingness to serve as one of our key informants. However, neither he nor any of the persons we interviewed for the study bears responsibility for the contents of the book or its conclusions.

Field interviews for the study were conducted mainly by us during 2016 and 2017. In the summer of 2017, Patricia Fernandez-Kelly traveled from Princeton to conduct extensive interviews focused on the city of Hialeah and its predominantly Cuban and Cuban American population. Patricia is the spouse of the senior author and an accomplished ethnographer and senior scholar. Her assistance, not only in conducting the interviews, but also in providing insights and wise advice during the writing phase of this project, is gratefully acknowledged.

At the University of California Press, executive editor Naomi Schneider enthusiastically responded to the idea of this book. We acknowledge her steady support during the successive stages of the project, as well as the reviews of earlier versions of the manuscript by Professors Bryan Roberts and Anthony Orum. Both Roberts and Orum gave us insightful comments, critical appraisals, and suggestions that guided the final thorough reorganization of the book.

In addition to the contributions of Bryan Lagae (of Florida International University), the study benefited from the assistance of a number of other people at the University of Miami, the University of Pittsburgh, and Princeton University. In Miami, Andrea Roca and Brandon Martinez provided valuable support in preparing and revising successive versions of several chapters, conducting internet searches, and arranging interviews with a number of key informants in 2016 and 2017. During the final months of the study, it also benefited from the valuable assistance of Maria Briz.

At Pittsburgh, Armony received extraordinary assistance from a talented group of young people that included Leo Schwartz, Martina Gesell, Ignacio Mamone, Rafael Khachaturian, and Danial Hoepfner.

Finally, at Princeton, Portes's longtime assistant and friend, Christine Nanfra, transcribed successive versions of each chapter and took on the onerous task of preparing the references, integrating the work of both authors. Her selfless devotion, experience, and integrity were central to the successful completion of the project. We are both in her debt.

Prescript

IN THE EYE OF THE STORM, 1992*

Waiting for a political cataclysm, a disaster of a very different kind struck. Not the end of Castroism but a huge storm that swept away everything in its path. The same fearsome natural event that has been the curse of these lands for centuries made its reappearance to remind everyone of the banality of human conflicts and the frailty of their outcomes. For centuries, storms have wreaked havoc on civilization in the tropics. They have done so with notable impartiality to the contenders of the day, scattering and sinking Spanish gold galleons and their French and English pursuers, trampling with equal fury on the colonizing ventures of competing European powers. The great wind of 1992 behaved in this time-honored way, impartially spreading destruction among peoples of different color, language, and political creed.

It is not the first time a storm has brought Miami to its knees. Forty-seven thousand residents were left homeless by the hurricane of 1926. It killed 113 people and flattened five thousand Miami dwellings.[1] That storm blew away not only the palm trees planted with so much care by

*Originally written as Postscript to Alejandro Portes and Alex Stepick, *City on the Edge: The Transformation of Miami* (University of California Press, 1993).

Collins and his successors, but also the reputation of the city as a carefree playground. For the next few years, it was not possible to give away the same land that, until then, had sold for millions. But every time, as calm returned and a new generation came of age, Miami renewed its illusion that disasters of such a magnitude could not happen there.

The first thing that strikes the observer in the aftermath of the August 1992 storm is how psychologically unprepared the city and its inhabitants were. Worried by everyday concerns, many people could not conceive that a catastrophe of an altogether different magnitude would hit them. Boats and houses were left unattended, utterly exposed to the wind's fury. Dade County did not even have an emergency evacuation plan for the hundreds of small craft in its docks and marinas. As a result, a good number ended up in the streets. Taught a lesson by Hurricane Hugo three years earlier, the Charleston, South Carolina, police department came barreling down Interstate 95 hours before the storm and managed to be in place in the worst-hit areas ahead of Dade County's own dazed officers.[2]

The vast destruction was not media hype. It was real. Eighty thousand homes destroyed or rendered uninhabitable; 160,000 people left homeless; 82,000 businesses destroyed or damaged; $20 billion in property losses. The miles and miles of wrecked properties and instant poverty added up to a defining moment in the history of the city. Thereafter, being a Miamian would mean having lived through the "worst wind."[3] Consequences will not be short-lived or easily forgotten. Yet, as with natural disasters elsewhere, they will not reverse but most likely accelerate the social and demographic trends already under way. Disasters of this order do not seem to stop social change; instead, they throw it into high gear.[4]

In the case of Miami, several such trends are apparent. The most important is the incipient progress toward a convergence of some sort between the city's polarized ethnic communities. Cultural and linguistic fragmentation is still dominant, but there are signs of a narrowing distance. The aftermath of the storm can accelerate this process. Two types of post-storm convergences must be carefully distinguished, however. The first is the well-publicized outburst of compassion, solidarity, and neighborliness in the initial wake of the disaster. Articles in the *Miami Herald* made much of how class and race barriers came tumbling down in the rush to rebuild half-destroyed neighborhoods and help hundreds of victims.[5]

The new blue-ribbon local committee put together at the initiative of President George H. W. Bush has been baptized "We Will Rebuild" and has also focused on the themes of unity and community solidarity.[6] The temporary suspension of ethnic animosities and heightened community spirit is a natural response, given the magnitude of the calamity. It would be risky to bet, however, that such altruistic behavior will be long lived. As things return to normal, established patterns invariably reassert themselves, and with them the social fragmentation and competing outlooks that have been dominant in the past.

There is, however, a more profound process of convergence. It is linked to the "defining" character of the cataclysm, the fact that hereafter the identity of the area will incorporate this experience. As San Francisco was marked by shaking earth and fire in the twentieth century's first decade, so have the winds imprinted Miami in its last. To local identities built on successive and competing images must now be added that of a land regularly ravaged by one of the most fearsome natural forces. The people who inhabit this land will incorporate that element into their outlook, whether they came originally from New York or Havana or were born in South Florida itself. As in other places similarly afflicted, the sense of identity derived from disaster cuts across ethnic lines.

It is this natural introjection of the experience into people's self-image rather than any display of immediate solidarity that can have the greater effect on long-term community building. This is because the new shared identity of formerly segmented groups can create a basis for forging a more unified discourse. The question remains, however, of what direction such convergence will take, since the process can incorporate, to varying degrees, elements from the competing definitions of the situation prevalent in the past.

Here the evidence is mixed. In an article published in the *Miami Herald* shortly after the disaster, a Florida International University sociologist argues that its demographic consequences would be significant:

South Dade [the area hardest hit by Hurricane Andrew] has been one of the few remaining areas of the county with an "Anglo" population majority. It has also been one of the few areas within Dade with affordable suburban housing. Other areas have experienced fast suburban growth. . . . But those are predominantly Hispanic. . . . For "Anglos" choosing to leave the hurricane-stricken zones, the areas that will prove attractive, in terms of housing prices and ethnicity, are not in Dade.[7]

If this analysis is correct, it would mean the acceleration of the process of Latinization of the city, as the outflow of the Anglo population to Fort Lauderdale and points north is augmented by the South Dade victims of Andrew. This trend would consolidate the political power of the Cuban American community. At the time of this writing, some changes in this direction, anticipated as the outcome of electoral reapportionment, have already materialized: Lincoln Díaz-Balart, a former state senator, has become the second Cuban American elected to Congress; the expected increases in Cuban representation in the state legislature have also occurred, to the detriment of Anglo politicians.

Such a trend suggests that the process of convergence will have a strong Latin undertone. *Acculturation-in-reverse* may spearhead the transition to a discourse focused on the city's unique Caribbean roots. Although participation in the political system will inevitably socialize Cubans into the institutions of the American mainstream, their local dominance can influence decisively the pace and character of the convergence process.

Hurricane Andrew also created a powerful countertrend, however. It is perhaps best symbolized by those Charleston policemen directing traffic in devastated South Dade: the aid pouring into Miami came from the rest of the country, not from the Caribbean. Baptist sects set up instant soup kitchens, the U.S. Red Cross and the Salvation Army distributed desperately needed water and clothing, caravans of volunteers came from as far north as Philadelphia and New York, and, a few days after the storm, the U.S. Army was setting up emergency tents for thousands.[8] This outpouring of national solidarity took Miami as by a second storm. It made evident that, whatever its quirks and foibles, it remained firmly an American town: "Miami, U.S.A.," not "Miami, Capital of the Caribbean," was the theme under which reconstruction was launched.

Reenergized, the old Anglo leadership took charge of directing the task. That perennial local brahmin, Alvah Chapman, was appointed chairman of the We Will Rebuild Committee, with other Anglo leaders occupying key posts. Ethnic figures were relegated to secondary positions, a fact that prompted the black attorney H.T. Smith, leader of the black boycott, to remark, "We must have the face of Miami, which is culturally diverse, making and executing the decisions."[9] To be sure, the Cuban-American National Foundation launched a vigorous relief effort, and thousands of Miami Cubans and other Latins contributed funds and worked as volunteers in the affected areas. But there was nothing in the "success story" discourse that could effectively integrate the tragedy and its aftermath. Instead, the themes of voluntarism and solidarity-in-crisis, so close to the core of American culture and so thoroughly practiced over many similar experiences, became dominant. The flattened Miami landscape was an American, not a pan-Caribbean, reality.

The storm made the city even more unique, if that was possible, and simultaneously brought it back into the national mainstream. Cubans and Latins will become increasingly influential, but in the storm's aftermath, it seemed evident that their local hegemony would be securely ensconced in a broader American framework. Undoubtedly, the cadences of Spanish, the sights and sounds of the Caribbean, and the ritual denunciations of Castro and his henchmen will be heard for a long time to come. But none of this will prevent a process of convergence, given a renewed impulse and a strong national focus by this natural catastrophe.

1 Introduction

A CITY IN FLUX

The 1960s movie classic *Midnight Cowboy* features a pair of New York hustlers at their wits' end. As winter sets in and one of them becomes increasingly ill, they set their hopes on escaping south. The healthy one robs an incautious businessman and, with the proceeds, buys a pair of bus tickets to Miami. The movie ends as the very sick member of the pair, played unforgettably by Dustin Hoffman, dies in the bus as it is about to reach its destination. In 1980 and again 1994, the Cuban government opened its ports, allowing anyone wishing to leave the island to do so. Tens of thousands of desperate people promptly took to the waters of the Strait of Florida in anything that could float.

Northerners wishing to escape freezing temperatures and southerners fleeing political oppression have nothing in common in terms of their ethnic origins or their history. Their only commonality is their destination, at the tip of Florida. These convergencies created a social and economic dynamic unseen anywhere else in the nation and, for that matter, in the world. The city in which they came together and which occupies us in this book is a strategic site for the study of urban change, less because of being representative or emblematic of other cities in the United States than because of the opposite, its radical uniqueness.

In the past, Miami has had its crop of serious and distinguished historians, but by focusing on how the city emerged and grew during the early twentieth century, they have been inexorably bypassed by the march of events. That fate was also that of the book published by the senior author in the early 1990s.[1] It attempted to trace the transformation of the city up to and including the crucial year, 1980, and its sequels. The diagnosis of that earlier study—that Miami was perched on a precarious "edge"—was valid at the time, but it has been superseded by events since then. Our focus in this new book is change during the last quarter of a century, not only as a logical continuation of the earlier study, but because this is the period that led decisively to the present social, economic, and political character of the city. The confluence of diverse populations in this single geographic spot continues to produce change without a blueprint, leading to surprising outcomes. Tracing them is the object of our investigation. Before launching into it, it is convenient to outline a set of conceptual guidelines framing our analysis.

THE STUDY OF CITIES

Since their emergence in ancient history, cities have been at the center of the evolution of humankind. This is because they are *loci, vehicles,* and *reflections* of what takes place in the broader society. From their very beginnings, they have served as administrative centers and places of refuge in dangerous times. To these functions was added their key role as a marketplace. That is why so prominent a figure as Max Weber defined the city as a market. The central place of commerce for the existence and growth of cities is no better reflected than in their shriveling to near-extinction in the Europe of the eighth and ninth centuries. As the French historian Henri Pirenne tells the story, the Islamic conquest of the Mediterranean deprived the continent of vital imports and key outlets for its exports; the urban system put in place since Roman times imploded as a result, and civilization had to take refuge in the countryside—in manorial demesnes and in feudal subsistence production.[2] Only the reconquest of the Mediterranean by the Crusaders two centuries later reversed the trend, setting the stage for the emergence of the great Italian commercial cities—Venice, Pisa, and Genoa—and farther north, the cities of the Hanseatic League.[3]

Thereafter, cities never lost their central role as marketplaces and as centers of administration in the West, these functions preceding and being more universal than their subsequent role as sites of mass production. The latter came into full force only with the advent of the Industrial Revolution in the nineteenth century. Thereafter, cities became primarily defined by the industrial goods they produced—cloth and apparel in Manchester and Birmingham; machinery in London; steel in Pittsburgh; ships in Philadelphia; and eventually automobiles in Detroit. But before that industrial turn, cities in ancient, medieval, and even modern times did not produce much of anything, serving primarily as markets and as sites for administrative coordination. In that capacity, they were the loci and the vehicle of the course of major events in human history, and their physical appearance stood as the reflection of such trends. The historical role of cities as sites of commerce and administration, rather than productive entities, must be kept in mind as we approach the city that is the subject of this book.

There are two additional features of urban life to be noted before going back to that story. First, urban phenomena are essentially *political*. They involve the interaction, conflict, and cooperation among interests backed by different amounts of power. This is not to say that such events do not take place elsewhere; but it is in the cities, by virtue of the concentration of large numbers of people in limited space, that the political interplay and struggles of interests and power become more visible and poignant. Contests for hegemony always culminate in cities, even if their origins lie elsewhere. Revolutionary armies can never claim victory until they have conquered the capitals of their respective realms; it is also in cities where political leaders claim office or are removed from it.[4]

Within cities, the competition for space inevitably triggers political confrontation. The wealthy always seek to influence politics in order to reserve for themselves privileged access to urban amenities and services. Everyday citizens, on the other hand, must band together in movements or parties in order to make their voices heard. Indeed, their claims do not become visible as "urban" issues until they enter the political arena. Above all, the most common political confrontation is spawned by the conflicting functions of cities as sites for human habitation and as centers for wealth accumulation. Competition among economic interests and their common wish to turn cities into profit-making entities inevitably clash with the desire of the working population for livable space. Industrial pollution, traffic congestion, ghetto areas right next to wealthy gated communities, inflationary "bubbles" in land and real estate are among the myriad problems issuing from this confrontation.

Second, urban phenomena are *spatial*. The attraction that the city has always had for generations of scholars is based on how clearly facts of social life are reflected in its physical configuration. It is often possible to "read" parts of the history of a nation, its present class structure, and its distinct culture by taking a leisurely stroll or a slow drive around its built environment. It is true that all social events tend to be projected into space. The unique feature of cities, however, is that the spatial reflection of social, economic, and political processes occur in a physically circumscribed perimeter. That makes them all the more visible and easier to understand.

Space in the city is more than land and the built environment. It is also a *resource* put to multiple uses by different actors. The result of the confrontation between private economic interests and the citizenry is often reflected in how much "free space" there is, how easily and cheaply one can travel from one place to another, and to what extent home dwellings in single plots are crowded out by land demands for multistory office and apartment buildings. Space can be used as a resource by upper-class families to escape the crowdedness and insecurity of central cities by moving into suburbs. In other instances, certain groups may deliberately choose to cluster in certain patches of urban space. Ethnic and minority groups frequently do so, albeit for different reasons: for some, the only way to maintain a precarious foothold in the city is by settling in its least desirable places; for others, it is the means to foster business growth by drawing on the in situ coethnic community as a market, a source of credit, and a labor supply.[5]

A view of cities as loci, vehicles, and reflection of broader societal processes and of urban phenomena as simultaneously political and spatial gives us the conceptual tools to approach the analysis of our topic systematically. With this theoretical spadework done, it is now possible to approach and understand better what has taken place in the city at the tip of the Florida peninsula.

THE EARLY NINETIES

It is appropriate to begin the story in 1992. The hurricane that practically wiped out the southeastern quadrant of Miami-Dade County took place that year, marking another decisive moment in the turbulent history of the city. Andrew, the "Big Wind," was not only a natural catastrophe; in then unrecognized ways, it marked the beginning of a new era. More than anything, it accelerated trends that were already in place and that moved the city away from the "edge" in which it had been precariously perched. *City on the Edge,* a book by the senior author with Alex Stepick, published one year after the catastrophe, summarized the social and economic conditions of Miami at that time as follows:

1. There is no mainstream. The hegemony of the old "upper uppers" has given way to parallel social structures, each complete with its status hierarchy, civic institutions, and cultural life. As a result, economic mobility and social standing have ceased to depend on full acculturation or on pleasing the elites of the old class order.

2. While the business class does exercise indisputable control in governing the city, it is increasingly composed of recent immigrants, rather than exclusively of "old" families or corporate branch executives.

3. The overlap of parallel social systems in the same physical space has given rise to "acculturation in reverse"—a process by which foreign customs, institutions, and language are diffused within the native population. As a consequence, biculturalism has emerged as an alternative adaptive project to full assimilation to American culture. Opponents of biculturalism must either withdraw into their own diminished circles or exit the community.[6]

These were extraordinary developments unique in the American urban landscape. Miami became loci, vehicle, and reflection of a clash of forces not seen anywhere else. The first chapter of the earlier book concluded by asking: How did it happen? How could a large American city be transformed so quickly that its natives often chose to migrate north in search of more familiar cultural settings? How could an immigrant group reproduce its institutions so thoroughly that a parallel social structure was established? And, perhaps most important, where would this process of change without a blueprint lead?[7]

The postscript about Hurricane Andrew and its aftermath, reproduced as a prescript to this book, adumbrated some of the answers by pointing to incipient trends that would consolidate over time. In the ensuing years, the process of convergence tentatively announced in those earlier lines accelerated, leading to a more solid and more transparent social order. That trend was not the result of a social "pact" between the warring ethnic communities of the past in order to cope with effects of the hurricane's destructive force. Instead, the demographic trends anticipated in that 1993 postscript did materialize: native whites continued to leave Dade County in droves, and Latins,[8] particularly Cubans, consolidated their hold, translating it into growing political and economic power.

The institutions of the old Miami establishment gradually gave way. The Non-group, an appropriately named entity, made up of local white brahmins who decided the course of the city behind closed doors, disappeared. Establishment leaders like that perennial figure, Alvah Chapman, publisher of the *Miami Herald*, faded from view, as did local politicians and journalists wedded to nostalgic images of what Miami had been. Private and public institutions that first ignored the presence of the Cubans and then resolutely confronted their rise were forced to yield and, in some cases, were taken over by the very people they had so fiercely resisted.

Of these institutions, none was more important than the *Miami Herald* itself—for years a power player in its own right and the voice of the local "Anglo" establishment. It is worth recalling what the confrontation looked like in the mid-1980s. Joan Didion, visiting the city at that time, remarked, "This set of mind in which the local Cuban community was seen as a civic challenge to be determinedly met was not uncommon among Anglos to whom I talked in Miami."[9]

An Anglo executive of the *Herald*, interviewed in 1987, remarked:

> We made a bet during the 1960s that the normal pattern of immigration that this country had seen over many years, when ethnic minorities came in large numbers and settled in different sections, would not be very different here; that within a reasonable number of years, English would become the dominant language. So we made a bet in 1960 that that would occur here in Miami as a large number of Cuban refugees came in, following Castro's takeover. That didn't happen as fast as we thought it would.[10]

A black civic activist of the time minced no words:

> In those days, I said to Cubans in a speech that there was going to be a time
> when white folks are going to try to treat you all like niggers. They're going
> to put you again in your place as they do with all minority groups. But unlike
> black Americans, Cubans had no history of being kept in their place, and, as
> a result, they responded differently. We black folks were saying to white
> folks, "Let us in." Cubans were saying to white folks, "Let us in so that we can
> take over."[11]

And a Cuban American banker summarized the high point of confrontation with the *Herald:*

> The conflict between the Cuban community and the *Herald* reached its peak
> when, after the resignation of one of the directors of the Cuban-American
> National Foundation, the newspaper started speculating, without basis of
> fact, about internal divisions in the organization. We decided to write an
> open letter, and it was published as a paid announcement in the newspaper.
> The *Herald* never expected that we Cubans would do something like
> that! . . . Richard Capen, the editor, called to complain, but, faced with the
> threat of a massive boycott, the newspaper relented.[12]

At the time, the Cuban-American National Foundation was running ads on radio and even in Miami city buses reading, "Yo no creo en el *Herald.*" (I do not believe in the *Herald.*) In the end, the defeat of the newspaper was complete. After a sustained confrontation with the president of the foundation, Jorge Mas Canosa, the publisher, David Lawrence, left his post. Shortly after, the *Herald's* parent company, Knight-Ridder, left Miami, not without appointing a new editor in chief for the paper, Alberto Ibargüen, a second-generation executive of Cuban and Puerto Rican origin. What traditional white leaders of Miami never fully grasped was the magnitude of the historical phenomenon that had appeared at their doorstep. Accustomed to run a tourist city for the benefit of Americans up north, the local establishment never paid much attention to events in its Caribbean backyard, or it regarded them with a measure of condescension.[13]

While the energies of the exiled Cuban upper class were initially devoted entirely to the overthrow of the Castro regime in Cuba, they knew how to react when local Miami elites, clustered in the Non-group and spearheaded by the *Miami Herald,* attempted to put exiles in their place as another ethnic minority, just as the black leader quoted above announced. Instead of accepting that role, Cuban leaders redefined Miami and then laid claim to it. This was "the Great Change" about which a Cuban banker of the time spoke eloquently:

> Before the "Great Change," Miami was a typical southern city, with an important population of retirees and veterans, whose only activity consisted in the exploitation of tourism during the sunny winters. No one thought of transforming Miami into what it is today. It is no exaggeration to say that the motor of the Great Change was the Cuban men and women who elected freedom and came to these shores to rebuild their homes and face with courage an uncertain future. . . . These last decades of the twentieth century have witnessed the foundation of a dynamic and multifaceted Miami over the past of a Miami that was merely provincial and tourist-oriented. Today, the level of progress has reached unanticipated heights, beyond the limits of anyone's imagination.[14]

When faced with opposition by the old Anglo establishment, Cuban leaders of the time turned their attention to electoral politics. Despite attempts by local nativist groups, such as Citizens of Dade United, to turn back the clock, the local political apparatus fell relentlessly into the hands of the Cubans. At the beginning of the confrontation in the early 1980s, the exiles' expectations were much more modest. Thus, a Cuban American county official of that period:

> The Anglo power structure is scared to death about the Cuban rise in this community. It has tried co-optation through an "interethnic relations committee" of the Miami Chamber of Commerce which is really a sham. There is now an embryonic organization promoted by the [exile] business leaders; the plan today is to try to elect a Cuban mayor of the city and perhaps one or two state legislators.[15]

Twenty years later, the mayors of Miami-Dade County, of the city of Miami, and of other large municipalities in the county were Cuban or Cuban American. So were three-fourths of the area's congressional delegation and over 70 percent of its state senators. By 2015, two Cuban Americans had been successively elected to the U.S. Senate from Florida, Mel Martinez and Marco Rubio. The latter even saw fit to run for president of the United States in 2016.[16]

Thus, the convergence foreseen in our 1993 Postscript did take place but not through compromise. Instead, it marked the near-complete triumph of one of the contending factions. As Aranda, Hughes, and Sabogal, authors of a more recent study of Miami, conclude, "Cubans no longer share power with Anglos . . . as they did in the late 1980s and early 1990s. Cubans politically dominate all other ethnic and national-origin groups in offices representing the larger constituencies."[17]

Looking back, the question still lingers: How could an immigrant minority, just recently arrived, lay claim to an American city and impose itself to boot? Immigrants, by the very character of their condition as foreigners, are defined and see themselves as guests of the host society and subordinate to its culture and preexisting social order. They are more likely to find themselves in the role of supplicants than that of claimants. Those foreign groups that eventually ascended to positions of political power in the past, such as the Irish in Boston and Chicago and the Italians in New York, took generations to reach that goal.[18]

The anomalous story of Miami can be explained by an unforeseen convergence of three facts. First, the Cuban upper classes that landed in the city as a consequence of the successful Communist revolution on the island were not only accustomed to power back home, but, in addition, were quite familiar with American politics and culture. They did not come from some remote Southeast Asian country but from what had effectively been, until 1959, an American protectorate only ninety miles from U.S. shores. They had reached their positions of wealth and power under American hegemony to which they readily acquiesced.[19]

Second, these groups did not see their departure and arrival in South Florida as a final outcome but only as a temporary expedient as they prepared for a seemingly inevitable return. The Communist victory in Cuba was seen as a political aberration that the nation claiming leadership of the Free World would simply not tolerate. Thus, the Cuban exile leadership lined up solidly behind the U.S. government in the global struggle against communism and, in particular, in the effort to defeat the dictatorship of Fidel Castro on the island. This situation gave Cuban exiles the status of allies in a common political endeavor, not refugees. The ignominious defeat at the Bay of Pigs in 1961 and the Missile Crisis of 1962—resolved by an agreement to refrain from any future invasions of Cuba in exchange for the removal of Soviet missiles from the island—were perceived by the exile leadership as unfathomable calamities.[20]

By the same token, however, and as an unforeseen consequence of these events, the status of Cubans in the United States was further legitimized. The failure of the U.S. government to deliver on its commitment to its fervent Caribbean allies left it, in a sense, obliged to them. Stranded in Florida through no fault of their own, they were entitled to both respect and assistance in the effort to reconstruct lives so unexpectedly shattered. This did happen, and federal support arrived in Miami in sufficient amounts to permit the exiled Cuban population to build its economic enclave in the next two decades.[21]

In this context, the attempt by some members of the local Miami elite to "put Cubans in their place" by sponsoring a referendum to forbid the use of Spanish in the city government was profoundly misguided. Proponents of that measure, mostly transplanted northerners, had no idea of the geopolitical drama they had stepped into. For the Cubans, the anti-bilingual referendum was the last straw. Having lost their island, they now confronted the prospect of also losing their adopted city. As we know, this did not happen. The Cuban leadership lost no time in marshaling its considerable resources, swiftly placing the hapless nativists in "their" place.

The anti-bilingual referendum thus accelerated what it had tried to prevent. Before the referendum, Cubans had never laid claim to the city, preferring instead an accommodation of sorts with what were perceived as friends and allies in the local establishment. That accommodation came to an end in 1980, with the former exiles steadily gaining political and economic power. It was not difficult to do so because of the third key fact at the time: the pre-1980 Miami establishment was rather feeble, lacking the historical roots of urban elites in other American cities, from Boston to Jacksonville.[22] Recent arrivals themselves, they did not possess the cohesion and resources to resist a determined onslaught. That made the Anglo attempt to marginalize the Cubans all the more pathetic. In a few years, local Anglo hegemony—including the lead role of the *Miami Herald*—became a thing of the past.

THE AFTERMATH

The transformation of Miami was, like all urban phenomena, essentially political. Spatially, it was reflected in the expansion of Cuban-owned enterprises, originally concentrated in an enclave in the southwest corner of the city, to the entire metropolitan area; the move of wealthy Cuban families to the exclusive Coral Gables municipality; and the renaming of city streets and parks in honor of Cuban heroes. More important is what took place afterward, that is, in the twenty-five years after Cuban elites took political control of the city. Contrary to the expectations of nativists, Miami was not pushed over the "edge," nor did it become a "banana republic."[23] On the contrary, Cuban leaders demonstrated a remarkable affinity to American capitalism, promoting domestic and foreign investments in what was now "their" city and seeking to convert it into a true global metropolis—the strategic center of trade and financial transactions between Europe, the United States, and Latin America.

Local interethnic battles took place under a resilient U.S. constitutional system that adjudicated impartially between winners and losers of electoral contests and that prevented extreme outcomes. Instead, under its new leadership, the city flourished, engaging in a momentous forward push whose consequences—physically reflected in its skyline—were unimaginable only a few years earlier. As Allman puts it in a 2013 afterword to his earlier study of the city:

By 2010, the decennial U.S. Census revealed Greater Miami had outstripped the Washington D.C. area in population. It also had surpassed what previously had been the South's dominant metropolitan region, Atlanta. . . . If, on election day 2012, you had driven from the center of Miami into what only recently had been the Everglades, you might have reached a restaurant done up in traditional "Latin" style. . . . Until very recently, there would have been no need to go inside to know what was happening. The winning candidate ranting about Castro, the Cuban flags waving, the political party of the victor would have been foregone conclusions. This time, however, the winner talked about other subjects: the environment, education, the need for all kinds of people to find common ground.[24]

Cuban American political leaders took firm control of the local Republican Party, seeking to use it as the instrument to move into state and even national politics. At the same time, the new economic leaders of the city engaged in a determined push outward, toward Latin America and Europe in a bid to make their city a true cosmopolitan center. As the banker Luis Botifoll had anticipated, they succeeded beyond all expectations. Specific reasons for that success are analyzed in a later chapter. For the moment, the key question is what consequences this unprecedented expansion had and how they have been reflected in the political arena and in the spatial layout of this metropolitan area.

Politically, the old-style Cuban elite that had been at the forefront of the ethnic battles of the 1980s and early 1990s aged and gradually relinquished power. It was replaced by a more acculturated Cuban American second generation that came to occupy increasingly prominent positions in the metropolitan economy and politics. These new leaders engaged with the rest of the country and looked for allies everywhere. If many older Anglos had left the city in frustration twenty years earlier, newcomers from the North now replaced them, ignorant of past battles and attracted by the city's dynamism, opportunities, and climate. They were joined by steady flows of migrants from the Caribbean and South America, to the point that by the 2010 census non-Cuban Latins came to rival Cubans in numbers. Both Haitians and West Indians also became important elements of the metropolitan population.[25] To these flows must be added a substantial number of Europeans, Russians, in particular, also attracted by the climate and the region's opportunities. The convergence of so many groups, combined with steady investments in real estate, financial services, and tourism, created an increasingly diversified and more cosmopolitan population. The old ethnic divisions did not disappear, but they were gradually submerged in this new urban mosaic.

So many new players and such diverse economic interests had the consequence of partially displacing the Cuban elite while preventing the rise of a new cohesive power structure. In welcoming major players in numerous economic sectors, Cuban leaders gradually lost hegemonic control of the city as power became diffused among several centers. The consensus among all well-placed informants is that no one governs Miami today, at least not in the way that the Non-group did in years past and that the

Cuban leaders who replaced it could have done. Instead, a number of important actors—from banking and trade leaders to sports and arts entrepreneurs—make their voices heard and seek to coordinate with elected officials in order to advance their interests. To be sure, Cubans and Cuban Americans still hold on to most of the important elective offices in the city and county, but they must now share authority with powerful actors in a number of other sectors. As a prominent Cuban American educator and longtime observer of the local scene concluded, "There is no mainstream in Miami now; power is diffused among multiple centers. As a result, anyone can come here and rise to a position of leadership in only a few years."[26]

The city is no longer on edge due to the confrontation between rival ethnic powers, but it faces the prospect of an increasingly amorphous social order, splintered among different interests and to which no one really belongs. As an Anglo educator and prominent civic leader puts it, "Miami today is a case of hyper-fragmentation: too many commissioners, too many voices, and no one really in control."[27]

Examples abound. The cruise industry that converted Port Miami into the largest facility of its kind in the world has a major say on anything traveling by water. The port itself and the airport have become power players in their own right, as they concentrate key international trade routes (see chap. 4). A major league baseball team, the Florida Marlins, changed its name to the Miami Marlins and, in exchange, persuaded the city to back a bond issue to build itself a spanking new stadium. Marlins Stadium was indeed built, but the controversy surrounding the bond cost the Cuban mayor of Miami-Dade his job.[28] He was replaced by another Cuban American, who then had to face another sports controversy: David Beckham, of soccer fame, came calling, wanting to bring a major league soccer team to Miami and build it a large stadium by Biscayne Bay. Faced with the determined opposition of the newly affluent residents of the area, as well as the city's mayor, Beckham relented. He did not abandon his plans, however, but transferred them to Overtown, a traditional black inner-city area, whose inhabitants lack the power to resist his plans.[29]

Similar dynamics are visible in the arts and culture world that has grown apace with the city's transformation. The organizers of Art Basel, a major show in Miami Beach, pretty much get what they want from city and metro authorities to facilitate their annual extravaganza. Well-heeled tourists arrive by the thousands during Art Basel, leaving behind significant sums. To anchor the art scene beyond Art Basel days, the city now features a new museum, the Pérez Art Miami Museum (PAMM), built, in part, with the donations of billionaire developer, Jorge Pérez.[30]

Not to be outdone, a pair of Jewish philanthropists, the Frosts, announced plans to build their own science museum next to the Pérez. Plans were approved by the County Commission, which also committed a substantial sum to the initial construction of the facility. However, private philanthropy fell far short this time, leading to the stoppage of museum construction. Miami-Dade mayor, Carlos Giménez, was then faced with the dilemma of committing additional tax dollars to forge ahead with construction or leave the museum half built. His decision was to proceed, despite the prospect of mass resistance from a taxpaying citizenry still smarting from the Marlins Stadium episode.[31]

Such controversies reflect both the growth pains of the city and the lack of a unified power structure. It is worth noting that the loci of controversies, when they occur, are all in the service sector, corresponding to the character of a resolutely nonindustrial city. As Allman noted in 2010:

> The metropolis built on a desire to escape freezing temperatures had overtaken such long established centers as Boston and San Francisco, as well as Rust Belt cities like Detroit ... and regional capitals like Denver and Minneapolis-St. Paul. . . . Miami still did not produce much of anything.[32]

Contrary to its industrial sisters up north, Miami adhered to the age-old historical roles of cities as markets and administrative centers. Its present socioeconomic profile curiously resembles those of medieval Italian city-states. As in Renaissance Florence and Genoa, trade and finance are the key businesses of the city by Biscayne Bay, with the proceeds invested in arts, recreation, and culture, which, in turn, have become major centers of capital accumulation on their own.[33]

TRANSIENCE AND INEQUALITY

The absence of a consolidated power structure and the still-evolving character of local culture are reflected in other urban features—from the relative feebleness of civic institutions to the mass of empty condominiums, bought as investments but not lived in by their proprietors. The geographer Jan Nijman made the "transience" of Miami's population the central point in his analysis of the city:

> Transience has always been Miami's *genius loci*—a constant coming and going of people dating back to the times of Ponce de Leon. It has only intensified in more recent, global times. Very few people here seem to plan a permanent stay. For most, the city is merely an interlude in their unfolding lives.[34]

The same author emphasizes the absence of "good government" coalitions in either the municipalities or the metropolitan area as a whole and the frequent incivility in public places, reflecting the lack of social cohesion. Whether this absence of a "we-feeling" is a temporary consequence of the city's rapid growth or whether it becomes entrenched as a defining character of urban life here is a concern to be explored in a later chapter. For the present, it is worth noting that the diagnosis of "transience" is not shared by everyone. Others see Miami, if not yet a consolidated global metropolis, at least as a city in the process of becoming one—including a nascent multiethnic philanthropic class. Thus, the Anglo head of a major university concludes:

> Miami is working toward becoming a global city—it has the feel of a place that is going to be great. The last fifteen years have witnessed the creation of great community-wide institutions—the Pérez Art Museum, the Adrienne Arsht Performing Arts Center, and the Miami Science Museum. Global cities require excellence, activity, and competition. Miami is developing this.[35]

And a former mayor of the city says:

> It is not true that there are no Miamians. More and more people feel that they have roots in this city. One sees this in the world of philanthropy. Wealthy people are making major gifts here instead of sending their money to New York charities as before. I myself am a true Miamian, growing up here and educated at the city's schools and the University of Miami.[36]

Finally, according to a Cuban American property developer and philanthropist:

Miami is becoming a serious city. In order for Miami, and any city, to be great and serious, people need to feel strong loyalty toward it. Miami is still considered a temporary place; however, loyalty is blossoming at universities like UM [the University of Miami]. This is a snowball effect which will help further fund-raising. . . . My own gifts to the city have been prompted, in part, to serve as an example for a new generation of Hispanic philanthropists. Legacy means what you leave behind, not how much money you are worth.[37]

Notice in the three preceding testimonies the sense of evolving toward something great but not being quite there yet. Nijman's diagnosis of transience may not yet be discarded. The bid for global status comes, however, with more serious pains than transience. There is real and growing inequality between different components of the metropolitan population. The glittering skyline of Miami's downtown and business district contrasts markedly with the vast dilapidated areas where most of the native black population and many immigrant groups live. One of our best-placed informants explains the situation as follows:

In the past, everyone who could, left the city so you had a homogeneously poor population. At present, a lot of well-to-do people are moving into downtown condominiums, Brickell Avenue, and other expensive areas. The tax base of the city has improved greatly, but inequality has also grown because the poor population—made up of African Americans and new immigrants—has also stayed here.[38]

The local developer and philanthropist we interviewed confirms the point:

Inequality in Miami is a huge problem. There is a massive distance between high-income and low-income areas. The "moderate-to-middle" class gets squeezed out, unable to find proper locations to settle in. The private sector can't deal with this alone, we need government programs.[39]

This collage of positive and negative views and predictions may leave us uncertain about prospects for the future. Looking back at the last quarter of a century, what is not uncertain is the amazing transition from a place ruled by a tight Southern-style elite to one where former exiles and their offspring gained the upper hand to one where that hegemony had to cede place because of the ceaseless arrival of capital and people from other countries and continents. That remarkable transition is reflected in the city's demographic expansion, a skyline unimaginable a few years ago, and levels of inequality surpassing those of other major cities.

THE "CAPITAL" OF LATIN AMERICA

It is a common saying that Miami is the capital of Latin America. It is also inaccurate. No Latin country is governed from Miami, and Miami has no say in political changes and policies in any nation. Its role vis-à-vis the Americas is both different and double. This dual relationship is examined in detail in a subsequent chapter. For the moment, it suffices to note its core features. First, the city is an economic entrepôt—the place where trade and financial flows from the global North and East encounter those from the South. There is no better meeting place to do business between Europe, North America, and South America than Miami. This is one of the reasons for the rapid growth of banks, foreign and domestic, here. It is also reflected in trade flows in and out of the city. In 2014, Miami's international trade reached $69.8 billion, of which almost half was with Latin American and Caribbean countries. Of the ten principal trading partners of the city, eight were Latin American nations.[40]

The second and key role of Miami with respect to Latin America is as a place of refuge. The instability and repeated political convulsions in Latin American countries invariably trigger flows of people and money to South Florida. The well-to-do in the region view Miami as a place to invest and save with security and in their own language. The city combines the safety of the American legal system with the ease of transacting real estate and banking operations in Spanish. As a former mayor of the city of Miami puts it:

> Every populist revolution in Latin America is a boon to Miami. When the rich in these countries have to move their money, where are they going to go? To Waco? This was the main reason why Miami got out of the financial and real estate crisis of 2008–9 faster than any other large American city.[41]

And an Argentine businessman now living in Miami Beach told us:

> Every morning when I wake up and open the newspaper, I give thanks to God that it is not going to say that the dollar has been devalued by half, that taxes on the rich will go up by 100 percent, or that their properties are going to be confiscated.[42]

Latin American revolutions that end up impoverishing their countries redound, almost inevitably, to the benefit of the city by Biscayne Bay. Fidel Castro showed the way, and the exiles of the Cuban Revolution, as they came to power in Miami, fully understood the dynamics at play. That is why they opened the city to the world and welcomed the flows of capital from Brazil, Argentina, Nicaragua, Venezuela, and Ecuador as each of these countries came, in turn, under the sway of populist regimes. Transient the city may be, but it is also secure. For those who come escaping political convulsions at home, it may be seen initially as a temporary refuge, but, with time, it can become home, especially as their children grow roots here.[43]

The definition of urban phenomena as "political" with which we started this chapter acquires in Miami a special character. This is not where winners of revolutionary struggles arrive to claim their prize but where the defeated classes come to secure refuge, comfort, and perhaps fight again at a later date. Miami has been the repository of these classes, and, out of their plight, it has constructed a vibrant economy and culture that, if still in transition and flawed in many ways, possesses exceptional dynamism. It stands as the promise of a global city built, in large measure, on the ashes of so many failed political projects in its backyard.

2 The Demography and Ecology of the City

THEORIES OF URBANIZATION

The French Canadian economist François Lamarche is arguably the most cogent theoretician of the dynamics of urban capital and the way that it organizes and molds urban growth.[1] Writing from a Marxist perspective, Lamarche differentiates types of capital by their sources of profit. Thus industrial capital derives its gain from the surplus value extracted from its labor force during production. Commercial capital does likewise by accelerating the transformation of surplus value into money through the sale of commodities and financial capital by facilitating access to credit to both industrial and commercial firms. There is, however, another type whose rents derive, not from industrial production, but from bringing together buyers and sellers and providing access by firms of different types to each other.[2]

What this additional type—property capital—sells is location. It deals in space but not any kind of space; it is space marked by certain qualities of desirability for prospective clients. For individuals renting or buying dwellings, these qualities include safe streets, a pleasant physical environment, and proximity to places of shopping and entertainment. For commercial firms, locations near sizable concentrations of well-heeled consumers determine the price per square foot of rents in shopping malls and similar facilities. For the headquarters of banks and other financial entities, a central location facilitating access to each other, as well as to a panoply of collateral services—legal and accounting firms, specialized consulting services, advertising and media companies—is decisive.[3]

Property capital does not derive its rents from the surplus value created by the construction of buildings itself. That surplus is appropriated by the construction industry, a form of industrial capital. Instead, property firms lease or sell space by the square foot based on its scarcity and desirability for other types of firms and for consumers: the more desirable and exclusive those locations are, the higher the price they command. That is why rents in the central business districts of major cities and apartments and houses situated near them or in other desirable locations reach extraordinary heights while those in poorer areas or in secondary cities are much lower and frequently fail to garner the attention of property firms.[4] While, for example, such firms abound in Manhattan and central areas of Chicago or Los Angeles, they are much less common in impoverished, minority areas of the same cities. There is no flourishing residential or commercial real estate in ghetto areas until and unless they undergo drastic renewal, involving, invariably, the expulsion of their previous tenants to create space for those able to afford the new facilities.

Property capital is a unique urban phenomenon precisely because it deals in that most urban of attributes, space. It derives its rent not only by bringing buyers and renters close to desirable, already existing locations but also by *creating* those locations where they did not exist before. These massive urban projects often involve the construction of large luxury condominium towers together with ritzy shopping malls, theaters, and other places of entertainment next door. Property firms sell to prospective condominium dwellers proximity to highly desirable commercial areas while at the same time these dwellers are "sold" to shopping mall merchants as a suitable mass of consumers. In this manner, property capital not only manipulates existing urban space, but molds it, fixing in the built environment the separation between the different functions of the city and the different social classes that inhabit it.[5]

Lamarche's analysis preceded by a decade the much better known *Urban Fortunes* by John Logan and Harvey Molotch that placed the "growth machine" at front and center of the forms that American cities took. For all practical purposes, Logan and Molotch's urban growth machine is the same as Lamarche's property capital, and these authors provide a host of illustrations of the dynamics at play.[6] Both theories highlight the perennial tension between the city as a site for human residence and the city as a profit-making center. Lamarche's refined analysis makes clear that while industrial, commercial, and financial capitals make use of the city for their own purposes, only property capital is distinctly embedded in urban space, this being the raison d'être for its existence and its source of profit.

These studies preceded in time and set the framework for the publication of the landmark work by Saskia Sassen, *The Global City*. Based on detailed analyses of urban trends in London, New York, and Tokyo, Sassen established definite criteria for characterizing cities as "global." Primarily, they have to do with serving as strategic nodes for a world-encompassing capitalist economy, concentrating its command and control functions. Borrowing a page from Lamarche, Sassen notes how physical proximity is fundamental at the heights of the world economy. Multinational corporations, global banks, and top law firms and other financial service providers need to be in close touch with one another in order for the entire capitalist machinery to operate smoothly.[7]

Sassen notes the irony that while top commercial and financial corporations control activities worldwide, their own internal coordination and decision making require tight spatial concentration. The few strategic locations selected for this purpose are global cities. Sassen complements her analysis with a fine study of the dynamics of urban classes in such places. As it turns out, the more they concentrate global coordinating functions, the less they produce by way of physical commodities. Industrial production leaves these cities to become dispersed worldwide. As a consequence, the classic industrial proletariat ceases to exist in them.[8]

In lieu of the old industrial proletariat, the urban labor force becomes employed exclusively in services. This service sector is increasingly bifurcated, however, in terms of function and class location. Financial and administrative services, concentrated in the central business district and other strategic locations, employ a highly paid labor force of executives, managers, technicians, and other skilled personnel. Their salaries allow them to command privileged access to urban facilities, such as luxury central-city apartments and other exclusive residential areas, as well as the most elegant shopping facilities. At the other end, manual services—many of them catering to the needs and tastes of the highly paid—are remunerated poorly since they require lower-level skills and benefit from intense competition among workers. These services include working in restaurants and supermarkets, clothing stores, home repair, domestic services, and other employment, for example, as porters and gardeners serving the buildings of the wealthy and animal walkers tending to their pets.[9]

The labor market of global cities resembles an hourglass, with demand concentrated at the top for professionals and other skilled personnel and at the bottom for manual service workers. As a consequence, economic and social inequality grows, as low-income workers are displaced from the central city and other desirable areas and forced to find housing in peripheral and dilapidated areas. A final feature of these labor markets is the rapid growth of an informal economy, with those unable to find minimally paid work devising their own solutions through invented employment. In turn, informal workers are useful to the well paid by providing a host of services at low cost; they also subsidize the consumption of manual wage workers by selling cheap goods and services accessible to a low-income population.[10]

This triad of theories provides a suitable framework for analyzing the dynamics of spatial, demographic, and economic change in metropolitan Miami. Using Lamarche, we can focus on the strategies of property capital to extract rent from space either by exploiting desirable locations or by creating them where none existed before. Relying on Logan and Molotch's metaphor of the growth machine, we can investigate to what extent the ecology of the city and the location of different sectors of its population have been determined by the strategies of accumulation of builders and property managers. Finally, adopting the lens of the global city, as described by Sassen, we may ask to what extent Miami fulfills the criteria to be classified as such and, if so, with what consequences for its inhabitants. An overview of demographic trends in this metropolitan area is an indispensable prelude to that inquiry.

DEMOGRAPHIC TRENDS: A GLOBAL
MAJORITY-MINORITY CITY

The Miami metropolitan area had a population of 2.7 million in 2015, having grown from 2.5 million in 2010 and 1.6 million in 1980. This steady growth has been relatively uniform across the county, though not among all age groups. The population 65 to 74 years of age increased by 21 percent during the first half of the decade (2009–14), and those 85 and older grew by 15 percent, while the population ages 19 and younger declined by 4 percent. As a result, the median age of county residents increased by one year, to 39.3, during this period.[11] The growth of the elderly population is due to the aging of the early Cuban exile population, most of whom have remained in the area, rather than to any recent migration of northern retirees. As discussed later, American retirees have mostly ceased to come to Miami, preferring instead the Florida Keys to the south. In Miami-Dade, meanwhile, the bulk of the population of working age, 20 to 64, also grew steadily, comprising about 1.7 million people and ensuring sufficient labor power for continuing economic growth.[12]

The population of the metropolitan area is ethnically diverse. By 2014, Hispanics made up the absolute majority, 66 percent, with blacks representing 16.7 percent and non-Hispanic whites a still lower figure, 14.7 percent, having declined from 61.1 percent in 1960.[13] If non-Hispanic whites represent the "mainstream" of the American population, then that mainstream has disappeared in Miami. Another way of saying this is that the index of dissimilarity, calculated for other American cities on the basis of how many minorities must move to "majority" (i.e., white) areas to eliminate spatial segregation, makes no sense in Miami since there are only a few, and diminishing, non-Hispanic white places to move to. Table 1 presents the evolution of the area's population in the past half century. The recent political history of the place, as told in the preceding chapter, is well reflected in this trend.

The mainstream in Miami-Dade County is now resolutely Hispanic, and this population adheres firmly to its own distinct and separate patches of urban territory. Together with blacks, this makes the area a majority-minority city, except that the two groups are quite distinct, maintaining separate social and geographic identities. To make the situation more

Table 1 Miami-Dade County, Population by Decade and Ethnicity

Year	Total (000s)	Hispanic (000s)	Black (000s)	Non-Hispanic White/Other (000s)
1970	1,268	299	190	782
1975	1,462	467	237	765
1980	1,626	581	284	773
1985	1,771	768	367	656
1990	1,967	968	409	618
1995	2,084	1,555	446	519
2000	2,253	1,292	457	534
2005	2,402	1,455	497	483
2010	2,551	1,621	526	442
2015	2,703	1,794	554	395
2020	2,858	1,972	583	342
		Percentages		
1970	100.0	27.6	15.0	65.7
1975	100.0	31.9	16.2	52.3
1980	100.0	35.7	17.5	47.5
1985	100.0	43.4	20.7	37.0
1990	100.0	49.2	20.8	31.4
1995	100.0	55.4	21.4	24.9
2000	100.0	57.3	20.3	23.7
2005	100.0	60.6	20.7	20.1
2010	100.0	63.5	20.6	17.3
2015	100.0	66.4	20.5	14.6
2020	100.0	69.0	20.4	12.2

SOURCE: Miami-Dade County, Dept. of Planning and Zoning, "General Statistical Data," 2015. U.S. Census of Population, 1970–2000.

remarkable, the foreign born now exceed half of the population (51.6 percent) of the county, making it the only metropolitan area in the United States to have a majority immigrant population. About 90 percent of the foreign born come from Latin America and the Caribbean, Cuba being the absolute largest source.

This exceptionality of the city's demographic profile contrasts with the apparent "normalcy" of everyday life in it, where English is still the unchallenged official and business language; where American economic, political, and judicial institutions are dominant; and where the standards of personal achievement and success are the same as elsewhere in the nation. One hears a lot of Spanish (and some Haitian Creole) in Miami, but the people who speak it accept that they live in an English-ruled world and that to succeed in it there is no alternative to full-fledged English learning and acculturation.[14]

The absolute demographic dominance of Hispanics and the rapid decline of the Anglo white population also means that an increasing segment of the class of property capitalists and of those leading and managing banks in Miami's financial district must be Latin. This is indeed the case, and that fact fits with the rise of the Cuban enclave economy in the 1960s and 1970s and the subsequent success of Cuban entrepreneurs and of their offspring.[15] While Anglo and, increasingly, European capitalists and executives are also found at the top of the business world, the Latin presence in these circles is indisputable.

Grouped in the powerful Latin Builders Association and the Latin Chamber of Commerce, Cuban and other Latin entrepreneurs have increasingly moved into the core of Miami's "growth machine." By contrast, blacks—whether native or foreign born—are mainly notable by their absence from these circles.[16] The history of the different groups composing Miami-Dade's current population and their distribution in physical space reflects these realities well.

TWO STORIES

Virginia Key, south of Miami Beach and the midpoint between the mainland and Key Biscayne witnessed a major confrontation in the late 1990s between property developers eager to cash in on its remarkable physical beauty and environmentalists fighting to keep it as an unspoiled wildlife reserve. There was, however, another important constituency struggling for Virginia Key's preservation. Black workers imported from the Bahamas and the Carolinas fought the swamp and jungle that South Florida was in the late nineteenth century to build a glittering playground for white tourists from the North. However, they could not set foot on what they had built. For decades, black residents of Miami could not swim in salt water, the beaches being the exclusive preserve of whites.

In 1945, a group of black community activists organized a "wade-in" in Haulover Park, north of Miami Beach, fully expecting to be arrested and, hence, setting up a legal confrontation with the prevailing Jim Crow laws. That legal battle did not take place because the County Commission, fearing bad publicity among northern tourists, relented and ceded then remote Virginia Key to the black population, turning it into a park for "coloreds only." Originally, there was no bridge to the key and beachgoers had to pay 75 cents, then a steep fare, for ferry transportation from the Miami River. But gradually, the Key acquired regular facilities and even places to stay overnight. Black Miamians turned it into their holiday playground, with big celebrations on the Fourth of July and other festivities.[17]

"It served its purpose," said John D. Johnson, a retired municipal court judge who remembers driving from black Overtown when the Rickenbacker Causeway was finally built in 1947. Now "it has a history behind it."[18] Thus, a place born out of racism and created as a vehicle to perpetuate segregation went on to become an important recreational and cultural center. Black celebrities like Nat King Cole and Jackie Robinson, who could not stay in Miami Beach hotels, came and stayed in Virginia Key as their only way to gain access to the sea. Up to the end of segregation days in the mid-1960s, the place was known as the "Black Beach" and was shunned by whites accordingly.[19]

In the late 1990s, however, property developers wanted the Key back in order to build hotels and apartment towers, but an alliance of environmentalists and African American activists resisted. The latter, in particular, wanted to create a memorial park honoring those who fought for their rights in the 1940s and who led the way for the area's subsequent transformation. Virginia Key looms large in black Miami's historical memory, and its leaders are determinedly set against its obliteration. For Athalie Range, the first African American Miami city commissioner, it's not "odd at all that blacks want to build a memorial to their struggle on the very site of their original exile."[20] The confrontation went on for some time; in the end, Virginia Key remained under the control of the City of Miami, which set up the Virginia Key Park Trust. No black memorial was built, but no hotels either, an exceptional defeat for the local growth machine. In 2002, Virginia Key entered the National Register of Historic Places.

By the time segregation was about to end, in the early 1960s, and not two miles away from Virginia Key, another very different drama was unfolding. Cubans escaping the early years of Fidel Castro's Communist dictatorship started arriving in Miami and settling in the modest southwestern fringe of downtown, only a few blocks away from black Overtown. Catholic to a person and despondent at the magnitude of their loss in the country left behind, these exiles had no house of prayer, at least none where they could come together and find support in their own language. There were no masses in Spanish and no place to celebrate them.[21]

Responding to this need, a Spanish priest, Fernando Ibarra, succeeded in renting the Tivoli Theater, right in downtown, for Sunday Catholic services. Yet Cubans attending mass and needing both spiritual and material support in the early years of exile could not be accommodated for long in this converted movie theater. The Archdiocese of Miami eventually recognized the situation and created a new parish, St. John Bosco, in 1962. Still there was no physical church. A Cuban priest, the Reverend Emilio Vallina, himself a recently arrived refugee, came to the rescue. In 1963, he received the keys to a rundown garage on Flagler Street, eight blocks from the old Tivoli. Parishioners renovated the building, which from then on became the spiritual and social center of the exile community. For people arriving with just their clothes on their backs, Sunday mass at St. John Bosco was "like a balm."[22]

Soon the parish was dispensing health and many other social services to its community. By the late 1990s, however, the old converted garage became too decrepit for use. It was torn down and replaced by a proper church, unsurprisingly baptized the "Exile's Cathedral." Yet, a decade later, a new turn in history took place: early Cuban exiles had prospered rapidly, learning English and creating their own businesses. As their fortunes improved, they moved away to middle-class neighborhoods and wealthier parishes. Their place was taken by Central American immigrants, primarily Nicaraguans, who came to occupy the same modest houses and low-rent apartments in what had become known by then as "Little Havana." Father Vallina retired in 2006, but St. John Bosco is still in place,

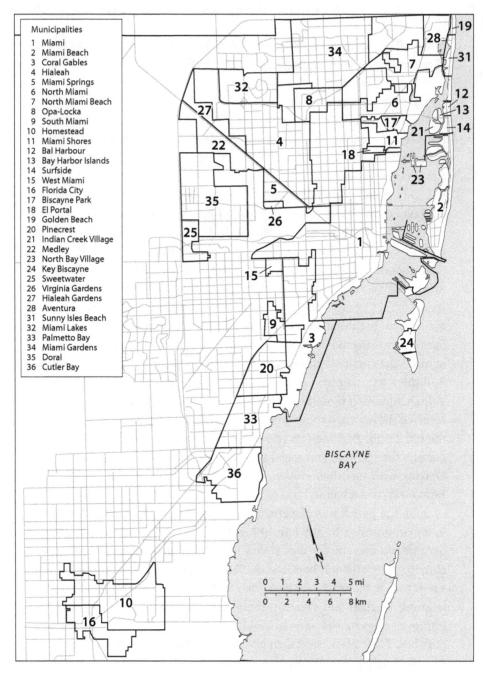

Municipalities
1 Miami
2 Miami Beach
3 Coral Gables
4 Hialeah
5 Miami Springs
6 North Miami
7 North Miami Beach
8 Opa-Locka
9 South Miami
10 Homestead
11 Miami Shores
12 Bal Harbour
13 Bay Harbor Islands
14 Surfside
15 West Miami
16 Florida City
17 Biscayne Park
18 El Portal
19 Golden Beach
20 Pinecrest
21 Indian Creek Village
22 Medley
23 North Bay Village
24 Key Biscayne
25 Sweetwater
26 Virginia Gardens
27 Hialeah Gardens
28 Aventura
31 Sunny Isles Beach
32 Miami Lakes
33 Palmetto Bay
34 Miami Gardens
35 Doral
36 Cutler Bay

BISCAYNE
BAY

N

| 0 | 1 | 2 | 3 | 4 | 5 mi |

| 0 | 2 | 4 | 6 | 8 km |

Map 1. The Miami Metropolitan Area and Its Main Municipalities, 2015. Source: Map from Miami-Dade County, Department of Regulatory and Economic Resources.

continuing to celebrate mass in Spanish and catering to the multiple needs of its newly arrived parishoners.[23] In recent years, a struggle similar to what took place in Virginia Key twenty years earlier is unfolding as property developers seek to push outward from downtown into Little Havana while older residents are resisting. The historical value of the area and the fact that many Cuban American elected officials grew up in it gives it a credible chance for survival.[24]

These two stories illustrate a point that can be exemplified by many others: the fragmented demography of Miami reflects the profoundly different histories of the ethnic communities making up its population. There is a lingering white city, with its triumphant history of struggles against jungle and swamp and subsequent, remarkable growth. There is a black Miami, descendants of those who did the actual struggling and who now revere Virginia Key as their place of refuge against decades of discrimination. And there is a Cuban Miami, with its memories of loss, adaptation, and eventual success and for which St. John Bosco is one of several iconic places distributed around the city. The ecology and demography of contemporary Miami is best read as a reflection of these divergent histories, struggles, and memories.

The ways that property capital has shaped the metropolitan area and the perennial struggle between the city-as-human-habitat and the city-as-growth-machine are best told at the level of its principal municipalities. Map 1 presents the Miami metropolitan area's political division, with its current thirty-six autonomous municipalities. The major ones are discussed next.

THE CITY OF MIAMI

The city that gives the metropolitan area its name owes its origins, according to legend, to some orange blossoms dispatched by a local resident, Julia Tuttle, to the railroad magnate and hotelier Henry Flagler in northern Florida. In 1895, a severe frost wreaked havoc with the citrus industry in the north and center of the state. The blossoms were sent as proof that ice never reached the southern tip of the peninsula. Persuaded, Flagler extended his Florida East Coast railroad to the Miami River, built a luxury hotel, the Royal Palm, where the river met Biscayne Bay, and shortly thereafter marched his "artillery" of Bahamian workers plus a few local whites to vote for political incorporation. The city of Miami was born in 1896.[25]

Indeed the raison d'être of the new city was its winter climate. The Bahamian and Southern black workers were promptly confined to barracks across the railroad tracks, today's Overtown, to keep them from view by the wealthy white tourists staying in Flagler's hotel and other accommodations. For decades, this white-black division, diligently enforced by the Miami police, dominated the racial/ethnic makeup of the city. It took Fidel Castro's revolutionary project to change that situation.[26]

By 2015, the city had 430,332 inhabitants, 70 percent of whom were Hispanic. The population had grown steadily and was now at par with Atlanta (pop. 456,000) as the South's largest metropolis. Blacks accounted for 19.2 percent and non-Hispanic whites, just 11.9 percent. Seventy-seven percent of this population spoke Spanish at home, and the foreign born constituted an absolute majority. Among Hispanics, Cubans were dominant, representing 34 percent of the total population—a fact well reflected in the current politics of the place. Not surprisingly, this majority-minority city with its large immigrant component has become relatively poor. Median household income was just $30,375 in 2014, more than $15,000 below the Florida figure.[27]

There are pockets of wealth around Brickell Avenue and Coconut Grove, the birthplace of the city, but the majority of the population earns low incomes. As Cubans prospered, they left their traditional areas of settlement in the city's southwest quarter for more prosperous municipalities. As seen above, Little Havana became increasingly Central American, populated by recent poor migrants from Honduras, El Salvador, and Guatemala.

The city of Miami and its environs fit well the classic configuration of a global city as described by Sassen. The central business district and adjacent Brickell Avenue house the banks, corporate headquarters, financial and insurance services, and high-powered law firms typical of this configuration. They also feature a rising number of luxury condominium towers housing the executives and other highly paid employees of these banks and property firms. Walk five blocks away, however, and you encounter the very modest one- and two-story houses now occupied by Central Americans in Little Havana. Walk a few more blocks west, and you are in Overtown, still the core black ghetto area left from the days of Flagler.

The wealth of the downtown, Brickell Avenue, and Coconut Grove residents is not enough to lift the average Miami income above near-poverty level, signaling the depth of inequality in this city. Beyond it, a few areas— targeted by the local growth machine—also feature exquisite residences and luxury shopping centers; the rest of the periphery is occupied by the working class, those laboring in the informal economy, and the fully marginalized. As in New York, London, and other global cities, the museums, performing arts centers, and other cultural symbols of prosperity coexist with abject poverty. Well-dressed operagoers must pass by clusters of homeless people on their way to the performance. As in similar urban places, the presence of the poor is simply ignored. In Coconut Grove, million-dollar residences are just blocks away from the "Black Grove," an impoverished ghetto area housing descendants of Flagler's Bahamian workers.

The dynamics of property capital, as described in Lamarche's classic text, are also quite apparent here. The decayed tenements of Overtown exist only so long as the growth machine does not claim the space for its own uses. The Marlins baseball park has already wiped out a large chunk of Little Havana, using vast amounts of public moneys for its construction. The older residents of that quarter are currently battling further expansion. Farther north, a consortium led by soccer star David Beckham is in the process of doing the same to Overtown, claiming the land for a new major league soccer stadium.[28] Tourists and sports fans are spared the spectacle of urban poverty by the high-speed thoroughfares and rapid transit systems designed for this purpose. The depth of inequality in Miami makes its newly found role as a global city a dubious honor. Indeed, it has become a hub for financial and commercial transactions spanning the hemisphere and beyond, but the new wealthy classes accompanying this transformation must share an urban space bifurcated by vast economic and social differences. Consequences of this polarization are examined in a later chapter.

MIAMI BEACH

The city of Miami has no beach. To access the Atlantic, you must cross Biscayne Bay toward the barrier islands east. Before there was a usable beach here, it was a tangle of mangrove and swamp uninhabited except by saltwater crocodiles and alligators. Taming this jungle took a great deal of effort, and it was not done originally to sell lots by the ocean but to grow coconuts first and avocados later for export to the north. The New Jersey horticulturist John Collins bought the entire barrier island that is today Miami Beach in the 1890s for his avocado plantation. He introduced the Australian pines that still grace the place to protect his avocado trees but to no avail: the land resisted, and the plantation promptly went bust.[29]

Collins's children eventually persuaded their father that the only way to make money out of his investment was to sell the land in lots to northerners. But to get the fruit out and the people in, some means of communication to the mainland had to be built. Collins strained his credit in New Jersey to build a wooden bridge across Biscayne Bay, only to see the project fail, a half-mile short, for lack of sufficient funds. Investing 100,000 1912 dollars in a bridge to nowhere was even a harder setback than the failure of the avocados. Collins had to sell his island, but his efforts are memorialized today in the main thoroughfare across it, Collins Avenue.[30]

The project was completed by an Indiana huckster and self-made millionaire by the name of Carl J. Fisher, builder of the Indianapolis Speedway, inventor of Prest-O-Lite, and promoter of the first cross-country highway. With the same energy displayed in these projects, he proceeded to finish Collins's bridge and clear the land, actually making more of it by the simple expedient of dredging the shallow bay. On top of it, Fisher put golf courses, Baroque hotels, and grand mansions.[31] Miami Beach soon became a smashing success and the favorite winter place to be and be seen by northeastern and midwestern elites who occupied Fisher's mansions and built others, invariably in the red tile and wrought iron Mediterranean style.

One of Fisher's few worries was to prevent Miami Beach from becoming another Atlantic City, dominated by New York's Jewry. To this end, signs reading "Gentiles Only" blossomed on properties for sale by the beach. Lots in Fisher's and other developers' projects were deeded with provisos that read: "Said property shall not be sold, leased, or rented in any form or manner, by any title either legal or equitable to any person or persons other than of the Caucasian race."[32] By one of the many ironies of history in this land, Miami Beach was to become, in due time, the most Jewish city in America. Jewish restaurants and synagogues proliferated in the 1940s and 1950s, and, when its time came, the main national monument in memory of the Holocaust victims was built there. For his anti-Semitic troubles, Fisher was relegated to a smallish bust virtually hidden in an out-of-the-way park. "He built a city out of a jungle," the caption underneath reads.[33] Practically no one knows of its existence.

While heavily Hispanicized at present, Miami Beach's Jewish heritage persists and is visible in multiple public buildings and synagogues. By 2015, the city had a population of 91,732, up 4.5 percent since the previous census. Hispanics are already a majority (53 percent), though less an overwhelming figure than in Miami proper. Forty percent of the Beach's population is still non-Hispanic white, with a heavy Jewish component.[34] The increasing Hispanic, predominantly Cuban influence is also reflected in the number of businesses owned by this group, 38 percent of the total. South of Lincoln Road, however, the city has experienced a notable influx of Europeans and Americans from up north attracted by the area's art deco architecture and its nightlife. South Beach, as the place is known, came back from decades of decay and oblivion to become one of the most glamorous winter resorts in the country.[35]

Unlike its cousin across Biscayne Bay, Miami Beach has no downtown and no center. City Hall is tucked away in an inconspicuous building on Washington Avenue and, otherwise, the city simply follows the Atlantic in a near-uninterrupted succession of hotels and condominium towers along Collins Avenue. As Nijman noted, many of these apartments remain vacant for most of the year, reaffirming the place's vocation as a tourist destination.[36] Nowadays, Miami Beach makes its living by selling luxury condominiums to wealthy foreigners and well-paid executives from downtown. Its newly found chic increasingly attracts tourists from the world over who come to play in the bars and nightclubs of South Beach and to shop in adjacent Lincoln Road.

Unlike Miami proper, the Beach has no business or financial center worthy of note, nor does it house a large working-class population. In the logic of property capital, its role is exclusively one of consumption.

Developers and hoteliers sell the beach by the square foot to the well-heeled buyers and tourists from everywhere and then sell this same population to store, restaurant, and bar owners catering to its every whim. As in Fisher's time, the poor and the working class do not live in the Beach, being confined to visiting publicly accessible parks. There is no area of concentrated poverty anywhere in the city. The current recovery of the place as a site for luxury consumption and property speculation is directly linked to the emergence of central Miami as a global city. One would not have happened without the other.

CORAL GABLES

Back on the mainland, Solomon Merrick's citrus plantation was no more successful at the turn of the twentieth century than Collins's avocado farm had been. Merrick's children, like Collins's, quickly saw the light and with outside backing began to develop the land. The exclusive residential city of Coral Gables netted its creators a profit estimated at more than 20 million 1910 dollars during its first five years alone.[37] The tycoons, hucksters, and visionaries who were mining gold out of the sands of Miami had something quite peculiar in common. Northerners all, it would have seemed reasonable for them to build a seaside resort on the model of, say, Newport or Atlantic City. That did not happen because, almost to a man, these Yankee developers were obsessed with the Mediterranean and, in particular, Spain.[38]

The tile and wrought iron mansions of the Firestones, Deerings, and other millionaires paved the way, but in Coral Gables the Merricks carried Hispanophilia to an extreme. It was to be not just a pleasant residential area, but the best resort in the world. It would boast, among other things, the grandest hotel and a prestigious university—today's Biltmore Hotel and the University of Miami. The impressive Andalusian façade of the Biltmore is capped by a replica of Seville's Giralda Tower, visible throughout the city.[39]

This Andalusian theme permeates every corner of the town. Even today, one enters Coral Gables through fake Spanish fort gates to face shaded streets named Granada, Almeria, Sevilla, Galiano, and Cordova. The Merricks' theme park came complete with Moorish minarets, a baroque frontispiece for the Congregational Church, and "Spanish" moss everywhere. The main thoroughfare in the city is Ponce de Leon Boulevard, making it appear as if the old Spanish sailor had conquered and settled the place after all.[40]

For the distraught and penniless Cuban bourgeoisie arriving on South Florida shores in the early sixties, the sight of those buildings and the names of the streets were an unexpected and welcome consolation. They knew these names, and although they could not afford to live in the exclusive city, they certainly set their sights on it. A decade later, Coral Gables was easily the preferred living destination among the upwardly mobile exiles, and it took only a few years for the city to elect its first and current Cuban-born mayor, Raúl Valdés-Fauli.[41]

Today, Coral Gables, the richest large municipality in the metropolitan area, has a population of 51,227 (2014), up 10 percent from the last decennial census. Cuban and other Hispanics are the majority (54 percent), with non-Hispanic whites still representing a sizable proportion, 40 percent; African Americans are just 3 percent. As in Miami Beach, the presence of Cubans is not only demographic but also economic. Cuban- and other Hispanic-owned businesses represent 46 percent of the total. The Merricks scarcely could have imagined that their Andalusian dreamwork would, in the end, return to its roots, being now settled by people whose ancestors, like Ponce, came from Spain.[42]

Coral Gables occupies a peculiar place in the property capitalists' map of the metropolitan area. It is not only the most desirable residential area; it is the place where local movers and shakers, including property developers themselves, live. Hence, unlike other areas of the county, it is nearly impossible to produce differential rent by the simple expedient of tearing down what exists and putting new residential towers and commercial plazas on the land. Any such attempt would be effectively resisted by both the municipal government and its powerful inhabitants. Unthinkable to put a baseball or a soccer stadium in Coral Gables.

There is an elegant commercial area, Miracle Mile, hugging City Hall and featuring expensive designer stores and restaurants. Next to it, a secondary banking and financial services center has emerged, supplementing Brickell Avenue and featuring the branches and regional headquarters of many foreign banks. These are located in pleasant and architecturally ornate buildings that do not mar the overall elegance of the city while simultaneously allowing executives and managers to live, work, and play in the same area. The resort that the Merricks built has thus become a protected enclave of privilege, hosting a not inconsiderable segment of the local upper class.

The main problem affecting Coral Gables today is not of its own doing. As the metropolitan area has grown, it has created new enormous suburban developments by the simple expedient of draining the Everglades. The middle and working classes who inhabit these developments often work in downtown Miami, and to get there, they must travel west through Coral Gables. The absence of a rapid transit system, a subject examined in detail in another chapter, means that these commuters must take to their cars, clogging not only the East-West Dolphin Expressway but also the avenues and even residential streets of Coral Gables. According to a former mayor, up to half of the traffic incidents and infractions recorded by the Coral Gables police do not involve local residents but commuters traveling east in the mornings and west in the evenings.[43]

HIALEAH

With 235,563 inhabitants in 2015, Hialeah is the sixth largest city in the State of Florida and the second largest in Miami-Dade. It is also one of the poorest, with a median household income of just $29,961, almost $20,000 below the comparable Florida figure. Twenty-five percent of the population lives in poverty. It was not supposed to be that way.[44] When Hialeah was incorporated in 1921, it was expected to be another playground for the rich and famous. The Hialeah Park Race Track was nicknamed the "Grand Dame" of horse racing, receiving visits by, among others, Winston Churchill and J. P. Morgan.[45]

Unlike the Merricks in Coral Gables, whose shaded trees and lovingly designed boulevards prefigured a brilliant future, Hialeah developers were in a hurry to get their money back. Led by Glenn Curtiss of aviation fame, they simply cleared the land and laid out streets in monotonous right angles. While Curtiss himself had great dreams, building an aerodrome nearby, supporting the race track, and even designing a mansion for himself, that vision contrasted sadly with the slapdash character of his creation. The big hurricane of 1926 and the arrival of the Great Depression in 1929 completed the destruction. The well-to-do abandoned the place in droves, lots were sold on the cheap, and urban infrastructure was thoroughly neglected.[46]

By the 1940s, Hialeah had become a gritty working-class city populated by factories, warehouses, garages, and modest one-story houses. The racetrack still functioned, but its surroundings became increasingly unfashionable. This was now redneck territory, with a notoriously corrupt city politics topping the derelict urban design. Despite its increasing ugliness, the place had some advantages. First, jobs became plentiful in the post–World War II period as the city concentrated whatever factory production there was in South Florida. Second, housing and living costs were among the cheapest in the metropolitan area.[47] Arriving first in the 1960s, Cuban exiles took note.

The exodus from Cuba thoroughly transformed Hialeah. Wave after wave of refugees found in the cheap housing and low-wage jobs offered by the city the first stepping-stone to life in a new land. Upper- and middle-class Cuban women who had never worked a day in their lives now found themselves sewing for Jewish contractors in Hialeah factories. As upper-class Cuban men regained their economic footing, they quickly pulled their wives and daughters out of the factories and out of Hialeah altogether.[48] Never mind, new waves of refugees—each of more modest origin than the last—took their place. Working-class Americans entirely quit the area, turning Hialeah into the most "Cuban" town outside the island itself.

Today, 95 percent of the city is Hispanic and 74 percent Cuban or Cuban American. Ninety-two percent of the residents report speaking Spanish at home. Upper- and middle-class Cuban and other Hispanic families do not live in Hialeah but in Coral Gables, Miami Beach, or the unincorporated southwest quadrant of Dade County. Hialeah remains the place of choice, however, for working-class Hispanics, including a steady flow of recent arrivals from Cuba.[49] Spanish and Latin music is heard everywhere, and Cuban restaurants, music shops, markets, and jewelry shops dot the area. Hialeah is still institutionally and politically an American city; socially and culturally, however, it could be a suburb of Havana.

Hialeah provides an exception to Allman's observation that Miami does not produce much of anything. Hialeah was and still is an industrial municipality, concentrating whatever in the way of productive activity exists in the region. In the logic of the growth machine, Hialeah's role is that of reserve labor. It is the place where industrial workers and those servicing the hotels in Miami Beach, the banks and condominium towers downtown, and the opulent residences of Coral Gables go at night. While efforts are being made to revive the grand Hialeah Race Track, no property developer worth his salt would dream of building a hotel or luxury condominium tower next to it at present.[50]

The garment shops that provided Cuban refugee women with jobs in the 1960s have mostly disappeared, but their place has been taken by new firms in electronics, high-tech equipment, and logistics. The city is also the center of a brisk export trade to Cuba and the Caribbean, much of it informal. It is perhaps due to that vigorous informal commerce that the city looks as it looks—modest but not poor. Despite its official high poverty rate and low average incomes, Hialeah teems with shopping centers, restaurants, and places of entertainment, suggesting a much more active (albeit concealed) trade and economy.[51]

Supermarkets and drugstore chains populate the streets, next to auto repair shops, cheap Latin restaurants, and the ever present *botánicas* selling folk remedies for everything—from muscular pains to unrequited love. Drab but vigorous Hialeah represents the counterpart to the economic transformation going on downtown. It reflects a process of "globalization from below"—informal and popular—complementing that "from above" spearheaded by the banks and the growth machine.

MIAMI GARDENS AND OPA-LOCKA

Hialeah is not the only urban invention owed to Glenn Curtiss's imagination. North of it and right next to the line with Broward County are another two of Curtiss's creations, also conceived with grand expectations. The city of Opa-Locka, in particular, was to be the site of a One Thousand and One Nights playground, with Arabian minarets and other suitable Eastern decor along a thoroughfare named Ali Baba Avenue. As in Hialeah, such dreams clashed with the realities of poor urban design and shoddy infrastructure. It did not take long for the city to decline in attractiveness and population, abandoned by its well-to-do earlier inhabitants.[52] Instead of a counterpart to Coral Gables to the south, Opa-Locka became increasingly poor and black, a refuge for an African American population displaced in growing numbers from Miami itself. Despite evident decay, Opa-Locka retains its icons from the past. Ali Baba Avenue still exists, along with Sultan Avenue and Sesame Street. The city boasts, to this day, the largest collection of Moorish revival architecture in the entire country. Many of these buildings are crumbling, and the desolate look along the town's main square is far more typical of an urban ghetto than of a suburban residential area.[53]

A similar transformation took place in the extreme north of the county in what is now the city of Miami Gardens. This is the youngest municipality in the metropolitan area, having incorporated only in May 2003. With a population of 112,265 in 2014, it is also the third largest city in Miami-Dade. Three-fourths of its inhabitants are African Americans, making it the largest city in Florida with a majority black population.[54] Predictably, the mayors of both Opa-Locka and Miami Gardens are African Americans. But unlike Opa-Locka, the economy of Miami Gardens has improved significantly in recent years. This is due, in part, to the resettlement of middle-class African Americans displaced from the city of Miami by the construction of Interstate 95. It is also due to the number of major institutions located in the area.

Miami Gardens is the home of two universities, Catholic St. Thomas and historically black Florida Memorial. The Sun Life Stadium hosts both the Miami Dolphins football team and the University of Miami Hurricanes. The city is also home to the Orange Bowl game and parade every year. At $42,040, Miami Gardens median household income is at par with that of the metropolitan area ($43,100). More than half (53.1 percent) of businesses in the city are owned by African Americans.[55] Undoubtedly, Miami Gardens has become the economic and social pivot of black Miami, counterbalancing Hispanic hegemony in the cities farther south. Black neighborhoods in Miami, like Liberty City, and the city of Opa-Locka still house a mostly poor population, but upwardly mobile African American families have increasingly found their place in "the Gardens."

Neither Opa-Locka nor Miami Gardens is on the local growth machine's mental map, nor do they house any of the functions and activities that have made Miami "global." Opa-Locka has deteriorated steadily, serving mainly as a depository of an unemployed and largely unemployable population. To this must be added a notoriously corrupt municipal administration. The deserted look of its streets and parks contrasts markedly with the hustle and bustle of Hialeah, less than a mile away.[56] Curtiss's Arabian Nights dream has deteriorated into one of the worst ghettos in the metropolitan area.

Despite its institutions and much more progressive character, Miami Gardens is also singularly unconnected to the activities of property capital downtown. The black middle class that has found refuge in it—government employees, small entrepreneurs, and others—appears more oriented to Broward County up north and even to Atlanta than to central Miami. Visitors to Miami go to the downtown and Brickell areas, South Beach, or Coral Gables; they seldom travel to the Gardens, and most do not even know of its existence. Though formally part of the metropolitan area, this vigorous black enclave could as well be in Georgia in terms of its relevance to locally dominant economic forces. Its sole relevance lies in the institutions it houses and the annual celebrations it hosts. Otherwise, the Gardens seldom garners much notice.

VIRGINIA KEY (AGAIN)

We last left Virginia Key in an uneasy impasse between the wishes of the black population to build a memorial to the days of segregation, the desire of property developers to put buildings on it, and the plans of the City of Miami to rebuild and reopen its Marine Stadium. None of these things has happened, but the struggle over the future of the Key serves as a telling microcosm of how complex decisions and initiatives can become in a global city. The City of Miami owns the Key, but Miami Metro owns the port, and the plans of the two do not always coincide. The city's desire to reopen the Marine Stadium and "develop" the area with new restaurants and hotels conflicts with plans by the county to expand the port in order to accommodate yet more cruise ships, as well as resistance from downtown hotel and restaurant owners to the new competition.[57]

On top of everything, Virginia Key is also the site of the city's main water treatment plant, which sends the treated effluent through an underwater pipe miles into the Gulf Stream. New State of Florida regulations will prohibit this; in search of alternatives, the city has hit upon the idea of digging miles underground and sending Miami's waste into the core of the earth.[58] Hence, while no buildings and no mausoleums are yet going up on the Key, its core is being ceaselessly dug by giant perforating machines. The future of Virginia Key may well be dominated by this treatment plant, as the struggle between city and county is compounded by the resolute opposition of another municipality, the Village of Key Biscayne, to further urban development.[59]

The two keys share the same and sole road to the mainland, the Rickenbacker Causeway. Key Biscayne is already full of expensive condominiums and homes built by the growth machine in the past. Its well-heeled residents naturally fear being confined to their village if Virginia Key, the midpoint between themselves and the mainland, also falls into the developers' hands. This new struggle again brings back into relief the perennial conflict between the profit-making and human functions of the city, made even more acute by globalization. Residents of Key Biscayne are mostly local, while property capitalists interested in cashing in on Virginia Key's unspoiled land are commonly foreign.

CONCLUSION

In the words of a longtime observer, there is not one "Miami" but multiple ones, in which each successive immigrant or ethnic group has created its own definition and vision of the city. The Miami of the remaining Jews in the Beach is quite different from Cuban Hialeah—the two groups seldom meeting anywhere. The same is the case with wealthy Hispanics and Anglos in Coral Gables and the African Americans in Miami Gardens. The amazing Moorish buildings in Opa-Locka remain a mystery to most residents of the metropolis for whom the area is just another depressed slum. The physical and social distances separating the various components of Miami's population are exceptional for a city of its size.

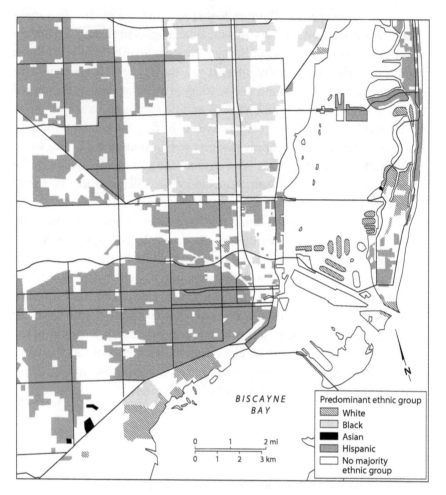

Map 2. Miami-Dade County Ethnic and Racial Composition. Image Copyright 2013
Weldon Cooper Center for Public Service, Rector and Visitors of the University of
Virginia (Dustin A. Cable, creator). Source: 2010 Census of Population Block Data,
2012.

Map 2 illustrates this diversity with an ethnic/racial map of Miami-
Dade County. Notice the near-disappearing non-Hispanic white areas, the
solid Hispanic dominance in most of the county, as well as the large, distinct black neighborhoods, mostly to the north. The historical trajectories
that brought these diverse populations to South Florida meshed with suc-

cessive attempts by the growth machine to cash in on its physical beauty and mild climate and then with the rediscovery by global capital of its geographic centrality to produce the present map. In the words of one of our informants, Miami today is a fragmented global city. This has important consequences as it faces major challenges at present and in the future, as will be seen next.

3 Between Transience and Attachment

> I can remember now, with a clarity that makes the nerves
> in the back of my neck constrict, when New York began for
> me, but I cannot lay my finger upon the moment it ended.
>
> —Joan Didion, "Goodbye to All That"

Joan Didion may have had New York in mind, but her words can be applied just as aptly to Miami. The duality she expresses—when a new place becomes home and when it ceases to be home—is crucial to understanding any city. Few cities are as defined by their transitory nature as Miami. As a city of immigrants, the questions, "Where do I belong?" and "Where is my home?," are ingrained in its culture. The debate rages as to whether Miami is a destination or just a stop on the way to somewhere else.

As seen in chapter 2, over 50 percent of the total population of Miami-Dade County emigrated from another country, most to escape political turmoil or economic troubles. An overwhelming majority of immigrants—about 90 percent—came from Latin America and the Caribbean. To some, the migratory nature of Miami is what makes it a home. When asked to reflect on his personal experience with Miami, the head of a prominent foundation said:

> For me, leaving Miami is not a realistic option. I don't fit anywhere else. My parents are Cuban, I go to Cuba, and they ask me why I speak with a Puerto Rican accent. I was born in Spain. I go to Spain, and they ask me if I'm from Venezuela, Cuba, or Puerto Rico. I go anywhere else in the United States, and they know I am a hyphenated American of some sort. I don't have to

explain myself in Miami, and there are increasingly larger numbers of people who feel that way here. This is our identity. . . . Attachment matters, because even if you go elsewhere you are going to be pulled back home.[1]

To others, the opposite is true. A billionaire real estate developer offered this comment on the same subject:

> People need to feel a strong loyalty to the city for the city to become a great city. Miami is a temporal place. You see that when you go to a Dolphins game. It is the only city where there are more people from the visiting team. We need to create a community vision; we need to create loyalty to the city.[2]

And yet attachment and transience are not only related to loyalty or a sense of belonging to the city; Miami's profound social and economic cleavages also define excruciating means of surviving—not just belonging—in the city. As an activist in a community organization working with vulnerable populations explained:

> Immigrants, particularly those without lawful status, move constantly within the city because of absence of roots, legal insecurity, and economic problems. The state of constant persecution, hostile political atmosphere, and racism impact their connection to the community. They live in constant movement—in a temporal nature but still with a certain sense of attachment.[3]

As an emerging global metropolis, Miami faces the challenge of generating a sense of belonging in a context marked by profound cleavages of race, ethnicity, and class. As we document throughout this volume, even compared to cities of similar size, the fragmentation, both physical and social, between groups is vast. The lack of cohesiveness undoubtedly shapes the sense of belonging to the city. In the course of our investigations, we interviewed a number of people from every walk of life. We heard countless times from our sources—in both the upper and lower echelons of society—that there is not one "Miami" but multiple ones defined by different groups with unique bonds to the city.

This multiplicity of bonds—some strong, some tenuous—expresses a fundamental feature of Miami: it is a city defined by a brittle balance between transience and attachment. This might differ from other American cities such as New York because of Miami's unique combination of a bifurcated class structure typical of global cities, a growth machine tied to the place's natural beauty and climate, and close geographic and cultural connection to Latin America and the Caribbean.

Understanding the character of urban life requires that we explore people's attachment to the city. Attachment to a place has a concrete psychological impact on individuals. It makes them feel comfortable, gives them a sense of security, and facilitates their involvement with the community. How we feel about the place where we live is a fundamental component of our lives. Conversely, how people experience attachment to a place is a fundamental component of the life of the city.

In the case of Miami, understanding community attachment requires that we examine the various ways in which people feel that they belong against the backdrop of transience. A city like Miami with such a degree of heterogeneity, constant migrant flows, and fragmentation faces a major challenge: How can it have meaningful community life? We need to go beyond the role of geography to understand other factors that attract people to this city and that enhance the connection that people experience with "their" Miami. We also need to understand what factors prevent people from developing attachment to a place and what factors push them away from it.

MIAMI AS DESTINATION AND PIT STOP

Miami is a city where extremes coexist in a delicate but stable balance. This is a city where old Cuban ladies with 1950s hairdos stroll down the sidewalk as young entrepreneurs blow past them, late for their next meeting. This is a city where Nicaraguan maids sleep in makeshift, windowless rooms in expensive homes in Palmetto Bay as Russian millionaires and their escorts make entrances at the most exclusive downtown restaurants. With people coming to Miami with such varying motivations—some to make money and some to flee economic chaos, some to create a new home and some to weather a political storm—how can we understand the sentiments people have toward the city?

To do so, we must define place attachment. Place is a point of reference—either natural or built—from which we can see our identity in the world. Attachment implies the desire to maintain closeness to that place.

From a sociological perspective, this is based on the web of relations we have with the place: employment, recreation, education, consumption, and so on. Place attachment has been linked to both positive and negative outcomes. On the one hand, place attachment is a source of individual well-being and community cohesion.[4] In their seminal article, "Community Attachment in Mass Society," John Kasarda and Morris Janowitz argue that the local community is a "complex system of friendship and kinship" into which new cohorts are incorporated.[5] Making a place home is key to the development of identity and the construction of a sense of belonging. Individuals with greater place attachment enjoy a better quality of life, including better physical and psychological health and more satisfying social relationships. At the public level, places with highly attached people are more likely to cooperate to achieve a desired outcome, such as improving specific features of their community.[6]

Place attachment can also have negative effects. Place attachment can become detrimental if it undermines people's judgment of alternatives or make them unlikely to leave, even when the place ceases to be livable. Furthermore, place attachment can lead to intergroup conflicts when new people move to a place with a high proportion of attached people, who will see newcomers as threatening to their way of life and to the physical and social characteristics of the place.[7]

Remarkably, existing research shows that the intensity of attachment to a place is not necessarily linked to having been born there.[8] This means that anyone can create a strong connection to their home, adopted or not, as the experience of Cubans has clearly demonstrated. Still, especially in a city with as many recent immigrants as Miami, it is fair to say that the bond does not exist immediately. It needs to be built. Creating this bond is part of a complex process shaped by individual, family, and community forces. Some key features of Miami, such as the continuous flow of people circulating through the city, shape this process in unique ways.

MIAMI'S MAGNETISM

Why are people coming to Miami? To answer this question, we must look first to Latin America and the Caribbean. The fates of Miami and Latin

America have been intimately connected for generations, most acutely in the past century. Miami in the second half of the twentieth century cannot be understood without focusing on the Cuban Revolution, and the same is true for Latin America as a whole. The Cuban Revolution and Miami are part of a continuum. Miami, as a new global city, can be seen as the unanticipated outcome of the Cuban Revolution. In some strange twist of fate, the anachronistic nature of present-day Cuba is mirrored by the modernity of present-day Miami. At the same time, the aspiration of creating a society based on equality in Cuba is mirrored by the emergence of a city marked by increasing inequality in South Florida.

The dramatic remaking of Miami began with the arrival of the Cuban immigrants, but it was strengthened by the subsequent arrival of Nicaraguans after the Sandinista Revolution, as well as newer flows from other Latin American and Caribbean countries. It continues today with growing immigrant communities from Venezuela but also from Europe, Russia, and India, along with new arrivals from East Asia. South Florida is an aggregation of places that re-create other places—the adopted homelands of those who came from Cuba, Nicaragua, Haiti, Colombia, Venezuela, and many other nations. These transplants often re-create their places of origin in Miami.[9]

An essential feature of this process is the reenactment of an experience that intends to replicate the familiar spaces of the homeland. However, the experience cannot fully duplicate the original one. Consider, for example, Graziano's Market on Bird Road, which sells meat in traditional Argentine cuts. The products are familiar to the Argentine customer, but the *experience* is familiar as well. The conversation with the staff at the meat counter is in Spanish. One needs to be alert: the attendant may try to give you subprime cuts if you do not pay attention. The experience is surprisingly close to everyday life in Argentina. However, there are palpable differences from the original experience. The staff's accents reveal different country origins, and the conversations that flow around the meat counter among customers never touch on the routine topics that are inevitable at a butcher shop in Buenos Aires: prices, inflation, and politics. While you may forget for a minute that you are not in South Florida, the reverie is soon broken. You are in the type of replicated Latin American space that could only exist in Miami.

These adopted spaces create an environment of diversity and sociability that reinforces people's feelings of connection to the city. This is a kind of place that "makes us feel unique, in control, good about ourselves, and consistent with our subjective ideas of who we are."[10] The existence of a "lived space" that feels "authentic" plays a vital role in helping individuals integrate the surrounding environment into their identity.[11] The experience, however, is even more complex. Because these spaces are slightly different, they have the impact of alienation as well.

As we examine in detail in the next chapter, a feature of Miami is that it is often a destination for those who were defeated—by revolutions, regime change, and tyrannies in Latin America and the Caribbean—and left to seek refuge. The city serves as a place that offers relief, new allies, access to resources, and, for some, a new life. For others, it is a place to regroup and attempt to return home in the near future. The *political* character of urban life acquires in Miami this singular twist as a place of refuge for social classes and groups defeated elsewhere. This is often a central dimension of transnationalism, as immigrants quickly organize to engage in long-distance activism back home.

BEYOND TRANSIENCE: LEGACY AND TRANSLOCALITY

In a city where more than half of the population is foreign born, one could easily diagnose transience as the explanation for lack of cohesiveness. As seen in chapter 1, Jan Nijman makes this the central point of his analysis of the city. He views Miami as a brief stop on the way to some other place.[12] Nijman compares the city's transient urban culture to a hotel, with people checking in, using the facilities, and checking out: "They show little interest in their neighbors, they do not invest in social relations, they come with a sense of entitlement, and they have no stake in the future of the place. The problem is not that people are coming. It is that most of them do not intend to stay."[13]

Still, Nijman's diagnosis is misaligned. Generational change and an emerging sense of legacy among the economic elite question his assertion. A core of former immigrants and refugees is staying in Miami. As the leader of an influential foundation observed, while this core may not have identified themselves as Miamians at first, there is a good chance their children will. As we also saw in chapter 1, several prominent informants took issue with the statement that "there are no Miamians." Most of those with firmer roots in the city are members of the second generation born and raised here.

This phenomenon is most apparent in the Cuban American community, as evidenced by a dramatic change in its attitudes. For the younger generation of Cuban Americans, the relationship with Cuba is not about a desire to return to establish residence in the island but about exploring roots and identity. Their views of U.S. relations with Cuba strongly indicate that they are not interested in a confrontational stance toward the island. As of 2014, only 8 percent of Cuban Americans ages 18 to 29 favored continuing the U.S. embargo against Cuba, as compared to 45 percent of those 30 to 64 years old and 60 percent of those 65 or older.[14]

Furthermore, new initiatives such as the CubaOne Foundation—a nonprofit founded by four second-generation Cuban American philanthropists (three of whom live in Miami) modeled after Birthright Israel—seek to promote new forms of connections with Cuba. Just as Birthright pays for Jewish youths to visit Israel, CubaOne offers young Cuban Americans free trips to Cuba to "explore issues of identity and personal heritage, and to build connections with the Cuban people."[15] Survey data and our interviews in Miami—as well as the emergence of organizations such as CubaOne—show that younger Cuban Americans reject the idea that "the real Cuba" can only exist in Miami. For them, the worldview built by their parents and grandparents—who believed that the island of Cuba had to be re-created in exile through language, storytelling, food, music, culture, and, of course, political discourse and activism—is no longer a valid proposition. They can find Cuba in both Miami and through cultural ties with the island.[16]

Still, not all older Cubans view Miami as a transitory place, at least in their imaginations. Other forms of change are happening even among older generation residents—the economic elite—who came from Cuba and other countries in Latin America. There is a growing interest in building a legacy that is closely connected to Miami. There has been a particular interest in art, from the privately owned de la Cruz Contemporary Art Space in the Miami Design District to the Pérez Art Museum Miami downtown. A new group of wealthy Cuban and Hispanic entrepreneurs uses the United States instead of Latin America as a point of reference to define their core values. Philanthropy is a key one, as Hispanic millionaires are taking their cues from the philanthropic legacy of the Gilded Age industrialist Andrew Carnegie and donating fortunes to the city. This first generation of "Hispanic Carnegies" is changing the notion of loyalty, pride, and positive outlook regarding Miami.[17]

The role that translocality plays in the lives of immigrants, meaning that "home" represents more than one place, is another dimension that questions the transience thesis. Often, people live their lives in more than one country.[18] With communication technology constantly advancing, residents coming from other countries build a daily routine that includes connection in real time with their places of origin. For them, home exists in both a physical and a virtual sense. Migration cannot be reduced to a one-way flow. Rather, there is a strong element of circularity, which is expressed in transnational networks that facilitate the movement of people, ideas, goods, and money. The relationship between immigration, economic development, and transnationalism in the nascent twenty-first century has challenged traditional approaches to migration. Immigrants are likely to participate in transnational organizations, engaging in numerous back-and-forth activities.[19] Individuals can develop attachment, simultaneously, to more than one place.

Such processes transform the economy, culture, and everyday life of both sending and receiving nations. When migrants' lives transcend national borders, they challenge long-held assumptions about group membership, development, and equity. As the sociologist Peggy Levitt and others argue, using a "transnational lens" to understand migration requires leaving behind the "methodological nationalism," or the expectation that social interactions take place within the nation-state framework. Understanding transnational migration calls for a distinction between ways of being (the actual social relations that individuals engage in) and ways of belonging (practices that signal identities of connection to a group). Movement and attachment are not necessarily linear or sequential but capable of rotating back and forth.[20]

"Transience" is thus a relative term: those who participate in these networks are not actually leaving a new destination for good if they move back to their home countries. They still maintain forms of attachment—

whether economic, political, or cultural—with their previous place of residence. A community of professional expatriates can potentially have a significant developmental impact on their home country while continuing to shape their previous place of residence. In this light, the "brain drain" (from both sending and adoptive countries) can be transformed into "brain gain."[21] As Anna Lee Saxenian explains in "Brain Circulation: How High-Skilled Immigration Makes Everyone Better Off," "The long-distance networks are accelerating the globalization of labor markets and enhancing opportunities for entrepreneurship, investment, and trade both in the United States and in newly emerging regions."[22]

New immigrant entrepreneurs usually take advantage of their connections to transnational communities. Indian immigrant engineers helped build Silicon Valley by linking U.S. businesses to low-cost software expertise in India. These entrepreneurs then returned to their home countries or alternate locations as part of their role in "coordinating the information flows and providing the linguistic and cultural know-how" that creates the basis for these social and professional networks.[23] As we saw in chapter 1 and revisit again in the next chapter, the economic engines driving Miami's transformation are not flows of retirees and pleasure seekers but the rise of a diversified and committed entrepreneurial class.

The city attracts businesspeople and entrepreneurs from Latin America who utilize their existing networks in the region to build bridges between South Florida and their countries of origin. From small businesses to commercial empires, we talked with many business leaders—primarily from Latin America and the Caribbean—who took advantage of their personal contacts in Florida and their sending country to establish profitable operations, often in the export-import sector. It is not uncommon to find that permanent Miami residents with secure financial situations own a second home in their home country and/or the country with which they conduct most of their business.

FRAGMENTED SOLIDARITIES

Research has shown that the emotional connection that people establish with a place is a fundamental factor in their inclination to stay there. Not

only does attachment make people less likely to leave, but it also underscores other feelings such as commitment to the place's future and a sense
that their personal future is tied to that of their community.[24] An examination of the social fabric that sustains people's sense of belonging to
Miami is important to understanding their ambivalence between attachment and transience.

Public opinion surveys offer a comprehensive window onto the factors
that link residents to their communities and, conversely, that persuade
them to move away. The Knight Foundation commissioned the Gallup
Organization to do one such study, titled "The Soul of the Community."
The project surveyed twenty-six communities around the United States
from 2008 to 2010 and collected about 48,000 survey responses.[25]

Contrary to Nijman's argument that views transience as the defining
characteristic of Miami, the mean score for Miami's collective community
attachment was significantly higher than those for a comparison group of
cities with high urban density and large populations, namely, Detroit and
Philadelphia. The picture that emerges from the Gallup study makes two
relevant points. First, if we consider how residents of Miami feel about
their city—from a sense of pride and connectedness to the likelihood that
they would recommend the place to others—Miami performs better than
comparable cities. Key factors contributing to attachment are the area's
natural attributes and geographic location, as well as entertainment and
high levels of tolerance for immigrants and the LGBTQ community. Good
higher education is a perceived asset as well. This general sentiment is
well reflected in the remarks of the top educator cited in chapter 1: "Miami
has the feel of a place that is going to be great."

However, there are other aspects that raise concern. One is that the city
is not seen as a place with strong social ties and solidarity. Three of four
respondents said that it is not a place where people care about each other.
Less than a third of respondents thought of Miami as a good place to meet
people or were positive about the availability of social community events.
Only about 20 percent believed that the city provides a good environment
for families with young children.

Community attachment is often correlated with civic participation.[26]
Thus, we want to know how engaged in public life Miami's residents are.
Data from the Corporation for National and Community Service Programs

show that participation rates in Miami are significantly lower than the national average when it comes to such forms of engagement as attending meetings (half the national percentage) and volunteering (14 percent in the Miami metro area; 25.3 percent nationally).[27] In this last category, Miami ranks 51st among the 51 largest metropolitan statistical areas. Other studies show that volunteerism is significantly lower in Miami compared to other metro areas such as New York, Chicago, Houston, and San Diego.[28]

We can learn about people's emotional connection with a place through their desire to stay or move away.[29] We analyzed data from the survey conducted by Gallup in 2010 to understand the reasons that drove some respondents to want to leave Miami. Our analysis showed that residents want to move either out of the city or out of the state at a rate 7 percent higher than the other 26 cities surveyed. Surprisingly, we found no meaningful difference in response for the amount of time a respondent had lived in Miami. Unsurprisingly, the same factors that people found troublesome about the area—for example, whether people care about one another—had an impact on their likelihood to leave or stay.

Respondents in the Gallup study emphasized the importance of healthy social connections and quality of place for families when they considered their relationship with Miami. In their view, the city did not perform well in these areas. These results are consistent with what we know already: the area's physical beauty and weather are major draws for those who choose to live here. However, when social offerings and social openness are considered, Miami suffers. It also may be fair to say that the attractions of the place—sun, beaches, and soft weather—entice people to come. Once here, though, they are much less inclined to establish bonds with each other than in grittier northern cities.

Social relations in Miami are also shaped by profound cleavages of affluence. This is especially true for immigrants arriving to the city who are not wealthy or securely positioned in the middle class. Many testimonies from immigrants, mostly from the Caribbean, stressed that even after years of hard work their economic situation remains fragile. The promised "good life" is not quick to materialize.[30] It is difficult for poorer residents (particularly undocumented immigrants) to develop a sense of attachment when conditions of unremitting economic troubles, relentless persecution, and job insecurity force them to constantly move from one section of the city to another. The city is a paradigmatic case of a bifurcated service sector. At one end, there are the well-paid professionals in the downtown and Brickell Avenue offices of banks and multinational corporations. On the other end, there are poor immigrants, most of whom work as restaurant and hotel employees, cleaners, landscapers, and other low-paid services.[31]

There are few places in the United States where the divide between rich and poor is as stark. Income for the richest quintile of the population is twenty times that of the poorest quintile, compared to about fifteen times nationwide. The median hourly wage in Miami was more than two dollars below the national average in 2015. Miami-Dade consistently ranks near the bottom in terms of median household incomes for counties of comparable size.[32] The percentage of households that are considered middle class is considerably smaller than that for the nation as a whole, with non-Hispanic whites being significantly more likely to belong to the middle class than Hispanics and blacks.[33] This inequality poses serious challenges to the prospects of making Miami a more inclusive community.

As discussed in chapter 2, Miami's neighborhoods are largely divided by class. The well-paid knowledge workers and creative classes are concentrated along the coastline, downtown area, and affluent municipalities such as Coral Gables, while the service classes are concentrated in Hialeah and other historically disadvantaged urban areas.[34] Unsurprisingly, equality of opportunities is marred by these vast divides. As an example, the quality of public education is closely related to the socioeconomic standing of the neighborhoods where they are located. If one examines a map of Miami-Dade Public Schools, one clearly sees a clustering of schools that received an "F" performance grade in lower-income communities, with no "A" or "B" schools in the vicinity.[35] As noted earlier, only one in five respondents in the Gallup survey viewed Miami as a welcoming place for families with young children. Residents did not have a positive opinion of public schools either; more than half of respondents rated the quality of K–12 public schools as poor.

As schools across the country increasingly emphasize a technology-heavy education, the digital divide in Miami becomes more pronounced. As of 2016, 42 percent of Miami-Dade residents did not have internet access at home.[36] Students are often forced to look for free Wi-Fi hot spots in fast-food restaurants and libraries and even on the Metrorail.

For low-income residents of the city, access to affordable housing and quality health care is limited. Basic necessities and services consume a disproportionate portion of their income. These challenges hinder their ability to benefit from growth opportunities available in the area, and, consequently, they have fewer chances to move upward economically. According to Gallup, 70 percent of respondents negatively rated the availability of affordable housing in Miami. This proved to be accurate, as the percentage of "cost-burdened households," or households that spend more than 30 percent of their income on housing, is considerably higher in the city than the national average. High unemployment and foreclosures have only aggravated access to affordable housing.[37]

Health care is another basic service in need of improvement. The percentage of uninsured individuals and families, as well as the average cost of health care, strongly suggests not only subpar performance in comparison to other American cities but also a strong association between the uninsured population and key socioeconomic indicators such as income, ethnicity, educational level, and legal status.[38] An earlier study of health care and immigration in the area assumed that since most mayors and other elected officials in Miami-Dade are Cuban Americans or Hispanics, they would "influence the health delivery system and display greater sympathy toward the needs of fellow foreigners."[39] However, the study concluded that the political capital held by Cuban Americans had benefited earlier exiles and older settled immigrants but had not yet addressed the needs of more recent arrivals, many of whom are undocumented Central Americans.[40]

Overall, public opinion surveys, socioeconomic trends, and qualitative evidence for sectors at different ends of the social hierarchy suggest that Miami is a place in which transience and attachment interact in unique ways. This is a city endowed with attributes that many other metropolitan areas would yearn to have. This diverse society has already experienced a process of "acculturation in reverse," demonstrated in high levels of tolerance toward groups such as immigrants. However, the city is still lacking in various aspects that are central to building strong attachment. If we want to understand social connectivity in Miami, it is important to consider the dynamics created by people dissatisfied with certain aspects of the community but content with multiculturalism and physical attractions. These contradictory results highlight once again the character of a city in flux—highly dynamic but still lacking a sense of collective "we-ness" among its various components.

INFLUX OF YOUNG PEOPLE

Cities see their future connected to their capacity to attract and retain well-educated Millennials, and increasingly Post-Millennials (Generation Z), whose entrepreneurial spirit and technological knowledge are considered important assets to stimulating innovation and urban renewal. Enticing them—and persuading them to stay—has become a central aspiration of the most dynamic cities in the United States and around the world.

As seen in chapter 2, retirees are no longer coming in large numbers to Miami, instead preferring other Florida locations. At the same time, Miami is attracting young people—mainly 25- to 34-year-olds with a college degree—in increasingly larger numbers.[41] Cities strive to attract young talent because this kind of migration can power economic growth. These workers are needed to meet the labor demand of an innovation-based sector; they fuel the growth of new companies, and they represent a consumer market that promotes the flourishing of cultural, gastronomic, and entertainment offerings. For young, well-educated professionals, the choice of where to live and work is considered as important as selecting a partner, a career, or a lifestyle.[42] These are all aspects that are expected to deepen people's connection to an urban space.

Miami's capacity to attract young talent is very much caught between two competing trends. On the one hand, the city is an overflowing melting pot of diversity and with it, new ideas. In the past few years, Miami has seen significant growth in incubators, accelerators, and venture capital.[43] Miami's "startup density" and its growth as a center of innovation are attracting national attention. On the other hand, the city still lags behind other major metropolitan areas in terms of technological growth and output. Businesses in Miami tend to agree that they face challenges when trying to hire young people away from top companies in other U.S. cities. Only three Fortune 500 companies are located here.

The effort to attract venture capital has so far yielded limited results. Venture capital investment in Greater Miami amounts to roughly 2 percent of all U.S. venture capital investment, a number that pales in comparison to New York (8 percent) and the Bay Area (45 percent).[44] While Miami is among the top destination metropolitan areas for Latin American students seeking a higher-education degree in the United States, the city ranks among the worst for graduating foreign students in science, technology, engineering, or math.[45] Overall, while Miami-Dade County is attracting more and more young professionals, the city's workforce still lacks the educational background needed for an innovation-focused economy and high-tech-oriented industries.[46] Hence, employment is concentrated in the service and retail sectors, which are characterized by a bifurcation between high and low wages.

Furthermore, Miami lacks a core institution that other technological hubs possess: a top-tier university. The Bay Area has Stanford, Boston has MIT and Harvard, but Miami does not have an equivalent. Universities of this caliber are often crucial to attracting the talent and money necessary to developing innovation in high tech. At the same time, Miami is exceptionally poised to take advantage of "push factors" such as limited professional opportunities in specific careers and depressed wages in Latin America and the Caribbean. Still, more than just attractive lifestyle options and good weather are needed to lure and retain a skilled workforce and build a strong ecosystem that sustains innovation.[47] As we discuss in the next chapter, the engines of the city's economy are banking and finance, international trade and transportation, construction, and real estate.

Beyond economics, young residents could play a relevant role in strengthening their community through active engagement. This is important for a city such as Miami, which is marked by highly fragmented social life. Despite its low levels of civic engagement, Miami-Dade County qualifies as a place with significant potential to improve its youth engagement. A new index (2017) that measures the quantity, equality, and impact of youth civic engagement across the United States (RAYSE, Reaching All Youth Strengthens Engagement) gives Miami-Dade County a five-star rating (out of five stars).[48] A strong RAYSE rating suggests a potential for growth in youth civic life. The rating takes into account such factors as the general education of residents, quality of life, level of political competition, relative size of the youth population and its degree of participation, and nonprofit-sector presence, residential stability, and charitable giving. Once again, the delicate balance between transience and attachment emerges as a constant in Miami's identity.

ATTACHMENT AND TRANSIENCE AT THE GLOBAL EDGE

> You're asked "Where are you from" within a minute of
> meeting someone, or you're doing the asking. "Here" is never
> a valid answer.
> —"How Do You Know If You Are a Real Miamian?"
> *Miami New Times*

As illustrated by the quote above, it is difficult to define what "here" is in relation to Miami. Miami's population is split by a combination of residency and translocality that defies traditional approaches to attachment. As a place of constant circulation, it is hard to pin down where the city's reach begins and ends.[49] The contradictions that we see in Miami are representative of a fundamental tension between "the benefits of 'diversity' and the costs of heterogeneity of preferences in a diverse multiethnic society."[50] Studies have shown that a diverse ethnic context produces a healthy array of experiences, skills, and worldviews that may increase productivity and innovative outcomes. On the other hand, clashes of cultural perspectives, biases, and conflicting preferences are likely to produce results— policy outcomes, for example—that are suboptimal for such communities.[51] As the president of one of Miami's universities explained to us, Miami's "hyperfragmentation" goes hand in hand with its extraordinary diversity. To think of the city simply as a pit stop misses its complexity and unique identity.

Miami possesses the characteristics of an emerging global city, as defined by Sassen (see chapter 2). It is a city that serves as a sophisticated hub for transnational corporations, as well as a regional center in which "the formation of globalized service management nodes coexists with traditional sectors, informal and marginal economic activities, deficient urban service, poverty, unemployment, and insecurity."[52] Understanding social life in such a place requires viewing it as a node of global circulation where different actors and interests produce a continuous flow of creativity, ideas, and wealth while recirculating inequality and diverse forms of exclusion.[53]

It is tempting to argue that the profound tensions between the city shaped by property capital and the one reflected by vast inequalities make cohesiveness unthinkable in Miami. It is also tempting to say that no one really belongs to the place. However, our evidence makes it clear that the city is in constant flux and that urban life is shaped by new social ties, opportunities, cultural expressions, and an emerging but palpable sense of attachment. People do belong, though in partial and sometimes incoherent ways. The city is continuing to find its place in the hemisphere and in the world. It provides a notable example of the contradictions, challenges, and energy unleashed by relentless globalization in the twenty-first century.

Still, while the connected world of the internet and cell phones and the ease of transportation greatly facilitates the construction of transnationalism, the spatial reflections of social, economic, and political processes, as noted in chapter 1, are still fundamental to understanding urban life. The physical world where we spend our daily existence continues to play a major role in defining who we are.[54] The argument that transience is a defining element of Miami is also challenged when we consider cultural expressions in the city, especially those that manifest sentimental attachment to a neighborhood. Space and cultural production are closely linked in a reciprocal way. Cultural production, in turn, expresses and shapes community attachment.

As a leader of one of Miami's top universities said, "There are things that are unique, persistent of who we are."[55] Of course, there are traditions like Three Kings Day Parade, Miami's response to New Orleans's Mardi Gras or Boston's St. Patrick's Day. The Three Kings Day Parade shuts down traffic on the legendary Calle Ocho as Miamians celebrate the anniversary of the three wise men visiting Christ. In true Miami fashion, the parade often features the music of Pitbull.

Then there are more atypical expressions of community attachment. A perfect example is a music video parodying Lynyrd Skynyrd's ode, "Sweet Home Alabama." The updated version, created by Miami radio hosts Enrique Santos and Joe Ferrero, is devoted to Hialeah, the second largest city in the Miami metropolitan area and an epicenter of the Cuban population.[56] The song's lyrics are intentionally controversial, but they clearly express the soul of a place that many identify as home:

> Sweet home Hialeah . . .
> *Dominó, cubilete y mucho chisme*
> *Corrupción, multas y accidentes*
> *Desempleo, escándalos y celulitis*[57]

In the words of the local poet and Hialeah native Yaddyra Peralta, *Sweet Home Hialeah* references all the staples of the community.[58] The video is also filled with a vocabulary unique to Miami and particularly Hialeah, like the instruction you might get on your prescription bottle from a local drugstore: "Aplicar to face dos veces al día."[59] *Sweet Home Hialeah* is a "Miami moment" that serves as a clear example of how attachment is expressed in concrete cultural terms.[60]

Migrant communities in Miami also experience attachment through the consumption of ethnic media. Mass media targeted to diasporas shape immigrants' adaptation to the new homeland. Consuming news and entertainment in the host community in one's language and cultural approach serves important functions to migrants: development of personal relationships, growth in personal identity, and fact-finding to learn more about the new environment.[61]

Miami hosts the major Spanish-language TV and radio networks in the United States. Univision, for example, produces and broadcasts its main telenovelas and sitcoms from its Doral studios. Dozens of radio stations around Miami serve commuters, pensioners, workers, and housekeepers with national and, most important, local news and sports events in Spanish and Haitian Creole. The print media have been very important for migrant communities, too. Cubans have forged a long-term relationship of collaboration and influence with the major newspaper in town, the centennial *Miami Herald* and its Spanish-language sister publication, *El Nuevo Herald*, shaping the way that mainstream media in Miami approach U.S. foreign policy regarding the island. Still, the experience is different for other, smaller migrant communities. A recent survey of ethnic print media outlets of the Argentine, Colombian, Peruvian, and Venezuelan diasporas shows that published stories serve an informational and educative function, blending fact, opinion, and advertising by coethnics.[62]

Media catering to the Haitian community, moreover, serve a distinctive function. A study by Sallie Hughes and other scholars examines the Haitian ethnic media in the context of media production among immigrant communities in Miami.[63] In a context of predominant Spanish-language media outlets, Creole- and French-language Haitian media are a key resource that help Haitians keep informed about and participate in what is happening in Haiti. As a community member summarized it, "It's only in Miami that you can hear every day what's happening in Haiti."[64] Thus, ethnic media enjoys a dual function, supporting a transnational mind-set and lifestyle while locating immigrants in their new place and their homeland, within their particular ethnic group.

However connected to both their places of origin and their new home, migrant communities cannot escape the processes of displacement that are transforming Miami from within. As a global city, Miami cannot avoid the tensions produced by two realities: hyperethnicity and hyperconsumption. The communities that we introduced before, with their ethnic clusters of residence, production, and exchange, are threatened by gentrification and conspicuous consumption.[65] The growth machine of real estate developers and the more affluent residents and visitors is displacing the African Americans, the Haitians, the Nicaraguans, and even the Cubans. Attachment is jeopardized by skyrocketing rent prices in newly gentrified parts of the city, all of which is more severe in the context of rising seas. Some call this trend "climate gentrification."[66]

Miami illustrates in compelling ways the coexistence of extremes, dictated by both local and global features. We have examined surveys, rankings, individual and collective experiences, and other data in order to capture the complex interaction between attachment and transience in Miami. However, beyond any empirical evidence, an impromptu reflection by the playwright Tarell Alvin McCraney—who cowrote the 2016 film *Moonlight*, set in Liberty City—during a "Cities for Tomorrow" conference encapsulates the reality of Miami: "There was something unreal about the beauty that surrounded our neighborhood."[67]

McCraney's home, Liberty City, was devastated by poverty, drugs, and violence, yet to him it was beautiful for its rich cultural identity. This is a place that was wrought with intensity but in painfully jarring ways. The lows of despair and blight and the highs of community and belonging created an almost unimaginable paradox.[68] His words about Liberty City express a larger phenomenon. They aptly describe the uneasy balance of Miami.

The counterpoint between community and transience is not unique to Miami, but it takes a particular character in this city. Miami's class structure and its ethnic mosaic are two key factors that play a role in shaping the relationship between attachment and transience. Miami is fast approaching the status of a global city and, as such, has its significant share of global entrepreneurs, executives, and owners of high-end real estate. These groups have a connection to the city that is strictly temporary. Transience is also experienced by those at the other end of the class structure, whose vulnerability forces them to roam the city in search of some fleeting sense of safety. Still, at the upper echelons of society and from there to the working-class communities, we observe manifold forms of community life that express a sense of place for many residents of Miami.

This is a city in which the majority is made up of ethnic minorities, where there has been an unprecedented transformation of the political order from an Anglo elite to Cuban émigrés, and where there is a rich culture that defines the city as simultaneously American, Latin American, and global. The result is a new global city with roots at multiple locations: an exceptional "Miami Experiment" at the edge of global transformations in the twenty-first century.

4 The Economic Surge

Muggy, insect-infested swampland was a poor medium of exchange for gold, oil, dollars, steel girders and all the other things you need to build a city. So right from the beginning Miami was fated to traffic in orange blossoms.

—T. D. Allman, *Miami: City of the Future*

Liberty Square is Miami's oldest housing project, built to accommodate displaced black workers from old Overtown. On a quiet afternoon, just before New Year's Day in 2015, mothers were sorting secondhand donated clothing and children were riding bikes in the park when gunfire shattered the much-needed respite from violence. Teenage shooters in separate cars sprayed bullets seemingly at random. One driver crashed into a light pole. According to Miami's then mayor, Tomás Regalado, this was the tenth random shooting in ten days, despite a vast police presence. The violence has no apparent purpose. It is random, pent-up anger by black teenagers who turn their fury on their own neighbors. And so Liberty Square sinks even deeper into isolation and misery, feared by its own inhabitants, who cannot even benefit from charitable gifts from better-off families in their city.[1]

Not a quarter of a mile away is Wynwood, a neighborhood where, according to Regalado, "walking during the day was dangerous and at night suicidal."[2] Traditionally a neighborhood housing Puerto Rican migrants, Wynwood deteriorated steadily through the 1980s into a collection of warehouses and abandoned buildings. Only some Korean import businesses selling cheap shoes wholesale existed there. In less than a decade, however, Wynwood has been transformed by the vision of a New York entrepreneur who combined two unlikely elements to make gold: the empty, decaying walls of the warehouses and the desire of angry minority teenagers to leave their mark.

Some do it with bullets, as in Liberty Square, but many others "bless the walls" with graffiti.[3] Instead of chasing them away, the new New York owner of the warehouses let them paint. Shortly thereafter, graffiti metamorphosed into "public art." Other owners, who had previously called the police on the newly empowered street artists, now let them act. As more and more tourists came to watch their work and be photographed next to it, new bars and jazzy restaurants emerged to cater to the new traffic. Then warehouse owners, including the Koreans, began *paying* graffiti artists to decorate their walls. As Wynwood fame expanded, artists from New York, Chicago, and other northern cities came down. Everyone wanted to have their work featured in those formerly forlorn streets. Things shifted, once again, and at present reputed artists must pay local owners for the privilege of placing their own work on display for the rising masses of visitors from the world over. Wynwood now rivals Coconut Grove and even South Beach in popularity among locals and tourists. A new plaza with walls covered by stunning artworks is at the center of the neighborhood. Its main thoroughfare is, predictably, Tony Goldman Street in honor of that New York visionary.[4]

The incident at Liberty Square is not exceptional. It is sadly repeated in inner city after forlorn inner city throughout the country. The story of Wynwood is truly exceptional and raises the question, how could it have happened? How could a derelict neighborhood be transformed, in a matter of years, into a world-class artistic attraction? The answer has many facets and involves many actors, but the fundamental underlying cause is the urban environment where it took place. Wynwood could not have happened without Miami—change in one encouraging and buttressing change in the other.[5] Before Wynwood attracted tourists from Europe and Asia, it was visited by the rising number of young, educated Miamians now inhabiting downtown condominiums and estates in Coconut Grove and Coral Gables. Artists and experts attending the Art Basel Fair in Miami Beach also made their way to the former modest Puerto Rican neighborhood. Wynwood would not have happened without a rising global city as a backdrop. In turn, Wynwood reinforced Regalado's observation that art is now big business in Miami.[6]

ORIGINS OF THE CHANGE

From time to time in the early twentieth century, one South Florida leader or another peered at the map and noted the obvious location of Miami, outward to the Caribbean and South America and at midpoint between key cities there and those of the U.S. North. The Miami Chamber of Commerce even drew concentric circles around the city to highlight its possible role as the "center of the hemisphere" and "Capital of the Americas."[7] But it was all hype; in reality, the city lived off its weather. Those orange blossoms that had first attracted Flagler and then brought the rich and famous to his hotels aboard his railroad later appealed to northerners of more modest means. They checked into beach hotels for a few days to escape the brutal northern winters, marveling at the greenery and the mildness of the climate. In due time, they made plans to retire there. By the 1950s, fulfilling Carl Fisher's worst fears, Miami Beach had become a city of Jewish retirees, its art deco hotels decaying in unison with its inhabitants.[8]

Retirees no longer come in such numbers to Miami-Dade. The rate of growth of the population 65 and over is slowing down. Of the three counties comprising South Florida, only Monroe County (the Florida Keys) reports a steady flow of retirees. As a result, the population of Miami-Dade is now younger than that of its neighbors. Its average age was 38.2 in 2010, compared to 46.4 in the Keys and 40.7 in the state of Florida as a whole. International migrants, most of them of working age (21–50), have replaced retirees as the main contributors to population growth in the city. That change both reflects and fuels the economic transformation of the area.[9] Young newcomers may not have as much money as retirees, but they come with plenty of energy and the American dream firmly implanted in their minds.

WHAT LED TO THE SURGE?

There are three fundamental causes that led Miami to pull ahead of other cities as the entrepôt of the Americas. The first is geography. Yet, as noted previously, the city was not born to serve as a commercial center but as place of refuge from winter. As late as the 1970s, the predominant business was the seasonal "snowbirds" and permanent retirees from the Northeast, Midwest, and Canada. The City of Miami, meanwhile, engaged in halfhearted efforts to attract labor-intensive garment manufacturing as a way to complement tourism and employ the black minority. Everyday life in the city and the scope of vision of its leaders remained exclusively domestic; practically no one looked South, much less East.[10]

The potential inherent in the city's geographic location had to be activated somehow, and the main factors were the other two causes of the transformation. The massive arrival of displaced Cuban elites had far-reaching consequences that could not have been foreseen in the 1960s and 1970s. At that time, locals in Miami regarded the exodus from Cuba with annoyance or bemusement—just another episode in the never-ending political fights of those Latins down South. If the Bay of Pigs invasion in 1961 had been successful, as the entire world expected, those early exiles would have returned to Cuba and the episode would have been closed. But the indecision and timidity of the Kennedy administration led to the failure of the invasion and, as a predictable consequence, the entrapment of the upper- and middle-class Cuban population in South Florida.[11]

Deprived of the option of return, these classes had to look for economic alternatives, and that they did with remarkable skill and energy. Cuban entrepreneurs activated their contacts in the United States and Latin America and marshalled their resources to create new firms. At first, these fledging enterprises served only their coethnics, but soon enough they started to engage in trade with the Caribbean and South America. The story of how the Cuban entrepreneurial enclave was created has been told often before. The important point here is that those early exiles began to reorient the economy of the city away from tourism from the North and toward trade with the South and East.[12] The meaning and significance of the word *Miami,* as it gradually became the center of intercontinental trade and, subsequently, of finance steadily gained an edge over competing southern cities. Cuban exile enterprises went from a few dozen in the early 1960s to literally thousands by the 1980s. These entrepreneurs could communicate easily with firms and businessmen throughout the hemisphere and, in the process, call attention to the fact that trade and financial transactions could now be conducted in Spanish in Miami and that, by dint of its diverse population, the city was increasingly cosmopolitan.

The third factor involved large transnational corporations and banks taking notice of these developments. The increasingly obvious advantages of Miami for these firms had three aspects: first, the privileged geographic location; second, the presence of an educated and fluently bilingual labor force, also an outgrowth of the Cuban exodus; and third, and of particular importance to banks, the fact that flight capital and investments from Latin America were increasingly attracted to this city because of its bilingual and cosmopolitan character.[13] Later we trace the evolution of the banking and real estate sectors in the metropolitan area. For now, the crucial point is that the role of the Cuban Revolution in activating the dormant economic potential of Miami represents, arguably, the most important unanticipated consequence of that event. As noted in chapter 1, the trauma and upheavals of political instability to the south paid off handsomely and long term for the city by Biscayne Bay.

The privileged geographic location of Miami had other, less palatable consequences. While the processes outlined above—consolidation of the Cuban enclave economy, its expansion outward, and the discovery of Miami by banks and multinationals—were taking place, much less desirable enterprises were making the same discovery. Close proximity to the Caribbean and the northern coast of South America made it the logical place for the transshipment of cocaine from Colombia and the laundering of cocaine proceeds back to that country. In the 1970s and until the mid-1980s, Miami had the dubious honor of becoming the drug capital of the nation. In the early 1980s, it was claimed that the value of drug sales and money laundering reached $10 billion, or four times the total legal trade between Florida and Latin America.[14]

Those were the years in which bank tellers in Miami received tens of thousands of dollars in deposits in the form of $20 bills packed tightly in paper bags. Area banks received so much money that they started charging a fee just to take in the deposits. In 1982, the surplus of South Florida banks (the difference between what they took in as deposits and what they lent) reached an estimated $8 billion, more than the combined surplus of all other banks in the United States. One nonbank, the World Finance Corporation, was nicknamed "Miami's Giant Drug Laundromat."[15] These money waves inevitably triggered a rise in violent crime, which turned the city into one of the most dangerous places in the country if not the world.

These were the days of *Miami Vice,* when "cocaine cowboys" moved openly and rival drug gangs battled each other in the streets. Eventually, the federal government reacted, appointing a South Florida Drug Task Force led by then vice president, George H. W. Bush. The U.S. Coast Guard, often in cooperation with its Cuban counterpart, began to effectively block the smugglers' air and sea routes into Florida. Banking regulations were tightened, preventing the indiscriminate acceptance of deposits.[16] As a result of these actions, the core of the drug trade eventually moved away from Florida to more hospitable Central American and Mexican routes. Many local banks in Miami that had thrived on cocaine money went under or had to drastically reduce their operations. Their names read like a Who's Who of area banking in the early 1980s: Great American Bank, Bank of Miami, Sunshine Bank, and Popular Bank and Trust Company.[17]

As Nijman accurately notes, not all the economic effects of the drug days in South Florida were negative. Not all hot money could be shipped back to Colombia, so much of it had to be invested locally. Lacking an industrial base, the logical investment outlets were luxury housing construction and tourist establishments. During the late 1970s and early 1980s, an estimated $1.5 billion of illegal money was laundered every year through real estate investments.[18] These investments, in turn, fueled a construction boom throughout the metropolitan area. Thanks to the illegal trade, Miami's construction industry became recession-proof. Up to 20 percent of new luxury apartments and houses were purchased in cash.[19]

Added to other traumatic events at the time, such as the Mariel exodus of 1980, the convergence of the drug traffic and money laundering reinforced dark premonitions about the future of the place. These were not only the days of *Miami Vice,* but the time when prominent national media, such as *Time,* pronounced the area "Paradise Lost" and anticipated its conversion into a pariah city.[20] It did not happen that way, because the other positive forces converging on the area eventually gained the upper hand. Clearly, drug trafficking and money laundering still exist in South Florida, but they represent a pale reflection of what they once were. While street crime is still present, as discussed in the next chapter, it is concentrated in low-income areas isolated from the urban core and tourist centers. Global trade and finances have taken firm hold of the place, turning Miami into one of its most dynamic hubs worldwide.

OVERALL TRENDS

According to the U.S. Bureau of Economic Analysis, the Miami-Dade County gross regional product in 2012 was $124 billion, having increased from $40.4 billion in 1982 and $50.9 billion in 1992. The region's own planning organization is much more optimistic, putting the gross domestic product (GDP) of the area at $175 billion in 2014, which represents 25 percent of the figure for the entire state of Florida, that, in turn, is the fourth largest U.S. state economy.[21] Throughout the 1960s, the tallest building in town was the twenty-eight-story courthouse; by 2010, there were fifty skyscrapers exceeding that height, forty-one built during the preceding ten years. The total number of high-rises built during that decade was larger than the combined total for the preceding forty years. The tallest buildings exceeded seventy stories.[22]

The motors of the regional economy are wholesale trade, transportation, real estate, finance and insurance, and health care. Together, these sectors accounted for almost half (48.3 percent) of the regional economy by the second decade of this century. By contrast the accommodation and food services industry, traditionally associated with tourism, represented just 6 percent of the metropolitan economy. An emerging high-tech sector offers promise of transforming the city into a center of technological innovation. So far, however, and for reasons examined in the previous chapter, this is still a distant prospect relative to other sectors. The most important are examined in detail next.

TRADE AND TRANSPORTATION

Miami's strategic geographic location finds practical application in two major engines of growth: the port and the airport. In 2012, the total volume of international trade (imports and exports) reached $125 billion, or more than double the total trade value in 2004 ($54 billion). In the same year, over 8 million tons of cargo passed through Port Miami. By 2015, the port was offering super post-Panamax gantry cranes capable of handling cargo ships up to twenty-two containers wide. Deep dredging of its ocean-going channel and technological innovations have made Port Miami the

Table 2 U.S. Airports Ranked by International Freight

Airport	Freight (in millions of tons)
Miami International (MIA)	1.82
Los Angeles International (LAX)	1.10
New York Kennedy (JFK)	1.06
Chicago O'Hare (ORD)	0.93
Hartsfield Atlanta International (ATL)	0.41
Dallas–Fort Worth International (DFW)	0.33

SOURCE: Miami-Dade Aviation Department, Miami International Airport Cargo Hub, 2014.

only logistical hub south of Virginia capable of handling fully laden post-Panamax vessels. These came into service after the completed expansion of the Panama Canal in 2016. By 2017, Port Miami was receiving six super post-Panamax vessels per week; only New York was in the same league.[23]

A new fast-access tunnel now connects the port with the U.S. interstate highway system. In addition, on-dock intermodal rail service in partnership with Florida East Coast Railway links the port directly with 70 percent of the U.S. population. Last, Port Miami is now the cruise capital of the world, hosting more cruise ships than any other location. In 2012, more than 4 million passengers traveled to Miami to embark on their dream vacation. The second largest cruise port in the world is just twenty-five miles north, in Fort Lauderdale.[24] Port Everglades, also just north of Miami, is also second in trade cargo. Together, the two South Florida ports currently account for over half of Florida's total seaport trade value.[25]

The annual freight trade at Miami International Airport (MIA) is equivalent at present to 96 percent of total air exports and imports for Florida. In terms of international freight tonnage, MIA ranks ninth in the world and is the only U.S. airport ranked among the top ten (table 2). Naturally, MIA's top trade partners are overwhelmingly Latin American countries. Brazil ranks first, with 19 percent of total air trade value. Of the top ten countries only two are nonhemispheric—Switzerland and China.[26] As shown in map 3, Colombia ranks first in terms of air tonnage, followed by Chile and Brazil. In terms of all perishable goods, such as flowers and agricultural products, MIA accounts for 71 percent of total U.S. imports,

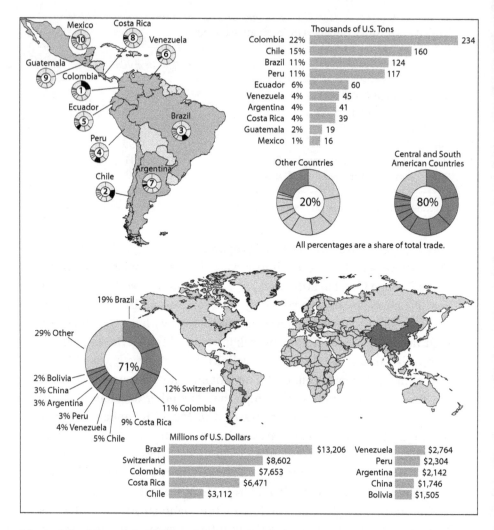

Map 3. Miami International Airport's Top Foreign Trade Partners, 2012. Miami-Dade Metropolitan Planning Organization, "Miami-Dade Compendium of Transportation: Facts and Trends Report," July 2014.

followed at a distance by John F. Kennedy Airport in New York (11.4 percent). Total air freight value in 2017 jumped 8 percent from the prior year, to $45.8 billion.[27]

In addition to sea and air transport, Miami-Dade Transit (MDT) operates the Metrorail, which, as of 2015, was the only heavy-rail commuter passenger system in Florida. The 72-mile Tri-Rail line extends from Palm Beach County through Fort Lauderdale and as far as Miami's international airport. Current plans are to extend the Tri-Rail to 82 miles—from Jupiter in the north to downtown Miami.[28] Another massive rail project, All Aboard Florida, will provide high-speed transport from Orlando to Miami, linking the two largest tourist hubs in the state. The aim is to capture fares for some half billion people a year across the corridor and to be complemented by new housing developments in the downtowns of all the in-between cities that it will serve. Completion is expected in 2018.[29]

REAL ESTATE AND CONSTRUCTION

Demand for new housing is propelled in Miami-Dade by two powerful forces. The first is steady population growth; the second, international investors and temporal residents from South America, Europe, and Asia. As seen previously, continuous political instability in Latin America prompts the wealthier classes to transfer capital and invest elsewhere. A logical place to do so is Miami, given its proximity, fine climate and quality of life, and the rule of law. A goal for many members of the middle and upper classes in Latin America is to own property in Miami; to a lesser extent, the same social classes in Russia and other parts of the former Soviet Union have started leaning in Miami's direction.[30]

In 2012, real estate and construction contributed $25.2 billion to the metropolitan economy, representing 23 percent of the nongovernmental regional product. Between 2000 and 2010, the housing stock grew by 24 percent, ranking first among large metropolitan areas nationwide. Still, housing prices remained moderate, which added to the attractiveness of the area for foreign investors. In 2012, the median price for a single family home was $187,238 and for a condominium apartment $146,221. These prices represent a considerable drop from pre–Great Recession levels in 2007 when single homes averaged $377,842 and condominiums $271,983. With economic recovery, housing prices are expected to increase steadily to prerecession levels. Indeed, by 2015, median house prices had reached $247,500 and median apartment prices $197,500.[31]

The investment opportunities offered by Miami real estate were not lost on foreign investors. According to the Miami Association of Realtors, Brazil topped the list of nations using its website portal, Miami.com, in 2014 and 2015. Brazilians also spent the most on Miami-Dade properties, with a median average price of $495,000, compared to $245,000 for all foreign buyers in the same year.[32]

The Case-Shiller Index Price for new home purchases was up 8.7 percent in the first quarter of 2015, year on year. This marked the thirteenth consecutive quarter increase, with the average rise being 10.2 percent.[33] Further construction and real estate growth at present are marked by several mega-projects, including the new "Green City Miami" in the southwest quadrant of the county. When finished, Green City will add 1,400 new homes, 1.36 million square feet of retail, 475,000 square feet for government and education, and 660 hotel rooms. A second such development is the Buena Vista Yards project, planned to revitalize a poor section of midtown Miami through the new Shops at Midtown and the construction of 3,000 lofts and 350 apartment units at an estimated cost of $1.2 billion. Green City is funded entirely by private investors; Buena Vista is a new joint venture between the City of Miami, Dade County, and private interests.[34]

BANKING AND FINANCE

> The exodus from Cuba continued with Operation Peter Pan.
> Approximately, 14,000 children were sent by their parents to
> the United States to escape communist Cuba. . . . Many of
> these "Peter Pan children" are today's successful community
> leaders, bankers, businessmen, and local, state, and national
> representatives. Some of the Florida International Banking
> Association's presidents were Peter Pan children.
> —Marcos A. Kerbel and Richard Westland, *Leading the Way*

The history of modern banking in South Florida can be traced to two key events: the establishment of a branch of Citizens and Southern Bank of Atlanta in Miami in 1969; and the arrival of Felix H. Reyler, a Cuban attorney and judge, as an exile in Miami in 1968. The Georgia branch was the first Edge bank created in South Florida. The Edge Act of 1919, named after New Jersey senator Walter Edge, allowed U.S. banks to establish subsidiaries in other states to engage exclusively in international business. That South Florida had to wait until 1969 to see the creation of the first such bank gives an idea of how provincial things were at that time.[35]

International business and banking took a decisive turn upward after that, and Felix Reyler was at the forefront of the movement. Hired first at Mercantile Bank, he created its first personal banking department specializing in Latin American clients. He then moved to Pan American Bank, assuming the leadership of its international division and traveling extensively to Colombia, Venezuela, and other countries promoting Miami as the place to do business in Spanish in the United States. Until then, wealthy Latin Americans had to travel to New York, where transactions were conducted in English with distant bank officials. Those wanting to establish accounts or invest in U.S. properties had no other way to do this. Reyler and his associates set up to change the situation. They established correspondent bank partnerships in Central and South America, allowing customers to open accounts in Miami without the need to leave their home countries. For those willing and able to make the journey, personal banking departments also proliferated.[36]

By 1981, Miami had a total of thirty-three Edge banks, more than any other city in the United States. By 1984, the number had grown to forty-three, again more than in New York, Chicago, or Los Angeles.[37] In addition to Edge banks and the new international departments of domestic banks, there was a third decisive development that altered the local financial scene. In 1976, Florida leaders realized that the State of Georgia was about to pass legislation that would give it a major competitive advantage in attracting international banking firms. To counter that threat, legislation was introduced to allow foreign banks to establish branches in Florida. Fearing competition from large foreign multinationals, many local bankers opposed the bill at first, and it failed that year. Felix Reyler and the Florida Bankers Association, led then by Michael Weintraub, came to the rescue. Their philosophy was that as more banks entered Florida, the state would become an international finance center attracting even more business and more investment.[38]

These efforts proved successful. In 1977, the Florida legislature passed and Governor Reubin Askew signed the Florida International Banking Act. It allowed foreign banks to establish offices in the state to serve U.S. subsidiaries of their home country corporations and assist their home clients with businesses in the United States. Eventually they were allowed to accept deposits from nonresident aliens. In the same year, Askew led a mission to Europe to entice foreign banks to come to Florida. Israel's Discount Bank became the first to receive a license under the new act. It was promptly followed by Bank Leumi, also of Israel, Bank of Nova Scotia (Canada), Standard Chartered (U.K.), and Lloyds Bank (U.K.).[39]

At Pan American Bank, Reyler and his associates supplemented this effort by persuading the correspondent banks in Latin America to also establish branches in Miami. By 1984, there were forty-five foreign banks with offices in the city, complementing the forty-three Edge banks from elsewhere in the United States, plus local firms. Miami had become an international banking center in less than fifteen years.[40]

By that time, Citizens of Dade United, a nativist organization, had succeeded in passing a county ordinance that prohibited "the expenditure of County funds for the purpose of utilizing any language other than English or any culture other than that of the United States."[41] These local reactionaries were clueless about the future, for Miami's rise to global status relied precisely on its skilled bilingual workforce and its character as a polyglot, multicultural city. The efforts of nativists to set back the clock of history were easily defeated. In less than ten years, the anti-bilingual ordinance had been repealed and its sponsors forced out of office by the newly empowered Cuban American electorate.[42]

A much bigger threat to the consolidation of South Florida as a financial center came from the South in the form of Colombian drugs and easy money. Drug dealers took advantage of the proliferation of international bank offices to concentrate their money laundering operations in the city. For a while at least, as Nijman noted, Miami's international business machine "kicked on cocaine."[43] It took the decisive efforts of a federal task force aided in no small measure by leaders of the Florida International Bankers Association (FIBA) to counter this threat. FIBA took steps to expel banks engaged in money laundering and actively supported new legislation at the federal level to counter illegal practices. These took the form of the Money Laundering Control Act of 1986, to which the USA Patriot Act of 2001 added a plethora of new controls and regulations.[44]

Eventually, the threat of narcotics subsided, although it never entirely disappeared. As seen previously, the flood of illegal drug money in the early 1980s did have some positive consequences for the local economy in the form of a strong stimulus to the real estate and construction industries. In due time, the dynamics of the global economy took over, displacing illegal laundering with much larger trade and financial enterprises. Edge banks established by such major corporations as Bank of America, Citibank, Chase Manhattan, and Bank of Boston came to Miami in the early 1980s in hopes of not only profiting from international transactions but also eventually entering the lucrative Florida domestic market. Finally, in 1997, banks from throughout the United States were allowed to enter Florida through the acquisition of locally based banks.

This legislation changed the local bank scene: Edge banks gradually declined in number, to be replaced by new "domestic" banks. By 2014, only four Edge banks remained, in contrast to seventy-one domestic ones and thirty-four foreign-owned branches. Their concentration in the Brickell Avenue area turned it into the largest banking center on the East Coast south of New York City. By the second decade of the twenty-first century, it was contributing $10 billion per year to the local economy and, in association with related sectors such as insurance and real estate, represented about one-fourth of the gross regional product.[45] Miami could not match San Francisco or Austin as a high-tech entrepôt; however, its economic dynamism was firmly grounded in geography and in an international finance sector initiated, in large measure, by exiled Cubans.

Felix Reyler was arguably the most prominent but not the only Cuban American banker to contribute to this transformation. Others included José Ramón Garrigó, also of Pan American Bank; Eduardo Benes, of Sun Trust; Sergio Masvidal, first head of the Irving Trust Edge branch; Gonzalo Valdés-Fauli, of Bankers' Trust; and Luis Botifoll and Aristide Sastre, of Republic National Bank.[46] These and others formed a core of highly skilled and internationally oriented entrepreneurs who made the difference in converting Miami into the financial hub of the hemisphere. Had they arrived in Tampa or New Orleans, the story would have been very different. The Cuban revolutionaries who expelled these people would have had gold in their hands had they made use of their talents to transform the island; instead, that transformation took place just north in a city that until the Revolution had served mainly, as the opening quote noted, as a place to grow orange blossoms in winter.

CONCLUSION

> In the United States, we have a clear monument to what
> Cubans can accomplish. It's called Miami.
> —President Barack Obama, speech in Havana, March 22, 2016

Maurice Ferré, mayor of Miami from 1973 to 1985, was one of the visionaries who played a leading role in the economic transformation that we have just chronicled. Commenting on the efforts of Citizens of Dade United to return the city to its monocultural and monolingual past, he wisely noted that those people had no clue about the future. Ferré was mayor in the midst of the battles with cocaine gangs and drug launderers, but he saw beyond that time and traveled often to Latin America to advertise Miami's economic renaissance. The scion of an upper-class Puerto Rican family, Ferré tried twice to gain reelection as Miami's mayor, but by the early 1990s, the Cuban American political machine had kicked in and no one of non-Cuban extraction had a chance at a major electoral office.[47]

Now, at the age of eighty-three, he is not bitter about these defeats and remains a keen observer of the city's transformation. He still lives in Miami. For Ferré, one of the most important changes taking place in the city in the past quarter of a century is the "Americanization of the Cubans" and the parallel Latinization of the white, non-Hispanic population. A good portion of this population is Jewish, and they have struck a tacit alliance with Cuban American elites, a pattern also noted by several other informants.

For Ferré, Miami politics is still ethnic rather than class based, but it is increasingly fragmented as new contingents of other Latin Americans and even Europeans make their presence felt. The Cuban hold on electoral politics is bound to weaken with the Americanization of the second generation. In unison with other local observers, Ferré believes that "no one really rules Miami" at present and that the proliferation of economic and political power centers is an indication of both the city's increasingly global character and its fragmentation.

The interview with Maurice Ferré took place in his elegantly appointed office in Coral Gables. One mile east, hundreds of tourists were preparing to board cruise ships for their dream vacations; two miles farther, South Beach was preparing for another night of mayhem in the midst of Spring Break. Turn west, however, and you would promptly find the site of another bout of teenage killings in Liberty City, accompanied by still another plea by the embattled public school superintendent to stop the violence. While Miami's economic engines churn on, its marginalized minorities shoot at and steal from each other in a desperate bid to cope with poverty and growing inequality. This is the other face of this history of urban transformation and progress; its causes and its effects are reviewed next.

The Miami Metropolis

A VISUAL OVERVIEW

Photographs by Zeinab Kristen Chatila

Plate 1. Downtown Miami.

Plate 2. The American Airlines Arena; in the background, Freedom Tower, a museum to Cuban exiles, built as a replica of the Giralda Tower of Seville and originally the headquarters of the *Miami News*.

Plate 3. The Pérez Art Museum Miami (PAMM); in the background, the One Thousand Museum Tower (under construction). Designed by the Iranian architect Zaha Hadid, it is the first exoskeleton building in Florida.

Plate 4. The Miami Beach shoreline; in the background, Biscayne Bay.

Plate 5. The Miami Marlins baseball stadium. The bond required to build it nearly bankrupted the city and led to the recall referendum of then Miami mayor, Carlos Alvarez.

Plate 6. The Hermita de la Caridad del Cobre Church. Built with the contributions of Cuban exiles, it sits on Biscayne Bay facing toward Cuba.

Plate 7. The Holocaust memorial, a monument in Miami Beach, the most Jewish community on a per capita basis in Florida.

Plate 8. The Carl Fisher Memorial, honoring Miami Beach's founder. The caption under the bust reads, "He Built a City out of a Jungle." Perhaps as retribution for his anti-Semitic leanings, the memorial sits in an out-of-the-way and seldom-visited park.

Plate 9. The Eternal Flame in honor of the fallen at the Bay of Pigs, S.W. 8th Street, Little Havana. The caption reads, "To the Martyrs of the Assault Brigade 2506. April 17, 1961."

Plate 10. Entrance to Domino Park, Little Havana, U.S.A.

Plate 11. Domino Park scene.

Plate 12. Brickell City Center Mall, completed in 2017, is the largest and fanciest commercial center in the city.

Plate 13. The Brickell Bank District.

Plate 14. The Ziff Opera House.

Plate 15. Opa-Locka City Hall. The arabesque building is heavily deteriorated and closed to the public.

Plates 16 and 17. Opa-Locka scenes.

Plate 18. Coral Gables City Hall, built in the neoclassical style with heavy use of the coral stone commonly found in South Florida.

Plate 19. Residential mansion in Coral Gables housing the Consulate of Spain.

Plates 20 and 21. Residential mansions in the Alhambra Circle, Coral Gables.

Plate 22. Caribbean Marketplace in Little Haiti.

Plate 23. Monument to Toussaint L'Ouverture, leader of the Haitian Independence Revolt, in Little Haiti.

Plate 24. El Yambo Nicaraguan restaurant in Little Havana.

Plate 25. Plaque in honor of fallen members of the Nicaraguan National Guard at El Yambo Restaurant.

Plate 26. The "Miracle Mile," Coral Gables's answer to Chicago's Magnificent Mile.

Plate 27. Florida International University.

Plates 28–30. Miami traffic scenes.

5 Crime and Victimization in Miami

In the opening chapter of his *Great American City*, Robert Sampson invites us to take a stroll with him through the city of Chicago. It starts at the "Magnificent Mile"—a district with skyscrapers, banks, high-end boutiques and department stores, and the famed Water Tower, among other landmarks. Then it moves south down Michigan Avenue toward Millennium Park fronting Lake Michigan with the buildings of the Loop as background. So far, everything is attractive, energetic, and brilliant, featuring an array of dazzling modern buildings not found anywhere else in the country. Then, south of the Loop, the scene changes dramatically. Down Michigan Avenue at 37th Street, Sampson shows us collapsing buildings, streets with broken glass, and no one to be seen except some furtive passersby. Then there is a wide, empty extension of land, not really a park, with a few black men huddled around a fire against the winter cold.[1]

Only a few years ago, this empty land was the collection of buildings known as the Robert Taylor Homes, a gigantic social engineering project where the city of Chicago attempted to warehouse its poor. Lack of maintenance and other factors made things so bad that this project had to be torn down: each of its twenty-eight sixteen-story high-rises was imploded with dynamite. Sampson continues his walk, surely relieved to reach Hyde

Park, home of the University of Chicago and a vital intellectual community. This sense of relief is short-lived, however, as he leaves Hyde Park for the struggling neighborhood next to it, around Washington Park: "Along the major thoroughfare of Garfield Boulevard stand burned buildings, gated liquor stores, and empty lots[,] . . . the inverse of Michigan Avenue north of the Loop; here we find empty spaces permeated by a sense of dread."[2]

We leave Sampson to continue his melancholy stroll around the vast poverty of Chicago's South Side, punctuated here and there by surviving but struggling black middle-class communities. What his walk demonstrates, among other things, is a point made nearly a century ago by another Chicago sociologist, Robert Park—that crossing a single avenue or park takes you into an entirely different world and that this urban "patchwork quilt" of wealthy and secure neighborhoods next to forlorn misery is, to most observers, incomprehensible.[3]

In Miami, you could not imitate Sampson's exercise. There are, to be sure, certain walks that one can rehearse: up and down Collins Avenue in Miami Beach; along "Miracle Mile," Coral Gables's answer to Chicago's Magnificent Mile; or due west on S.W. 8th Street along the interminable blocks of Little Havana. But none of them would transport you abruptly from one social world into another. For this, you need a car. Like other new cities in the American South and West, Miami is not as compact as Chicago or the former industrial cities of the Eastern Seaboard. Instead, it uses space to render inequality and abject poverty invisible or nearly invisible. Since Flagler's day, the city's growth machine has taken care that Miami's outward appearance does not resemble that of Chicago or Cleveland.

So we need a car and a map to drive deliberately to the other side of Miami's glitter. We also have to be careful: a wrong turn on the interstate can land you in the midst of Overtown, still a dangerous area. Driving deliberately into Liberty City brings you straight into Liberty Square at 12th Avenue and 67th Street, where gang encounters and random shootings have become an almost daily occurrence.

In this chapter, we look at urban crime as the flipside of globalization and economic progress. Crime is not homogeneous; there are several distinct types, each with its own etiology and consequences. Homicide, for example, is related to but emerges from causal configurations different from those leading to property theft or money laundering. Below we review leading theories of urban crime in order to develop a framework into which our empirical findings can be fitted and understood.

THEORIES OF URBAN CRIME

Structural Interpretations

Arguably, the best known theory of criminal deviance is Robert Merton's typology in his classic essay, "Social Structure and Anomie."[4] Written more than seventy years ago, the essay places the causes of deviance at the individual level, in the gap between cultural desirable ends and legitimate means to attain them. While desirable ends, such as cars, fashionable clothing, and elegant homes are wanted by almost everyone, the means to attain them are scarce and not within the reach of many. The logical consequence is a search for alternative paths to attain these goals. "Innovators" is the label that Merton applies to those who follow this course.[5] Criminals of the most varied types fall under this rubric.

This simple, "by hook or by crook" theory is subject to a number of caveats. First, desirable goals and the strategies to attain them may vary greatly. This variation gives rise to a typology of different types of deviance, as discussed shortly. Second, searching for deviant means to achieve desirable ends is not the only path available to enterprising individuals; other paths are legitimate inventions and innovations and even rejection of the goals of a consumerist society and embracement of alternative life ends (Merton labels followers of this path "rebels").[6]

Third, and most important, opportunities for innovative behavior, including deviance, are contingent on the social context in which one finds oneself. Institutions of the state and social controls created and enforced by communities set limits on what isolated individuals can do. Social disorganization theory, almost as well established as Merton's, holds that the main structural reasons for crime lie not with the individual but with the community: loss of social controls—brought about by residential instability, a weak presence of state institutions, and other causes— is what gives individuals the opportunity to engage in deviant behaviors of various kinds. "Broken windows," a modern version of classic social disorganization theory, argues that not only purposeful "entrepreneurial" deviance is rife in disorganized communities; other forms of criminal behavior, including irrational impulsive violence, can become common.[7]

Unlike organized "rational" deviance such as that fostered by Mafia families, youth gangs often engage in shoot-outs with one another motivated by alleged slights and personal rivalries that have little to do with the attainment, by systematic means, of wealth and power. Indeed, these seemingly random shootings by gang members have become more terrifying to the average citizen than the "normal" activities of established crime syndicates.

Exceptional instances exist of communities that are not disorganized but organized on values, norms, and social hierarchies at variance with those of mainstream society and, hence, likely to foster various forms of deviance. Immigrant communities in advanced countries have often been at the forefront of such instances. Irish immigrants in Boston and New York, for example, gave rise to well-organized crime syndicates engaged in various sorts of illegal activities—from protection rackets to bootlegging at the time of Prohibition. Italian migrants followed suit, importing from Sicily and other southern regions organized crime groups such as the Mafia.[8] Chinatowns have long been known for hosting various forms of illegal gambling, as well as other prohibited services such as prostitution.[9]

Thus social organization, as well as social disorganization, can foster deviance. The key lies, as we will see next, in the values and norms sustained by different types of communities. For the common citizenry, disorganized violence in the form of random shootings and the seemingly inexplicable murder of children and teenagers in the streets is what comes to mind when one talks about urban crime. But other forms do exist.

Cultural Interpretations

A different family of theories focuses less on gaps between means and ends and structural opportunities for deviance than on the culture predominant in different communities. Culture consists of the complex of values, norms, and behavioral repertoires held by particular collectivities and transmitted to new members via the socialization process. Mainstream culture upholds values, norms, and behaviors deemed right and necessary for the survival of society and normal, peaceful interactions among its members. Along with it, different types of deviant subcultures can exist. The concept of deviant subculture is different from that of social disorganization because it does not imply disorder but rather order patterned along different lines and organized by norms and behavioral repertoires contrary to those of mainstream society.

The anthropologist Oscar Lewis became famous (and simultaneously infamous) by advancing the concept "subculture of poverty."[10] According to this view, urban poverty is a self-reproducing consequence of values and behaviors at variance with those of middle-class society that prevented the poor from breaking out of poverty. The concept was promptly attacked as "blaming the poor" to the neglect of the structural barriers arraigned against them by lack of employment opportunities and spatial segregation.[11] Along similar lines, Daniel Patrick Moynihan argued passionately that the racial configuration of American cities and a "tangle of pathologies" kept slum dwellers, overwhelmingly black Americans, in their subordinate and marginal place generation after generation.[12]

Moynihan's argument was also attacked as a blame-the-victims approach. However, Moynihan was careful to point to the concatenation of historical developments leading to the tangle of pathologies confronting inner-city residents. "Three centuries of injustice," he wrote, "have brought about deep-seated structural distortions in the life of the Negro American. . . . [T]he cycle can be broken only if these distortions are set right."[13]

There is no question that deviant subcultures exist and that they tend to be associated with specific patches of urban territory. However, the question is where these subcultures come from. In the case of domestic minorities, specifically black Americans, they come, as Moynihan emphasized, from a history of discrimination and disadvantage, severely constraining the chances for economic, residential, and upward status mobility of those so labeled. In the case of some immigrant groups, they arise from collective efforts to bypass and overcome the structural disadvantages associated with foreignness and lack of opportunities in the host society.[14]

Put in other words, *culture devolves from structure.* Situations of advantage and disadvantage, of opportunities and lack of access to them give rise to adaptational behaviors that, in time, become crystallized into norms and eventually values. What originally were contingent responses to specific situational constraints become normative—"the thing to do" and, ultimately, "what ought to be done." At that point, deviant patterns, as described by Lewis's "subculture of poverty" or Moynihan's "tangle of pathologies," take over, becoming explanatory mechanisms on their own.

A TYPOLOGY OF DEVIANCE

ANOMIC CRIME

> For the first night since February, children were playing outside the Blue Lake Village apartments, a cluster of three-story yellow buildings in Miami Gardens where 6-year-old King Carter was killed in front of a playground. . . . [T]hen on Monday, gunfire erupted again. Kids fled again. A woman was shot in the head and a man in the shoulder.[15]

The apparent cause of the new incident was a fight over a boyfriend. The aggrieved woman grabbed a knife and slashed the tire of her rival's car; then she shot her and the boyfriend. Santonio Carter, the father of the boy killed in February 2016, had been organizing a movement called Save Our Kings, a grassroots attempt to stop random violence in this corner of Miami Gardens. According to the *Miami Herald,* the community lost 35 children and teens to gunfire in 2015. In the past decade, 335 teens and children have been assassinated in the area by guns.[16] The new shootings on May 9, 2016, were the last straw for Santonio Carter; he packed up his family and left Blue Lake. He is still keen on promoting Save Our Kings and organizing street marches for the cause but from somewhere safer in the city.[17]

The dire situation at Blue Lake Village serves as a suitable introduction to the different types of crime coexisting today in metropolitan Miami. Not all of them follow the rational entrepreneurial path anticipated by Merton's structuralist model; they seem to reflect more closely Moynihan's "tangle of pathologies." At the bottom of the crime hierarchy, we find random violence that does not yield any material benefit. People are hurt or killed out of petty rivalries or by having the misfortune, like little King Carter, to be in the wrong place at the wrong time when three youths, ages eighteen, seventeen, and sixteen, opened fire at a perceived rival over a feud that had been taking place on Facebook.[18]

On April 25, 2016, another five people were struck by random gunfire near Liberty Square in Miami. The attack was similar to repeated ones in the same neighborhood during the previous years. In June 2014, only ten blocks away, nine people were shot and two killed; the attackers were never caught. In June 2016, Tremelle Raymond Sr. had two of his sons, ages 16 and 18, ambushed and killed by gunfire and his other two children, ages 11 and 13, wounded. Raymond Sr. had planned to move out of Liberty City because "too many children were getting shot" over what family members called "foolishness"; but he was unable to do so before unidentified attackers killed two of his children in what, he speculated, was retaliation for something as trivial as a disagreement at school.[19]

This kind of violence is what fills the urban citizenry with horror. It has two characteristics in common: it is consistently committed by adolescent and young minority males; and it is concentrated in poor, mostly black neighborhoods where the "pathologies" originally described by Moynihan are most evident.[20] In Miami, the police have succeeded in encircling this type of crime, concentrating it in certain identifiable areas. The average resident of Coral Gables, Brickell Avenue, or Miami Beach sees these incidents in the evening news but is never confronted directly with them.

This first type of crime may be labeled "anomic," because it stems from the breakdown of the normative order restraining violence against others and because it has no evident rational purpose, yielding no material benefit to the perpetrators. When interviewed by police, more than one teenage perpetrator of random murder have responded that they did it to see what it was like to kill someone.

This kind of crime may be contrasted usefully with the protection rackets organized by ethnic mafias in the past, where local merchants were shaken down for protection money to the benefit of gang leaders. That type of "business" organized in the past by Italian, Irish, and Chinese syndicates in cities like Boston, New York, and San Francisco is not visible in Miami. At the bottom of the crime hierarchy in this city, purposeful violence has largely disappeared.

PETTY ENTREPRENEURIAL CRIME. On the next rung of the crime hierarchy are activities deliberately committed for gain on a small scale and without individual victims. The complex set of grassroots transactions known as the "informal economy" belongs here. They involve the nonviolent provision of goods and services that avoid taxation and other legal rules. The principal "victim" of such crimes is the state, although participants can also be defrauded because of the absence of formal protections against deceit and malfeasance. This vast category includes such activities as the street sale of contraband goods, unlicensed house construction and home repairs, unregulated medical and dental practices, and domestic work paid in cash.[21]

In the absence of formal protections, trust grounded in social networks within the community is the sole guarantor against guile and deceit in these informal transactions. Without it, buyers of contraband goods might easily find themselves with worthless or even dangerous items such as food and drugs bought under the table, and day laborers may be cheated of all or part of their pay. Only common social bonds provide a measure of protection against these and multiple other violations of expectations in the informal economy.[22]

In Miami, a vast informal sector exists in working-class areas such as Hialeah, Little Havana, and Homestead. These areas are populated by the same minorities—mostly of various Hispanic nationalities—and a common ethnic bond provides the necessary minimum trust to make informal exchanges possible. Transactions of all kinds without receipts or sales taxes are an integral part of daily life in these poorer communities.[23] Wealthier areas are not exempt from informal activities, usually involving the provision of goods and services for cash. Domestic service is the most common; but construction, home repairs, gardening and landscaping, and unregulated care of children and the elderly are also widespread. Nevertheless, informal transactions are clearly subordinate to the regulated formal economy in middle- and upper-class neighborhoods.

Another type of activity also classifiable under the same category of grassroots crime involves more direct and serious violations of formal rules. For example, a May 11, 2016, article in the *Miami New Times* reported:

> Opa-Locka-Hialeah Fruit and Produce Market didn't just sell fruits and vegetables. Instead, owners allegedly used their produce stands to bilk the government out of $2.4 million. . . . The US attorney for the Southern District of Florida said . . . these owners were among 22 people charged in "Operation Stampede," organized to bust business owners . . . who allowed customers to use their government-issued EBT food stamps card as a means

to get cash, in exchange for a cut. In total, there were more than 13 million dollars in fraudulent food stamp transactions from markets throughout South Florida, the largest food-stamp take-down in US history.[24]

The article goes on to name a long list of busted business owners, almost all of them with Hispanic names. It is worth noting that these are "victimless" crimes insofar as buyers and sellers agree to the transaction. The only victim is the state or, at least, the federal food stamps program that is supposed to provide food assistance, not cash, to needy recipients. Note also the location of the first police bust under Operation Stampede: the Opa-Locka-Hialeah Market, right between the two minority cities. One can well surmise what goes on in the place: Cuban small traders from Hialeah boost their income by servicing the needs of inhabitants of the nearby slum, mostly African Americans.[25] The business logic of these transactions accords with Merton's structuralist theory of deviance: recourse to illicit means in order to gain access to desirable cultural ends. Modest produce-stall owners in Hialeah can thus be seen driving late-model cars, frequenting expensive restaurants, and even owning small yachts, courtesy of the generosity of Uncle Sam diverted to their own purposes.

PROPERTY CRIME. The previous type of "victimless" crime contrasts markedly with those that are the bread and butter of police work, namely, the taking of other people's property, with or without violence. "Larceny" is a common-law term developed by the royal courts of England in the seventeenth century to denote theft in nonviolent face-to-face encounters. It differs from robbery, which involves some measure of violence. When a deadly weapon is used or the victim suffers injuries, the robbery becomes "aggravated assault." Finally, burglary, like larceny, involves the taking of others' property via surreptitious entry into private residences or places of business, without personal violence. Auto thefts can be classified as a particular form of burglary.[26]

All of these activities are committed by single individuals or by gangs. The latter may be pickpockets or purse snatchers or organized bands of bank robbers. The intent is always the same: to gain by illicit means what cannot be gotten by legal ones by depriving others of their property. However, the level of rational planning required for that purpose varies widely. In 2015 in Miami-Dade County, a total of 116,311 crimes were reported by police. The crime rate was 4,383 per 100,000 inhabitants, representing a significant decline (6.8 percent) from the prior year.

By far, larceny (nonviolent personal theft) was the most common crime, numbering 76,400 cases in 2015, followed by burglary, at 14,534 cases. Hence, the two forms of nonviolent thefts accounted for over 90,000 cases, or about four-fifths of all reported crimes. Motor vehicle theft, a specific form of burglary, numbered 8,800 cases. The three forms combined represented 86 percent of the total. By contrast, violent theft, including robbery and aggravated assault, numbered 15,304, or about 13 percent. Nonentrepreneurial crime, including forcible rape, accounted for the remaining one percent.[27]

With the exception of motor vehicle theft, the total number of property crimes in Miami-Dade County has declined steadily in recent years, a pattern that corresponds to that for Florida as a whole. Thus, the crime rate in Miami-Dade dropped by almost 1,000 cases per 100,000 population between 2012 and 2015.[28] When pitted against the enforcement resources of the state, the ability of individuals to victimize others to appropriate their wealth appears increasingly limited. Naturally, major variations exist across the metropolitan area, both in absolute numbers and in trends over time.

In Opa-Locka, which has a population of 17,528, there were 105 robberies and 279 cases of aggravated assault in 2015; the corresponding figures in Coral Gables, whose population is almost three times as large, were one and zero, respectively. The crime index in Florida City, a predominantly poor African American municipality south of the metropolitan area, reached a remarkable 12,029 per 100,000, or more than four times the figure in Hispanic Hialeah and three times that in wealthy Bal Harbour and Coral Gables. Violent thefts are concentrated in the same areas as anomic violence. Thus, Liberty City, a relatively small area in the city of Miami, reported 349 charges for violent crimes, or about 18 percent of the total for the entire metropolitan area; the figure for Miami Gardens was 473, or 24 percent.[29]

These results do not mean that other areas in the metropolitan area are crime-free but rather that illegal activities adopt forms other than violent property theft. Hence, Hialeah with a crime rate of just 2,720 per 100,000 in 2015, is known as a hub for informal economic transactions and fraudulent schemes of the sort described previously. This may be reflected in the gap between arrests for violent thefts in this municipality, just 252 in 2015, and the total number of arrests for all illegal activities, 7,950.[30] Moynihan's "tangle of pathologies" is clearly more closely associated with violent crime, random or purposeful, than with more rational forms of deviance. The latter do not take place only in working-class Hispanic areas; they occur in wealthier parts of town as well.

MIDLEVEL ENTREPRENEURIAL CRIME. Exchanging food stamps for cash is a simple, basic level of fraud, but other, more complex schemes are found higher up in the crime hierarchy.

> Angel Castillo, a high school dropout, pleaded guilty . . . to running eight medical equipment companies under others' names and submitting more than $48 million in false claims to Medicare. . . . While his bogus businesses raked in about $8 million in 2006–07, he personally pocketed more than $2 million. "A lot of people are getting into this business," Castillo said. "You see it as white collar. There's not a lot of risk." Fraudulent medical equipment suppliers use patients' Medicare number without permission. In effect, they steal the patients' Medicare IDs. . . . In a new congressional report, investigators said Medicare paid an estimated $92 million to medical equipment providers that improperly used the identification numbers of 18,240 dead doctors in Miami and other major cities between 2000 and 2007. Many are still listed as active Medicare physicians, even though they died 10 to 15 years ago.[31]

> In September, a trio of FBI agents showed up at a Hialeah dental office looking for Pedro Torres. Torres slipped away before they could arrest him[,] . . . a suspected mastermind of a ten-chain pharmacy ring that bilked Medicare for millions; he escaped to Cuba along with three other members of his organization. Authorities say they pulled off the multimillion-dollar racket by forging doctors' signatures for medication that was either unnecessary or not provided. Medicare and private insurers failed to detect the fraud after paying out millions. "Unfortunately, South Florida remains ground zero for this type of scams," said William Maddalena, assistant special agent in charge of the FBI Miami office.[32]

Many other examples can be cited. This type of crime is also "victimless" and, for that reason, seldom appears in police statistics, which focus on personal theft and violent crimes. This higher level of illegality involves much greater knowledge of the operation of federal and state social programs and a much more complex set of operations designed to defraud them. Setting up fake medical equipment firms or pharmacies requires a certain level of start-up money, knowledge of the billing process, and a network of trusted associates. Illegal entrepreneurship of this sort is ingenious and complex, not within the reach of everyone.

Another relevant example is the laundering of cocaine trade proceeds in order to pay Colombian drug suppliers. The years when Miami was the drug capital of the Americas are mercifully past, but it still remains a center for transactions involving proceeds from the trade. Colombian drug cartels generally want to be paid in pesos, which is the currency in which they operate. Several ingenious schemes have been devised to change dollars into pesos. One involves a network of confederates who deposit cash proceeds from street sales into dozens of U.S. bank accounts. The deposits are made gradually, and for relatively small sums each time, to avoid raising suspicion.

Legitimate Colombian businesses selling electronics, sound equipment, TV sets, and the like place their orders with Miami exporters, who commonly have their warehouses in Hialeah. When one such order arrives, exporters arrange the legal shipment of goods to Colombia and receive payment in the form of wires from the multiple bank accounts fed by street drug sales. Colombian merchants receiving the imported goods then turn around and pay the equivalent value to designated representatives of the drug cartels, which thus receive their profits laundered and in pesos.[33]

The networks of people involved and the levels of trust required in such operations are usually cemented by a shared history and group solidarity. Recent Cuban refugees have frequently been involved in Medicare and insurance fraud schemes. While earlier waves of upper- and middle-class Cuban exiles were at the forefront of Miami's economic renaissance, as seen in chapter 4, recent arrivals come from more modest social and economic backgrounds. Born and raised under a Communist regime and an economy of scarcity, they were schooled to survive in ingenious ways. The Cuban expression *resolver*, meaning "to solve economic difficulties in any way possible," stems from that permanent context of scarcity.[34]

Recent refugees have translated this expertise to address the challenges of economic survival and progress in the United States. While most do so legally, others resort to informal business activities, just as they did in Cuba, or even to elaborate fraudulent schemes. The relative ease with which some of these gangs manipulate the Medicare system may be related to their experience in dealing with the omnipresent Communist state on the island. That experience also creates the basis for solidarity among recent arrivals and, hence, mutual trust as they organize complex operations directed against federal agencies.

Hialeah, where many recent refugees settle, is an ideal place for such ventures given its dominant Cuban population and long experience with the informal economy. Doing business "under the table" is common in Hialeah, and while most of these transactions are relatively innocent, involving home repairs and otherwise legal goods and services, they set the groundwork for more serious violations.[35] Defrauding the state through various schemes is one such practice. Several known "Medicare millionaires"—successful fraudsters—have escaped to Cuba and are currently living there, and well, courtesy of U.S. federal largesse. The frequency of such scams is the prime reason that recent Cuban refugees have acquired a negative reputation, even among their earlier compatriots. The increasing social and economic distance between both sectors of the Cuban community, discussed in the next chapter, is directly related to the proliferation of these forms of crime.

HIGH-STATUS CRIME. The wealthy areas of the city, downtown, along Brickell Avenue, and in the "condominium canyons" of Miami Beach, are commonly the scene of more complex and ever more ingenious forms of crime involving millions of dollars. The flipside of Miami as the place of refuge for legitimate wealth escaping political instability in Latin America is that it plays the same role for corrupt politicians and businesspeople in the region, as well as in Russia and elsewhere in Eastern Europe.

High-level criminality in Miami generally involves the laundering of money from corrupt or illegal practices elsewhere and its use, once transformed into legal capital, for local investments. Thus, Paulo Octávio Alves Pereira, former governor of the city of Brasilia, after being indicted for corrupt dealings at home, approached a law firm in Miami for help getting his money out of Brazil. The Miami lawyers then contacted a specialized enterprise, the Panamanian firm Mossack Fonseca, which creates offshore companies in places like the British Virgin Islands where company owners can remain anonymous. The Miami law firm subsequently created a Florida company legally owned by the offshore enterprise. It then bought several million-dollar apartments in Miami Beach and Coral Gables with money transferred by the offshore. The Brazilian investor now owns these properties through a Florida company owned by the anonymous Virgin Islands firm. The money is now properly laundered, and when these properties are sold the flow of capital reverses, eventually ending in the Brazilian's pockets as "clean" profit.[36]

A still more complex scheme involved Giuseppe Donaldo Nicosia, a shady Italian businessman with ties to former Italian prime minister Silvio Belusconi. Nicosia is now accused of masterminding a $48 million tax fraud in the United States. One of his plans involved setting up a network of offshore shell companies through the same Panamanian firm, Mossack Fonseca, and the Miami law firm Roca González. One of the offshores, called Darion Trading, established a branch in Delaware, where the identity of owners can remain opaque. The Delaware company then bought Nicosia's New York apartment for $2 million. The money, wired by Darion Trading, was deposited by the Delaware outfit, called Amadocia, in Nicosia's bank account. In effect, he sold the apartment to himself and, in the process, established a paper trail that legalized the $2 million. The money could then enter the legal banking system for further investment.[37]

These schemes, involving foreign banking firms, exclusive law offices, and developers specializing in multimillion-dollar properties are not possible for the common criminal. They seldom appear in police statistics since they tend to escape the reach of local law enforcement. Federal agencies, such as the FBI and the IRS, are the only ones capable of tracing the complex paper trails of these operations. Federal officials pursuing these cases are not pitted against common criminals but highly trained lawyers and banking professionals.

High-level criminal enterprise partially disconfirms Merton's structural theory of deviance because the perpetrators are not poor individuals deprived of the means of acquiring culturally desirable goods. For the most part, such goods are within reach of these people, but they want still more. Their aim is to legitimize gains from political corruption, drug trafficking, and the like such that this capital confers on them the opportunity to engage in consumption of luxury goods and a high-status lifestyle. Thorstein Veblen's concept of conspicuous consumption comes to our assistance here. What corrupt politicians, top drug dealers, and shady businessmen want is not to escape poverty—they did so long ago—but to gain social prominence and legitimacy. Theirs can be labeled "status crimes." If they can get away with them, they and their families will figure prominently on the social register and move easily within the circles of the rich and powerful locally and nationally. If the FBI or the IRS catches up with them, they will end up disgraced and perhaps in prison. But, for such types, the prize is worth the risks. Wealthy areas of Miami and Miami Beach are full of these status aspirants.[38]

CONCLUSION

The typology of urban crime, summarized in table 3, is applicable not just to Miami, but to every major American city. It has been developed here for two reasons: First, to highlight the fact that not all urban crime occurs at street level or involves personal victims. Second, to note the physical association between different forms of crime and locations in urban space. As noted in the first chapter, urban phenomena are, first and foremost, spatial and crime is no exception. Sampson's walk through the streets of Chicago, at the start of this chapter, illustrates this dimension, as well as the major differences than can exist between one neighborhood and the next. However, that exercise fails to note that other wealthier areas of town are not crime-free. They are sites for different forms of crime—more complex, apparently "victimless," but at times more insidious than the street varieties.

Table 4 presents the most recent available data, at the time of writing, on crime levels in Miami-Dade and its principal municipalities. The table illustrates the overall decline in street crime levels during recent years, as well as the significant differences across areas of the metropolis. In contrast to Chicago and other major U.S. cities, Miami is unique in three respects. The first is the overwhelming presence of an immigrant, mostly Hispanic population, which, as noted in chapter 2, has become the effective "mainstream" of the city. The second is the recency and internal

Table 3   A Typology of Urban Crime

Type	Examples	Location
1. Anomic violence	Random street killings	Ghetto and poor urban areas
2. Petty entrepreneurial	Street selling and informal transactions (e.g., food stamps for cash)	Immigrant enclaves
3. Crimes against property	Larceny, robbery, burglary, aggravated assault, auto theft	Ghetto areas, other poor and working-class neighborhoods
4. Midlevel entrepreneurial	Medicare fraud, identity theft, petty money laundering	Immigrant enclaves and working-class neighborhoods
5. High-level entrepreneurial	Corruption, tax fraud, large-scale money laundering	Downtown government offices and businesses, luxury residential areas

diversity of that foreign population, which conspires against a sense of collective "we-ness." In this environment, social cohesion and social networks tend to be limited to migrants of the same nationality and cohort who share a sense of common history.

The third is the transience of most of the city's economic elite. With the exception of old-style Cuban bankers and established Jewish businesspeople, most of the wealthy and powerful in elite areas are relatively recent arrivals who come and go according to their economic fortunes. Many use the city as a repository for capital and assets at peril elsewhere or as a place to make a quick profit in real estate or the tourist industry. Despite the growth of a stable population with firm roots in the city, mostly the children and grandchildren of earlier refugees and immigrants, transience continues to be a trademark of a good part of the population of South Florida.[39]

In such an environment, it is understandable why, instead of violent street crime, fraudulent schemes, tax evasion, and money laundering flourish. Many of those involved in these activities see nothing intrinsically wrong with them. They are, after all, victimless activities whose main

Table 4 Crime in the Miami-Dade Metropolitan Area, 2013–2015

Annual Report	Year	Population	Total Crime	Percent Change 2014–15	Murder	Rape	Robbery	Aggravated Assault[a]	Burglary	Larceny	Motor Vehicle Theft	Crime Rate/ 100,000	Percent Change 2014–15	Percent Cleared
Miami-Dade County	2013	2,582,375	127,034		229	813	3,370	9,827	18,935	82,528	8,332	4,919.3		18.3
	2014	2,613,692	122,943		212	801	5,706	10,183	17,115	80,448	8,478	4,703.8		18.4
	2015	2,653,934	116,311	−5.4	217	756	5,366	10,238	14,534	76,400	8,800	4,382.6	−6.8	18.4
Municipalities														
Miami-Dade Police Dept.	2015	1,160,457	43,093	−5	86	379	1,661	4,053	5,380	28,314	3,223	3,713.7	−6.1	19.9
Coral Gables Police Dept.	2015	49,397	1,748	−15.3	1	11	22	41	219	1,371	83	3,538.7	−16.3	19.3
Hialeah Police Dept.	2015	233,053	6,341	−13.4	7	30	265	465	680	4,174	720	2,720.8	−14.3	16.8
Homestead Police Dept.	2015	69,533	3,567	−6.7	7	39	312	535	600	1,911	163	5,129.9	−10.7	22.0
Miami Police Dept.	2015	439,509	23,601	−5.1	75	80	1,681	2,637	3,109	13,721	2,298	5,369.9	−7.6	13.6
Miami Beach Police Dept.	2015	91,714	10,000	−3.1	2	54	418	524	698	7,680	624	10,903.5	−3.2	13.8
North Miami Beach Police Dept.	2015	43,533	1,950	−2.1	5	16	112	156	323	1,191	147	4,479.4	−2.7	8.6

(continued)

Table 4 Continued

Annual Report	Year	Population	Total Crime	Percent Change 2014–15	Murder	Rape	Robbery	Aggravated Assault[a]	Burglary	Larceny	Motor Vehicle Theft	Crime Rate/ 100,000	Percent Change 2014–15	Percent Cleared
Doral Police Dept.	2015	55,600	2,126	–0.7	0	7	10	65	151	1,782	111	3,819.6	–5.7	35.1
Opa-Locka Police Dept.	2015	17,528	1,416	–9.6	6	5	105	279	268	649	104	8,078.5	–13.0	16.9
Hialeah Gardens Police Dept.	2015	23,004	814	–8.6	2	4	13	25	80	625	65	3,529.5	–10.4	42.5
North Miami Gardens Police Dept.	2015	62,380	3,107	–8.2	5	35	169	277	477	1,887	257	4,980.8	–8.8	15.2
Sweetwater Police Dept.	2015	20,793	898	30.1	0	0	10	29	54	757	48	4,318.8	–27.3	33.4

SOURCE: Florida Department of Law Enforcement, 2016 Crime in Florida, 2015 Florida Uniform Crime Report. FDLE, Tallahassee.
a. Includes figures for the metropolitan area and for municipalities of at least 15,000 population.

target is the state. Law enforcement finds it difficult to identify and prosecute mid- and higher-level criminals in this setting, given relationships of "complicity," especially if they belong to the same nationality and historical cohort. Miami's growth machine—its property capitalists—while not directly involved in Medicare fraud or money laundering—has often depended on the success of such activities for the sale of its buildings.

Luxury condominiums and palatial estates have become favorite investments for the wealthy of other countries, whether bringing legitimate capital to Miami or not. As seen in this chapter, such investments are also favorite vehicles for money laundering. Cash purchases of expensive properties in Miami Beach or Coral Gables by shell companies are a common occurrence, as is the frequent sale and resale of such properties for profit or as a means to launder money. The sparkling buildings along Biscayne Bay and the Miami Beach skyline are simultaneously the product of the city's rapid ascendance in the global economy and of a shadier side that it has not managed to leave behind. The dual character of the "Magic City" is well reflected in its reputation in Latin America and the rest of the world, as shown in a later chapter. While anomic ghetto violence is largely the same everywhere, the unique mix of types of crime in South Florida is a direct consequence of the history of the area and a reflection of its character as a fragmented global city.

6 A Bifurcated Enclave*

THE ECONOMIC EVOLUTION OF THE CUBAN
AND CUBAN AMERICAN POPULATION OF MIAMI

Of all the major ethnic groups making up metropolitan Miami's population, Cubans have pride of place, not only because of their demographic
dominance, but also because they played a pivotal role in the area's economic and social transformation. As seen in previous chapters, the earlier
waves were the builders of the enclave that gave their children and later
arrivals a decisive platform for entrepreneurial ascent. Subsequently, they
were central to Miami's entry into the global scene by building up the city's
international banking sector and attracting capital and investments, first
from Latin America and then worldwide.

But all is not well with the Cuban "success story," as it was labeled in the
1970s by the early leaders of the enclave. Beginning in the 1980s, things
took a rather different turn for the Cuban population of the United States.
By 2010, its average income had descended below that of other Latin
American groups and its poverty rate exceeded by a significant margin the
national average. The decisive turn of events took place around the Mariel

* This chapter is a revised version of a keynote address delivered at the IX Conference of
Cuban and Cuban American Studies, University of Miami, May 2013. An earlier version of
this chapter was published in *Cuban Studies* 43 (2015). Earlier version coauthored with
Aaron Puhrmann.

exodus of 1980 and its aftermath. A disagreement with the Peruvian government that year led the Castro regime to remove the police guard around the Peruvian embassy in Havana. In a matter of days, the embassy grounds became overcrowded by hundreds of Cubans desperate to escape their grim lives on the island. The spectacle of the human wave in and around the embassy was broadcast around the world, proving highly embarrassing to the Cuban regime. True to form, Fidel Castro did not negotiate or apologize but changed the rules of the game. The Cuban government announced that it would ready the port of Mariel, west of Havana, so that all Cuban exiles in the United States who wished to come and retrieve their families from the island would be able to do so.[1]

Wishing to rescue their families from communism, dozens of exiles in Miami and elsewhere bought or rented boats and set out for Mariel harbor. But then Castro played another of the political tricks for which he became justly famous. In lieu of relatives, many boat owners were forced to take onboard common criminals, mental patients, and others that the regime deemed "undesirable." The spectacle of the Mariel flotilla bringing to Florida boatload after boatload of such people made a deep impression on American public opinion. While the majority of Mariel refugees were legitimate relatives of those who came to fetch them, the minority who arrived straight from jails and mental hospitals stigmatized the exodus. In Miami, their arrival led to near-chaos, with a quantum rise in robberies, burglaries, and assaults.[2] Cuban refugees who until that time had been portrayed by the U.S. media as a model minority and the "builders of modern Miami" instantly became one of the most unpopular and undesirable groups in the nation. Newspapers as far north as Columbus, Ohio, spoke of "Mariel criminals" coming north in droves and wreaking havoc.[3]

In reality, disorder in Miami streets lasted only a short time, as the federal government stepped in and moved Mariel refugees to military installations away from South Florida. But the damage was done. The Mariel episode produced two lasting consequences. First, it shifted the mode of incorporation of new Cuban arrivals in the United States from positive to negative. President Jimmy Carter's declaration that the United States would continue to receive all new Cuban escapees "with open arms" represented the last gasp of the previous policy of an unrestricted, tolerant U.S. government stance. Realities on the ground proved too much, and the official attitude shifted to denying Mariel arrivals permanent settlement. Instead, a new and more ominous legal category was invented for them: "entrants, status pending."[4]

Second, the abrupt change in its public image led the old exile community to also shift its stance—from welcoming the new arrivals to creating distance from them. The derogatory term, *marielito*, made its appearance about that time.[5] For displaced pre-Revolution Cuban elites whose sole source of comfort in exile had been their cozy relationship with Washington and the welcoming attitude of the American public, the stigma brought about by Mariel was intolerable. The successful anti-Spanish-language referendum held in Miami-Dade County following the Mariel episode became the last straw. These events marked the beginnings of the bifurcation of the Cuban expatriate population into two distinct communities, with significant consequences for its economic and political future.

The reaction of the old Cuban upper and middle classes to the anti-bilingual referendum and the stigma of Mariel took two forms: a political shift from an exclusive concern with overthrowing the Castro regime to domestic mobilization in self-defense; and a parallel closing of the networks of the enclave to the new arrivals. Following the events of 1980, Cuban exile businesspeople who had believed themselves integrated into the Anglo mainstream in Miami began to withdraw from its organizations and create ethnic associations. The Mesa Redonda, Facts about Cuban Exiles (FACE), and the Cuban-American National Foundation (CANF) were founded around that time. Plans were made to run candidates for local office. More important, and as discussed in chapter 1, a new discourse began to emerge that portrayed the exile community itself as the solution to Miami's problems and the vehicle for a positive transformation of the city.[6]

The new refugees, settling mainly in working-class Hialeah and impoverished sections of Miami, were not the beneficiaries of the networks of solidarity that had allowed earlier exiles to find jobs in Cuban enclave firms, move ahead, and eventually become entrepreneurs themselves. The "character loans" that had given earlier Cuban businesspeople access to start-up funds solely on the basis of their known reputation in Cuba were unavailable to the new arrivals.[7] Other forms of coethnic solidarity were also withdrawn. From the viewpoint of earlier and better established exiles, Mariel and post-Mariel refugees were different: raised under the Revolution, they lacked the work ethic and the principled anti-Communist political stance of their predecessors. They could not be trusted. According to a Cuban American social worker of the time, the "quality" of Cuban refugees who arrived in the 1960s and 1970s was very different from those who came in 1980: "About one-third of the 125,000 Marielitos are trash—delinquents, homosexuals. Their effects on Miami have been terrible."[8]

If Mariel had been an isolated episode, perhaps its consequences would have dissipated over time. But it was not. Cubans kept escaping from the island by whatever means possible. Most of them eventually reached Miami, where they were met with the same unwelcoming attitude inflicted on Mariel arrivals. The reasons for the continuous influx had to do with the failure of the U.S. government to repeal the Cuban Adjustment Act, a relic of the Cold War that granted near-automatic asylum to any Cuban arriving in the United States and put him or her on a path to acquiring U.S. permanent residence in just two years (eventually shortened to one).[9]

Failure to repeal the Cuban Adjustment Act and the closure of the enclave's networks to newcomers worked at cross-purposes. On the one hand, the act functioned as a siren call for more Cubans to escape the island; on the other, once in the United States, Cubans were deprived of the forms of assistance that had allowed earlier arrivals to succeed economically and socially. Older exiles tended to paint new arrivals with the Mariel colors. The latter did not come to join the fight against the Castro regime but to take advantage of the economic opportunities offered by the United States in order to support their families back in Cuba. Regular remittances to relatives and frequent return trips to the island characterized these new arrivals; they were not, therefore, political refugees but economic migrants, on a par with other impoverished Latin American groups.[10]

The Cuban population of Miami became divided into two distinct blocs: older Cubans, the creators of the business enclave and their American-born children, on the one hand, and Mariel and post-Mariel arrivals and their offspring, on the other. Like all urban phenomena, this bifurcation had a spatial dimension. The homes of the old Cuban bourgeoisie and their children are mostly in Coral Gables, Kendall, Pinecrest, and other high-income areas of the city; Mariel and post-Mariel arrivals cluster in Hialeah, Little Havana, and other working-class cities and neighborhoods.

Post-1980 arrivals also tried their hand at entrepreneurship, exhibiting high rates of self-employment.[11] However, the economic payoff of their businesses was disappointing for two reasons: the continuous outflow of remittances to families on the island drained capital resources when they were most needed for business start-ups, and the new enterprises lacked support from more established Cuban firms and banks that regarded post-Mariel Cubans as no different from other immigrants. Economic returns to Cuban enterprises after 1980 declined, and many new arrivals had to avail themselves of jobs in the informal economy. Under-the-table trade practices thus came to flourish in Hialeah and other areas where Cuban recent arrivals concentrated, further tarnishing their reputation.

This bifurcation took place silently and without major confrontations between the two Cuban communities. The Cuban Adjustment Act had been seen as a badge of pride among earlier exiles, singling them out as privileged allies of the United States in the global struggle against communism and making them the only foreign group with ready legal access to American shores. Until very recently, the Cuban American political leadership refrained from attacking the Cuban Adjustment Act, despite its perceived abuse by new arrivals, because of its symbolic value to the older community.[12]

For their part, Mariel and post-Mariel arrivals were decidedly nonconfrontational toward their wealthier compatriots. Arguably, the experience of growing up under a totalitarian regime instilled in this population an aversion to politics, leading them to concentrate on rebuilding their lives and supporting their relatives back on the island. In effect, they became a silent majority, ceding political representation of the community to the older exiles and their offspring. This silent and growing population also added demographic heft to the Cuban community while benefiting established enclave firms—banks, insurance offices, supermarkets, and drugstores—by steadily expanding their consumer base. Without this growing population, Cuban and other Latin-oriented stores and firms would have steadily lost their market as older exiles died off and their children acculturated to American ways.

Thus, a tacit agreement developed between the two segments of the Cuban community of Miami: older exiles and their offspring were able to consolidate their political and economic hold on the city, and the mass of post-Mariel refugees expanded the labor force and the Latin market. At election time, Mariel and post-Mariel Cubans who had become U.S. citizens lent support to their coethnics, although they have also shown a marked preference for candidates advocating a less confrontational stance toward Cuba.[13]

TRANSNATIONALISM: RESCINDED, REBORN, RESURGENT

The historical ties between Cuba and the United States were effectively eliminated with the advent of Fidel Castro's Revolution. Thereafter, only a few brave souls dared to go back after being granted asylum in the United States. It was, in novelist Heberto Padilla's words, a "world in black and white," where the confrontation between the revolutionaries and the old Cuban upper and middle classes left little space for dialogue, much less for regular visits.[14] In subsequent years, extremists on both sides of the Strait of Florida tacitly supported each other, as the Cuban revolutionaries based their claim for political legitimacy on their struggle against Yankee imperialism and the "Miami mafia" and older exiles consolidated their political hold on Miami on the basis of intransigent anticommunism.[15]

With the advent of new communications and transportation technologies, other immigrant groups proceeded to build dense transnational networks with their home countries. They transferred economic resources, know-how, and cultural innovations and received, in turn, the affection of kin and local communities and, eventually, the recognition of their home states. Cubans were different. The exiles of the 1960s and 1970s would not partake of these practices, and those who dared break ranks were ostracized if not physically attacked. Cuban transnationalism was effectively rescinded.

The aftermath of Mariel started to transform this situation because the new refugees saw their departure as an economic strategy on behalf of their kin on the island rather than as principled opposition to the Revolution under which they had been raised. Militant anticommunism declined, and family solidarity took its place. Discreetly, the new refugees found ways to send money and goods to their families and friends and to return to the island frequently to enjoy the recognition garnered by their generosity. Their outlook and behavior did not differ much from that of other Third World immigrants. With time and growing numbers, Cuban transnationalism was reborn. It emerged, however, in a bifurcated context in which the older, richer, and more politically connected segment of the community strongly disapproved of these practices.

Until 2017, the U.S. government tacitly collaborated in the reemergence of Cuban transnationalism in various ways. First, it did not repeal the Cuban Adjustment Act and continued to grant Cubans who set foot on American shores quasi-automatic asylum. Second, it did not pursue vigorously those who returned to the island or the commercial agencies that organized these trips. Even at the height of more restrictive regulations during the second Bush administration, post-Mariel refugees continued to send remittances home and travel there via third countries. Penalties for doing so were exceptional and were all but eliminated by the Obama administration. The effect of these policies was to allow, unwittingly or not, the emergence of a new dense traffic across the Strait of Florida and a growing dependence of Cuban families and local communities on the generosity of their kin abroad.[16]

The next phase of this saga began when the Cuban government gained full consciousness of what was taking place and began to actively promote rather than just allow departures. For years, it had been selling the services of Cuban doctors, physical education instructors, and musicians to other countries. The idea, however, that the mass of refugees abroad, especially in the United States, could become a significant economic resource took hold only gradually. This new phase culminated in the decision of the Cuban government in 2014 to grant passports to anyone wishing to leave the country and to extend the period of legal residence abroad to two years, not coincidentally about the time it would take a newly minted Cuban refugee to gain legal permanent residence in the United States.[17]

The arrangements that facilitated the continuation of the Cuban inflow came to an end only in January 2017, when the departing Obama administration put an end to the near-automatic acceptance of Cubans arriving in the United States under the "wet foot, dry foot" policy.[18] The end of this policy, which was presented by the Obama administration as part of its effort to normalize relations with Cuba, put would-be Cuban asylum seekers in the same position as asylum seekers from other countries. Although the Cuban Adjustment Act was not repealed, the end of the wet foot, dry foot policy had essentially the same effect, barring Cubans from ready entry into the United States. Those who were seeking to make their way to American shores at the time the policy was rescinded found themselves stranded in other countries. Tellingly, no one in power in Miami made a move to help them. The bifurcation of the Cuban enclave came into full view as Cuban American political leaders did not lift a finger on behalf of their unlucky compatriots.[19] The Obama administration's move thus brought to an end the second great wave of Cuban migration that had started with the 1980 Mariel exodus.

THE ECONOMIC EFFECTS OF POST-1980 CUBAN EMIGRATION

Cuban-owned firms grew nationwide from an estimated 919 in 1967 to about 37,000 in 1982 and 61,500 in 1987. Most of these were located in the Miami metropolitan area, where 75 percent of the Cuban-origin population concentrated. Although most such enterprises were small, aggregate receipts of Hispanic firms in Miami reached $3.8 billion in 1987, a figure that exceeded by $400 million that of second-ranked Los Angeles and was three times that of third-ranked New York, despite the fact that these cities had much larger Hispanic populations. By 2000, the national rate of self-employment per thousand population was 93.5, while for Cubans it was 127.3. In 2001, there were 125,273 Cuban-owned firms in the United States, with receipts of over $26.4 billion. Again, most of these firms were located in the Miami–Fort Lauderdale area.[20]

These and related figures attest to the significant economic dynamism created by the Cuban enclave since its origins in the 1960s and 1970s. But then something worrisome started to happen. In 1979, Cuban families in the United States had a median household income of $16,326 (in 1978

Table 5 Median Annual Household Incomes and Poverty Rates
of Largest Immigrant Nationalities, 2010

		Income	
		MEDIAN HOUSEHOLD	POVERTY
Region/Country of Birth	*Persons (N)*	INCOME ($)	RATE (%)
Total native born	269,393,845	50,541	14.8
All immigrants	39,955,854	46,224	18.9
Above U.S. Average (above $60,000)			
India	1,780,322	94,907	6.8
United Kingdom	236,840	84,819	5.8
Hong Kong	199,971	84,657	9.3
Philippines	1,777,588	78,692	6.0
Taiwan	358,460	76,893	13.0
Canada	798,649	64,478	8.9
Close to U.S. Average (between $45,000 and $55,000)			
Vietnam	1,240,542	52,522	15.1
China	1,601,147	52,187	17.3
Poland	475,503	51,943	8.4
South Korea	624,538	50,786	15.2
Colombia	636,555	47,485	14.2
Peru	428,547	47,214	12.3
Below U.S. Average (below $43,000)			
El Salvador	1,214,049	42,515	19.0
Haiti	587,149	40,969	21.5
Guatemala	830,824	38,778	24.8
Mexico	11,711,103	35,254	28.1
Cuba	**1,104,679**	**34,919**	**19.6**
Dominican Republic	879,187	32,253	24.3
Somalia	82,454	18,391	52.9

SOURCE: U.S. Census Bureau, *2010 American Community Survey.*

dollars), a figure at par with that of the U.S. population as a whole. By 1989, the median household income of the Cuban population was $27,292, or $3,000 dollars below the national median; the poverty rate for Cubans that year was 14.7 percent, well below that for the Mexican population, the largest Hispanic minority, but 2 percent above the national average.[21]

By 1999, the median Cuban household income had reached $40,085. This, however, was almost $10,000 below that for the native-born population and more than $3,000 below the Colombian immigrant population. The Cuban poverty rate crept up to 18.2 percent, 3 percent above the national average. In 2010, the downward trend accelerated. As shown in table 5, the median Cuban household income in that year was $34,919, $15,000 below that for native-born households and at par with the Mexican-origin population. The much-vaunted Cuban economic advantage relative to other Latin immigrant groups had effectively disappeared. As the table also shows, the Cuban household poverty rate now exceeded by a full 5 percentage points the native-born average.

This downward trend is due to the lower average levels of education and occupational skills of the post-Mariel refugee population as well as to the little support and guidance received from its coethnics. By failing to involve the new arrivals in its economic networks, the Miami Cuban community accelerated its own economic and social bifurcation. This trend is seen more clearly when we examine patterns of entrepreneurship and its consequences in recent years.

The U.S. Census Individual Public Use Microdata Sample (IPUMS) files for the year 2000 provide data for 66,955 adults, ages 18 to 65, who earned more than $500 in the Miami–Fort Lauderdale Metropolitan Statistical Area (MSA). This large sample can be divided, in turn, into the categories non-Hispanic white, non-Hispanic black, Cuban, other Hispanic, and other. The Cuban-origin sample is composed of 12,004 cases that can be further subdivided into pre-1980 (pre-Mariel) arrivals, Mariel entrants and later arrivals, and the U.S.-born second generation. The data for 2000 are convenient because they include a sizable number of pre-Mariel Cubans still in the labor force and because adult second-generation Cubans in that year were overwhelmingly the children of these early exiles. Table 6 presents personal and family incomes for these ethnic categories.

Table 6   Personal and Family Incomes of Racial and Ethnic Groups in Miami–Fort Lauderdale Metropolitan Area (Adults 18–65), 2000

| | Total MSA | Non-Hispanic White[a] | Non-Hispanic Black | *Cuban* | | | *Other Hispanic* | *Other* |
				PRE-1980 MIGRANT	1980 OR AFTER MIGRANT	U.S. BORN		
Personal income	37,407	49,812	26,642***	45,218**	23,961***	34,971***	27,671***	32,724***
Family income	68,720	84,842	51,361***	82,589	51,071***	78,739**	56,371***	59,674***
N	66,955	25,383	12,003	4,914	5,021	2,069	14,546	3,019

SOURCE: Public Use Microdata Sample (IPUMS 2000).

a. Non-Hispanic white is the reference category for all comparisons. Significant differences from this category are noted by asterisks.

**Probability of non-significant difference less than one in 100.

***Probability of non-significant difference less than one in 1,000.

Results show that non-Hispanic whites (N = 25,387) occupied the top of the economic hierarchy, with incomes higher than any other group. All others had average personal incomes that were significantly lower but of these only pre-1980 Cubans and the U.S.-born Cuban second generation had incomes that exceeded the average for the metropolitan area. The trend was the same when we consider family incomes. In this case, only non-Hispanic whites and pre-Mariel Cubans exceeded an annual income of $80,000, with the Cuban second generation shy of that figure by little more than $1,000. By contrast, refugees arriving during the Mariel exodus and after had not succeeded economically. Their personal and family incomes were lower than those of other Hispanic immigrants in the area and not statistically different from non-Hispanic blacks, the bottom ethnic category.

It could be argued that the category "1980 or after Cuban migrant" is too broad because it does not distinguish between Mariel entrants and arrivals in the next few years from Cubans coming later whose characteristics could be quite different. To examine this possibility, we subdivided this category into Cubans arriving in the United States between 1980 and 1989 and those coming after 1990. Results do not support the idea that there are significant differences in the entire post-Mariel period. If anything, the economic profile of the most recent Cuban migrants is worse: the average personal income of post-1989 Cuban migrants in the Miami–Fort Lauderdale metropolitan area was $21,313, compared to $26,330 for those arriving during the Mariel exodus and its aftermath. The low incomes of more recent arrivals may be due to their recency in the country and, hence, their lower U.S.-acquired work experience. We examine this possibility below.

Table 7 disaggregates the figures further into the categories self-employed and wage earners among adult males (there were not sufficient numbers of self-employed females to permit interethnic comparisons). The same ethnic hierarchy observed earlier holds, with non-Hispanic whites at the top, pre-Mariel Cubans close behind, followed by their children and everyone else below. As repeatedly found in earlier studies, entrepreneurs (the self-employed) enjoy a substantial economic advantage in terms of personal and, especially, family incomes.[22] Non-Hispanic white and pre-1980 Cuban entrepreneurs were the only groups to exceed

Table 7 Personal Incomes and Family Incomes of Working, Self-Employed, and Wage/Salaried Males by Racial and Ethnic Group in Miami–Fort Lauderdale Metropolitan Area, 2000

| | Total MSA | Non-Hispanic White[a] | Non-Hispanic Black | Cuban | | | Other Hispanic | Other |
				PRE-1980 MIGRANT	1980 OR AFTER MIGRANT	U.S. BORN		
Personal Income								
Working adults	45,010	61,712	18,929***	56,541***	26,918***	29,265***	32,414***	37,383***
Self-employed	64,968	80,948	39,255***	71,302 n.s.	28,250***	65,594 n.s.	49,033***	57,369***
Wage/salaried	41,639	57,474	28,244***	52,523**	26,647***	35,983***	30,254***	34,429***
Family Income								
Working adults	70,500	88,226	53,078***	87,404 n.s.	50,109***	77,688***	55,409***	58,974***
Self-employed	90,618	106,667	60,443***	105,921 n.s.	53,545***	94,683 n.s.	71,671***	79,990**
Wage/salaried	67,102	84,162	52,589***	82,363 n.s.	49,410***	75,569**	53,294***	55,868***

SOURCE: Public Use Microdata Sample (IPUMS 2000).

NOTE: Universe includes adult males ages 18–64 who were not unemployed and whose annual income was greater than or equal to $500. Person-weights used.

a. Non-Hispanic white is the reference category. Significant differences from this category are noted by asterisks.

** Probability of non-significant difference less than 100.

*** Probability of non-significant difference less than one in 1,000.

n.s. = non-significant difference.

an annual family income of $100,000 in 2000, with the difference between both groups just shy of $1,000. They were followed, at some distance, by second-generation Cubans (children of the earlier exiles) and then all others.

Differences among wage and salaried workers followed exactly the same pattern: there was no statistical difference between the average incomes of non-Hispanic white and pre-Mariel Cuban workers, while all other groups fell significantly behind. This result indicates that Cuban workers who arrived at the time that the ethnic enclave was built had done rather well economically, whether or not they were employed in Cuban firms.

The difference is stark in the economic performance of Mariel and post-Mariel refugees whose income levels were at the bottom of the ladder for both the self-employed and the wage or salaried workers, in terms of personal as well as family incomes. Noteworthy, in particular, is the poor performance of entrepreneurs from this group; their economic rewards were the lowest of all ethnic categories. It is clear from these results that the original advantages conferred on entrepreneurs by the Cuban enclave did not extend to post-1980 arrivals. This disadvantage was due in part to their recency, a possibility that we examine next. However, second-generation Cubans entered the local labor force at about the same time; that is, they were also "recent" workers with little work experience. Yet their economic performance as both entrepreneurs and workers far exceeded that of their Mariel and post-Mariel compatriots.

This lack of success was not for lack of trying among recent arrivals. Table 8 presents self-employment rates for all adult males in the Miami metropolitan area by ethnic categories in 2000. Two trends are apparent in these results. First, pre-Mariel Cubans were the most entrepreneurial group, with a rate significantly higher than even non-Hispanic whites. This result accords with the historical role of this group as builders of the original enclave. Second, Mariel and post-Mariel Cubans were strongly inclined to follow that route, with self-employment rates not significantly lower than non-Hispanic whites. However, as just seen, their efforts did not pay off.[23]

The average interethnic differences observed previously are suggestive but are subject to the objection that they reflect differences in levels of

Table 8 Self-Employment Rates among Males by Racial and Ethnic Group in the Miami–Fort Lauderdale Metropolitan Area (Adults 18–65), 2000

| | Total MSA | Non-Hispanic White[a] | Non-Hispanic Black | *Cuban* | | | Other Hispanic | Other |
				PRE-1980 MIGRANT	1980 OR AFTER MIGRANT	U.S. BORN		
Self-employment	0.14	0.18	0.06***	0.21***	0.17n.s.	0.11***	0.12***	0.13***
N	35,285	13,780	5,430	2,398	3,077	1,051	7,872	1,677

SOURCE: Public Use Microdata Sample (IPUMS 2000).
NOTE: Universe includes adult males ages 18–64 who were not unemployed and whose annual income was greater than or equal to $500. Person-weights used. a. Non-Hispanic white is the reference category. Significant differences from this category are noted by asterisks.
*** Probability of non-significant difference less than one in 1,000.
n.s. = non-significant difference.

Table 9   Regressions of Family Income on Ethnicity and Selected Variables
(Adults 18–64), 2000[a]

	I	II
Ethnicity:[b]		
Cuban	−9511.28***	
Pre-1980 Cuban		212.53 n.s
1980 or After Cuban		−23552.77***
U.S.-born Cuban		114.91 n.s
Black	−21608.99***	−21912.73***
Hispanic	−19352.02***	−19680.03***
Other	−19793.26***	−20046.82***
Female	−1925.97***	−2342.27***
Age	392.40**	442.76**
Age Squared	−0.93	−1.79 n.s
Self-Employed	14167.01***	14133.69***
N	66,995	66,995
R^2	0.12	0.12

SOURCE: Public Use Microdata Sample (IPUMS 2000).
NOTE: Universe includes adults ages 18–64, who were not unemployed and whose annual income was greater than or equal to $500. Raw N values included; person-weights used.
a. Controlling for levels of education.
b. Non-Hispanic white is the reference category.
** $p < .01$.
*** $p < .001$.
n.s. = non-significant difference.

human capital, including education and work experience. Reasonably, it could be argued that pre-Mariel Cubans represent an older and, hence, more occupationally experienced population and that this is the root of their superior economic situation. To address this possibility, we conducted a series of statistical analyses controlling for levels of education and work experience, as well as gender and self-employment.

Results of the first of these analyses, indexing work experience by the conventional indicators of age and age squared, are presented in table 9. Two main findings emerge from this analysis. First, it confirms the income disadvantage of females and the significant income advantage of

Table 10   Regressions of Family Income on Ethnicity and Selected Variables
Substituting Work Experience for Age, 2000[a]

	Adults (18–64)	Males (18–64)
Ethnicity:[b]		
Pre-1980 Cuban	2023.88 n.s.	3849.55*
1980 or After Cuban	−14956.88***	−16442.62***
U.S.-born Cuban	−222.71 n.s.	−372.66 n.s
Black	−19062.42***	−17100.27***
Hispanic	−14163.78***	−15565.28***
Other	−14091.57***	−15856.60***
Female	−2408.99***	
Work Experience (U.S.)	940.46***	934.68***
Work Experience (U.S.) Squared	−15.81***	−13.00***
Self-Employed	14869.66***	15281.24***
N	66,955	35,285
R^2	.13	.15

SOURCE: Public Use Microdata Sample (IPUMS 2000; 5% microsample).
NOTE: Universe includes adults ages 18–64 who were not unemployed and whose annual income was greater than or equal to $500. Raw N values included; person-weight used.
a. Controlling for levels of education.
b. Non-Hispanic white is the reference category.
* $p < .05$.
*** $p < .001$.
n.s. = non-significant difference.

entrepreneurs (i.e., the self-employed), even after controlling for levels of education and work experience. When compared to wage or salaried workers with the same training and experience, females earned about $2,000 less per year, while entrepreneurs had a net income advantage of about $14,000.

Second, all ethnic categories earned significantly less than non-Hispanic whites, even after controlling for education, gender, and self-employment. These differences are statistically significant in the first model but disappear when the Cuban-origin sample is disaggregated. Pre-Mariel Cubans and the U.S.-born Cuban second generation now exhibit incomes that are actually higher than comparable non-Hispanic whites, although the differences are not statistically significant. In contrast, post-Mariel Cubans continue to experience an income disadvantage that is higher than that suffered by any other ethnic category, including African Americans. The income gap relative to statistically comparable native whites was a startling $23,000 for this segment of the Cuban population in year 2000.

A possible objection to these findings is that age is not a good indicator of U.S. work experience. Mariel and post-Mariel entrants of the same age as pre-1980 Cubans may have had much fewer years of experience in the U.S. labor market because of their recency of arrival. In order to take account of this possibility, we substituted actual U.S. work experience for age across all ethnic groups. For the native born, work experience is computed in standard fashion as age minus education minus six. For adult immigrants, it is years since U.S. arrival minus y, where y is 0 for those who arrived after the age of 18 and (18−age at arrival) for those who arrived as minors. Table 10 presents the result for the adult universe and for males only.

With U.S. work experience directly entered into the equation, results are still more powerful than before. The Cuban second generation remains statistically indistinguishable from non-Hispanic whites, although they receive slightly lower average incomes. On the other hand, pre-Mariel Cubans males now exceed the incomes of the reference category by a significant margin. Net of work experience and other control variables, earlier exiles displayed an income advantage over native white males of almost $4,000 in 2000.

By 2010, the number of pre-1980 Cubans in the Miami metropolitan labor force had dwindled considerably and the figures for the U.S.-born second generation were no longer limited exclusively to their children. Still, the trends noted for 2000 held. Table 11 presents family incomes for the same ethnic categories for the Miami–Fort Lauderdale MSA in 2010. The same rank order among groups is evident. For the adult male population as a whole and for the self-employed, pre-Mariel Cubans are next to non-Hispanic whites in annual incomes, and the difference between the two groups is statistically insignificant. The U.S.-born Cuban second generation follows, then everyone else. The "Other" category, comprising

Table 11 Family Incomes of Working, Self-Employed, and Wage/Salaried Males by Racial and Ethnic Groups in Miami–Fort Lauderdale Metropolitan Area, 2010

				Cuban				
	Total MSA	Non-Hispanic White[a]	Non-Hispanic Black	PRE-1980 MIGRANT	1980 OR AFTER MIGRANT	U.S. BORN	Other Hispanic	Other
Working Adults	79,797	101,697	63,147***	98,508 n.s.	56,887***	90,820**	64,349***	83,937***
Self-Employed	83,357	115,401	60,929***	95,179 n.s.	56,549***	88,291*	64,543***	89,049***
Wage/Salaried	78,051	98,004	63,394***	99,471 n.s.	56,987***	91,283 n.s	64,318***	83,337***

SOURCE: U.S. Census Bureau, 2010 American Community Survey; Public Use Microdata Sample (IPUMS).
a. Non–Hispanic white is the reference category. Statistically significant differences are noted by asterisks.
* p < .05.
** p < .01.
*** p < .001.
n.s. = non-significant difference.

Table 12 Regressions of Family Income on Ethnicity and Selected Variables
Substituting Work Experience for Age, 2010[a]

	Adults (18–64)	Males (18–64)
Ethnicity:[b]		
Pre-1980 Cuban	1156.69 n.s.	2367.85 n.s.
1980–89 Cuban	−14301.99***	−14851.41***
1990 and after Cuban	−30636.59***	−30803.23***
U.S.-born Cuban	4687.64*	638.53 n.s.
Black	−24230.51***	−22658.45***
Hispanic	−19709.82***	−22159.07***
Other	−10918.04***	−14375.35***
Female	−4887.57***	
Work Experience (U.S.)	431.46***	510.35**
Work Experience (U.S.) Squared	−8.14**	−10.50**
Self-Employed	3035.84*	3957.43*
N	27,192	13,537
R^2	.14	.15

SOURCE: U.S. Census Bureau, *2010 American Community Survey.*
a. Controlling for levels of education.
b. Non-Hispanic white is the reference category.
* p < .05.
** p < .01.
*** p < .001.
n.s. = non-significant difference.

mostly Asians, had slightly higher self-employment incomes than the Cuban second generation. Hence, despite the additional decade that elapsed since 2000, post-Mariel Cuban refugees still trailed by a wide margin. Their annual incomes were slightly more than half those of their older compatriots and lower than those of African Americans.

Table 12 presents results of a parallel analysis of determinants of average incomes in 2010 on the same set of predictors used previously. In this case, however, we broke down the Mariel and post-Mariel category into Cubans arriving during the 1980s and those coming in the 1990s and after. With U.S. work experience controlled, results are clearer than before, showing that post-1989 Cubans had the lowest average family incomes. Mariel and post-Mariel arrivals also continued to display a significant disadvantage. Pre-1980 exiles were not statistically different from native whites, but, as indicated previously, their numbers have been dwindling rapidly. Among adults, the Cuban second generation, born in the United States, performs significantly better than native whites. However, as "Americans," second-generation Cubans do not count on the average census statistics for the Cuban-born population of the country as a whole. This is reflected in the dramatic decline in the economic position of this population, as seen in table 5 above.

THE CHILDREN

Consequences of the bifurcation of the Cuban-origin population extend beyond the first generation. The socialization process of their offspring also reflects these differences. The exiles of the 1960s and 1970s created a system of private schools in Miami by transplanting the best-known ones in pre-Revolution Cuba; most of these schools were operated by religious orders. The purpose of this system was to promote selective acculturation by combining the learning of English and academic subject matters with the preservation of Spanish and key elements of Cuban culture. Few children of Mariel and post-Mariel refugees attended the private schools created by earlier arrivals. For the most part, they enrolled in public schools, most of which were located in poorer areas of metropolitan Miami. Attendance to private versus public schools by Cuban American children can thus serve as a reasonable proxy for their parents' period of arrival.

In 2002, the final survey of the Children of Immigrants Longitudinal Study (CILS) was conducted.[24] The study followed a large, representative sample of children of immigrants from early adolescence, at the average age of 14, to early adulthood, ten years later. Included in this study was a sizable sample of second-generation Cubans, divided between those who attended private bilingual schools in Miami and those enrolled in public schools in the same city. By age 24, the adaptation process of these youths had begun to "harden" into a series of objective outcomes likely to determine the future course of their lives. These outcomes include educational achievement, occupation, and family income, as well as indicators of a downward assimilation course—such as adolescent childbearing, unemployment, and incidents of arrest and incarceration.

Table 13 presents results of the study for the principal nationalities represented in the CILS South Florida sample. In every case, they favor the children of pre-1980 exiles. Only 8 percent of these youths had abandoned their studies with a high school diploma or less, a figure tripled by their public school counterparts. Early school abandonment by public-school Cuban youths was higher than among second-generation Haitians and Jamaicans—the two poorest immigrant nationalities in the CILS Miami sample.

The average family income of Cubans attending private schools in 2002 was $104,700, the only nationality to surpass six figures. The average family income among their public school peers was 40 percent lower. Levels of unemployment at average age 24 reflected similar trends, with the public school Cuban unemployment rate double that of their private school counterparts. Only 3 percent of the offspring of earlier exiles had had children themselves during adolescence; the figure was about six times higher among public school Cubans. Adolescent parenthood is an indicator of problematic adaptation, because it saddles young people with adult responsibilities that commonly prevent them from moving ahead in the educational system or labor market.

The CILS data also contain incidents of arrest and incarceration obtained not only from self-reports, but from official data. The data on incarcerations are public information available from the website of the Florida Department of Corrections. As shown in table 13, males were far more prone than females to be incarcerated, but there were significant differences among them. Only 3.4 percent of male children of pre-1980 exiles suffered that fate, a figure tripled by their public school counterparts. Hence, one in ten male children of post-Mariel Cuban refugees was in jail by average age twenty-four.

These differences demonstrate that patterns of relative economic and social advantage and disadvantage associated with the history of immigration and settlement of Cubans in the United States are resilient and tend to consolidate over time. As with other immigrant groups, the fate of the

Table 13 Characteristics and Adaptation Outcomes of Second-Generation Immigrants in South Florida, 2002

	Education		Family Income		Unemployed[a] (%)	Has Had Children (%)	Incarcerated	
Nationality	AVERAGE YEARS	HIGH SCHOOL OR LESS (%)	MEAN ($)	MEDIAN ($)			TOTAL (%)	MALES (%)
Cuban (private school)	15.32	7.5	104,767	70,395	3.0	3.0	2.9	3.4
Cuban (public school)	14.32	21.7	60,816	48,598	6.2	17.7	5.6	10.5
Haitian	14.44	15.3	34,506	26,974	16.7	24.2	7.1	14.3
Jamaican/West Indian	14.63	18.1	40,654	30,326	9.4	24.3	8.5	20.0
Nicaraguan	14.17	26.4	54,049	47,054	4.9	20.1	4.4	9.9
Other (Asian)	15.2	9.1	58,659	40,278	4.5	11.4	6.7	9.5
Other (Latin)	14.4	25.5	43,476	31,500	2.2	15.2	6.4	18.8
Other	14.55	20.8	59,719	40,619	7.3	16.4	4.9	8.3

SOURCE: Children of Immigrants Longitudinal Study (CILS), third survey, 2002–3. Results corrected for third-wave sample attrition. $N = 1,765$.

a. Respondents without jobs, whether looking or not looking for employment, except those still enrolled at school.

ethnic groups created by new migrant flows will be determined by what happens to their children, the second generation. In the case of Cuban exiles, that destiny is decisively bifurcated.

CONCLUSION

The trends noted in this chapter—resurgent transnationalism among Mariel and post-Mariel Cubans and the deteriorating economic averages of the Cuban-born population of the United States—seem irreversible. Older exiles are dying off, and their offspring are becoming more thoroughly integrated into the U.S. social and economic mainstream. Recent Cuban arrivals refugees have continued engaging with their families on the island, remitting as much as they can to them. These transfers, plus the absence of support by established Cuban firms, ensure that most entrepreneurial ventures started by recent refugees will be poorly capitalized. For its part, the Cuban government appears content with allowing the present situation to continue. The aging revolutionary leadership, now diminished by the death of its supreme leader, has come to rely on the economic contributions of its young population not by employing it but by exporting it. The new facilities for leaving Cuba starting in 2014, coupled with the continuation of quasi-automatic entry into the United States, translated into new and significantly larger waves of refugees in 2015 and 2016.

The sudden termination of the wet foot, dry foot policy in the waning days of the Obama administration put an end to this flow. Thereafter, only recipients of legal resident visas—limited to twenty thousand per year—and the immediate relatives of those who have managed to acquire U.S. citizenship can be expected to arrive. With rare exceptions, those claiming political asylum will be turned back. Yet the end of sustained migration from the island leaves the bifurcated pattern described previously in place. That situation leads to the notable paradox that Miami presents today: as the city pursues its new global economic and cultural vocation, its inhabitants include large numbers of escapees from a failed regime whose economic role in the world has become increasingly irrelevant. As noted previously, the two sectors of the Cuban population of Miami have reached an accommodation of sorts, but the difference is stark when one compares the areas of the city where older exiles and their offspring work and live to those where new refugees from Cuba have clustered.

These differences can have significant results for the growing Cuban second generation, as the findings presented above suggest. Unless the established Cuban leadership of Miami reverses course, the future of post-Mariel children of immigrants can be very different from that of their predecessors, confining them to the status of another underprivileged minority. The end of large-scale migration from the island, following the shift in policy of the U.S. government, should gradually improve the economic situation of the Cuban-origin population as a whole, but this will be a slow process at best. The rapid success of the original builders of the Miami enclave and the fast entry of their children into positions of political and economic power are unlikely to be replicated by most post-Mariel arrivals and their offspring in the near future.

7 Miami through Latin American Eyes

Latin America has never truly freed itself from the unrelenting presence of the United States, a country that leaves an imprint—real or imagined—on the lives of people throughout the region. Of course, the dynamic is not unique to Latin America. The influence of the United States on global affairs is commensurate with attitudes toward the country expressed around the world. The intensity and diversity of these beliefs is so strong that an entire field of study has emerged in international affairs to understand dispositions toward the United States, along with their sources and implications. It is no coincidence that the field is largely defined as the study of "anti-Americanism."

However, this growing body of research has shown that beliefs about and attitudes toward the United States are multidimensional. They express tensions, paradoxes, and often ambivalence. Individuals display both positive and negative identification with different dimensions of the United States, and their attitudes result from an accumulation of "considerations, predispositions, and information" that combine "cognitive, emotional, and normative elements." The diversity of anti-Americanisms is a function of the diversity of the United States.[1]

In their work on anti-Americanism, the political scientists Peter Katzenstein and Robert Keohane emphasize the difference between "what the United States is" and "what the United States does."[2] The difference between essence and action speaks to the difference between immanent and temporary attitudes among individuals. Studies have indicated that access to information and personal contact with the United States are vital in shaping people's dispositions because these concrete interactions have a direct impact on individuals' conceptions about the United States.[3]

Research has also demonstrated that anti-Americanism in Latin America is shaped by ideology and national context.[4] Furthermore, the anti-Americanism of political leaders and that of the average citizens reinforce each other. Migration has visible, mixed effects both in terms of its economic consequences back home (e.g., remittances) and in terms of the stories of success and failure associated with those who migrate to the United States. Failure, of course, is often associated with the experience of illegality.[5]

However, as influential as the United States is in Latin America, Latin America has one outpost in the United States where its presence is just as strong: Miami. The real Miami cannot be fully grasped without understanding the city that lives in the minds of Latin Americans. Miami has become an extension of Latin America and the Caribbean, where the culture is as influenced by Cubans, Haitians, Venezuelans, and other Latin groups as it is by the sophistication and allure of New York City and Hollywood.

"THE UNITED STATES IS MIAMI"

When polls ask people about their views on the United States, their construct is mostly processed through concrete experiences. These experiences are likely to be tied to a specific place. Many Latin Americans look at the United States through the prism of Miami, which is loosely defined and often encompasses other cities such as Orlando and Fort Lauderdale. Miami figures prominently in the everyday experience of Latin Americans through the media, migration, tourism, consumption, investment, and countless other ways.

As one Argentine writer put it, "For most Argentines, the United States is Miami. For some, New York. For just a few, the rest of the country."[6] For instance, Miami is the preferred destination for tourists from Argentina (56.3 percent of all Argentines traveling to the United States went to Miami in 2015–16; only 30.2 percent went to New York City). It is also the primary destination for Colombians (50.3 percent went to Miami, 35 percent to Orlando), a close second for Brazilians (36.9 percent of all tourists went to Miami, while 39 percent went to Orlando), and a favorite among others from Latin America and the Caribbean.[7]

Miami's reputation as the "gateway to the Americas" is reinforced by the level of activity registered at Miami International Airport, which, as the largest U.S. gateway to Latin America and the Caribbean, receives 15 million passengers annually from the region. New York's JFK is a distant second to MIA, with 7 million passengers to and from Latin America and the Caribbean. MIA's top five international markets are Brazil, Colombia, Mexico, Venezuela, and the Dominican Republic. Nonstop flights connect MIA with over seventy cities in the region.[8] As a marketing specialist at Miami International Airport noted, "If an Argentine is going to meet with someone from Lima, Peru, chances are they will both fly to Miami to meet."[9] Miami is considered a premier center for doing business in the hemisphere, not only because of its location and ease of international transportation, but also because transactions (banking, investment, etc.) can be conducted in Spanish.

Miami as a preferred destination to do business is also driven by its image as a city that is becoming increasingly global and cosmopolitan. As an article in one of Argentina's most influential newspapers, *La Nación*, put it, "Miami attracts and Miami fascinates, and it's not only because of its beaches of turquoise water or for the adrenaline created by its incredible sales. While it's a preferred destination for tourists, it also seduces businessmen. It has the clear and established rules of a developed nation but the idiosyncrasies of a Hispanic one."[10] Indeed, according to *América Economía* (2014), Miami is consistently ranked the Best City to Do Business in Latin America. It is also the only non–Latin American city that appears on the list.[11] For many businesses in Latin America, international expansion must start in Miami.

Economic exchange is a significant form of interdependence that results in a concrete, material experience for Latin Americans, especially through consumers seeking lower prices and a greater variety of goods. The consumption of imports shapes individual perceptions of other countries because imports offer direct benefits to consumers, and brands communicate their foreign origin. Four of Miami's top five trading partners are in Latin America and the Caribbean: Brazil, Colombia, the Dominican Republic, and Chile. Two of the top three exports from Miami to Latin America and the Caribbean are landline and cellular phone equipment and computers, which are the kind of consumer products that have significant visibility, convey social status, and shape people's everyday lives.[12]

For a subset of Latin Americans, real estate is another concrete connection to Miami, which is the U.S. city that sells the most properties to international buyers. According to a 2015 survey by the Miami Association of Realtors, international sales accounted for 36 percent of residential sales (dollar volume). Buyers from Venezuela, Brazil, Argentina, Colombia, and Canada represented 62 percent of international sales (units). Latin American buyers, particularly Brazilians, dominated the luxury property market.[13]

DOMINANT THEMES

Miami's high visibility in everyday life throughout Latin America and the Caribbean facilitates personal encounters, circulation of information, and the diffusion of ideas, practices, and behaviors. Like the United States as a whole, Miami generates loyalty and animosity in equal parts among Latin Americans. This tension is fundamental to the city's identity.

The magnitude of identification or rejection varies greatly among individuals and groups. Miami exercises a strong psychological attraction as a prototypical example of a Latin, modern metropolis. Simultaneously, the city stands as a sort of "black hole" that "sucks people . . . into its bland hodgepodge of hotels and shopping malls"—a place that exercises a toxic influence on Latin America.[14] Few other cities in the world—and probably no other ones in the western hemisphere—generate such contrasting reactions.

Two dominant themes convey the most impactful forces of Miami in Latin American society: consumption and ideology. Both have positive and negative valences, expressing both affinity and aversion. More important, they are inextricably interrelated.

In terms of consumption, Miami is seen as a "mecca of prosperity," a place in which consumption, social aspirations, and a model of successful capitalism are effectively realized. Simultaneously, Miami is perceived as a city that embodies the obscenities of the market and the false promise of the United States as a land of opportunity.

The city is also a site of ideological contestation. As explained in chapter 1, it is essentially a political hotbed, where contests for hegemony take manifold expressions. Miami is a site where political groups defeated at home come to retreat, often to reorganize in order to regain power in their countries. This is a place frequently perceived as the bedrock of anti-Left ideology in the Americas, both by those who champion leftist agendas and those who oppose them. Unlike any other city in the Americas, Miami is a focal point of both sides of the ideological spectrum in Latin American politics.

Miami is as much a Latin American settlement in the United States as a manifestation of U.S. influence in Latin America. It is the perfect lens through which to view Latin American attitudes toward the United States. Miami provides a unique perspective informed by an intense, two-way interaction between the city and the rest of the Americas.

I, CONSUMER

Conspicuous consumption plays a crucial role in emerging economies, where people strive to achieve status through products and brands. In other words, enjoyment comes from a display of social status rather than the actual use of the good. The consumption of products becomes the reflection of images that project social prestige. Individuals engaged in conspicuous consumption experience material possessions as the gateway to happiness.[15]

As discussed in chapter 2, the emergence of metropolitan Miami as a global city is linked directly to its rise as a site for luxury consumption and property speculation. Both exist in tandem. In the logic of property capital, the city's role is singularly one of consumption. The sale of location is intertwined with the desirability offered by mild weather, a beautiful physical environment, safety, and proximity to shopping malls and entertainment. Our analysis in chapter 2 notes that property capital has played a fundamental role in Miami by molding urban space to cash in on the area's physical beauty and pleasant climate. The resulting urban growth machine—using the concept advanced by Logan and Molotch—shapes the ecology of the city and the distribution of the population according to the strategies devised by real estate interests.[16]

Miami as a capital of consumption is central to its image in Latin America. The city is primarily experienced by the wealthy and the middle classes in the region. Still, its allure is also meaningful to the urban lower class, who relate to the "bling lifestyle" through the consumption of cheap imports and mass media. The symbolic meaning of Miami is steeped in materialism and conspicuous consumption: success (admiration for people who own expensive material possessions such as cars, clothes, homes, and even beautiful bodies), social standing (envy of those who can buy whatever they want and those who consider themselves superior to average people), pleasure (the feeling that luxury and goods bring satisfaction and happiness), and "blingness" (being brand savvy and knowing how to consume in style).[17]

The role of Miami on the mental map of Latin Americans as a mecca for consumption reinforces its importance as a global city. Most of the global growth in consumption in the next decades will come from about one hundred cities, and a third of those cities will generate a quarter of the world's total growth for the period 2015–30. The confluence of two factors—the fact that Miami is among the twenty metropolitan areas with the highest consumption totals and the fact that Latin America's working-age consumers are one of the groups of global consumers to keep an eye on—underlines the reality that the city will continue to reinforce its image as a magnet of consumption for Latin Americans in the years to come.[18]

Home ownership is another form of conspicuous consumption. While in other global cities home ownership frequently means a mansion in an elite neighborhood, in Miami home ownership generally means owning a condo that serves as a permanent vacation home. Owning real estate in Miami—which is not a phenomenon restricted to the ultra-rich—offers several advantages to Latin Americans who can afford it: social status, security of capital, insurance against political or economic calamity, and, for some, the option to embrace an "astronaut" lifestyle (i.e., furthering children's education in a developed country while maintaining residence in the home country).[19] The internet and communication technology have significantly facilitated the option of living simultaneously in different places.

Exclusivity of locations is a fundamental dimension of global cities. As Sassen explained, by virtue of their tight spatial concentration, global cities offer a strategic location that gives real estate a premium value.[20] In Miami, trade and finance are the main businesses, with the proceeds invested in other areas as well: arts, recreation, and culture. These sectors have become major centers of capital accumulation on their own and have, in turn, shaped other areas of the city by virtue of spatial, demographic, and economic change.

A STUDY OF THREE COUNTRIES

We can draw information about perceptions on Miami from newspapers, which illustrate the relationship between Miami's image, consumption, and politics. We collected and analyzed news stories and op-eds printed in six major newspapers in Argentina, Brazil, and Colombia—the top three Latin American countries in terms of bilateral trade, tourism, and real estate investment in Miami. An analysis of this collection of articles, columns, and editorials allows us to tap individual attitudes and collective beliefs over a period from the mid-2000s to the mid-2010s.

Our sample includes 3,098 articles from *La Nación* from 2005 to 2016 and 3,817 articles from *Página/12* from 2002 to 2016 (Argentina); 2,968 articles from *O Globo* from 2005 to 2016 and 1,505 from *Folha de São Paulo* from 2005 to 2012 (Brazil); and 1,550 from *El Espectador* from 2008 to 2016 and 1,390 from *El Tiempo* in the same period (Colombia). In turn, we drew subsamples consisting of 40 to 100 unique articles from each newspaper on the basis of content related to significant aspects of Miami, in eight categories: local politics, sports, international news, entertainment, arts, society, business, and tourism.[21]

We first identified main topics by analyzing the distribution of keywords in the titles and bodies of articles and op-eds. The more frequently certain words are mentioned in the sample, the more likely the newspaper is to put a strong focus on that topic. Raw word counts yield very consistent results across newspapers and countries.

Dollar is one of the most frequently used words we found. A constellation of words built around *dollar—money, peso* (Argentina, Colombia), and *real* (Brazil)—is associated with other keywords such as *exchange rate* and *prices*. The topic of exchange rate and the value of the dollar vis-à-vis the local currency appeared frequently in the newspapers across the three countries. As often reported, variation in the exchange rate is important because it affects consumption and makes Miami more or less attractive for Latin Americans.

Looking at the sample of articles over time shows how fluctuations in the exchange rate have an impact on the appeal of Miami to the average tourist/consumer. The possibility of maximizing one's local currency generates excitement about the opportunities offered by Miami's stores, outlets, cheap shopping venues, and sophisticated malls. The strong rise of the dollar makes these types of tourists consider other options (e.g., Ciudad del Este in Paraguay for Brazilians and Argentines). When a favorable exchange rate is back, Miami is again the tourist destination with great deals to offer.

Another constellation of words that emerges from the study also revolves around consumption: *shopping, market, goods, tourism, real estate,* and *investment*. A more focused analysis of selected articles reveals significant emphasis across the three countries on the consumption of images and glamour. Miami is presented as synonymous with wealth, beauty, luxury, and exclusivity. The narrative emerging from the publications portrays the city as a place that generates appeal and admiration. Many articles tell stories about ordinary Latin Americans who think of Miami as the paradigm of happiness. New arrivals from Latin America—often entrepreneurs, businesspeople, athletes, or artists—are featured as examples of individuals who succeeded beyond all expectations, thanks to Miami.

SAFETY, GLAMOUR, AND SOPHISTICATION

An important thematic thread that emerges from our study revolves around safety and predictability. On this perspective, the reason Miami became a magnet for many wealthy Latins is because "things work there." More specifically, the so-called *organización gringa* (the American way of organizing society) creates an environment that does not exist in Latin America. Examples in the articles and editorials reflect facets of everyday life: lines are orderly, people don't throw trash on the street, traffic has clear rules, theft is under control, justice is effective, women can go to the supermarket (even with their maids) without being afraid of being robbed, and children of wealthy families can play with friends on the street or at the park without fear of being kidnapped.[22]

Articles emphasize the importance that tourists give to the freedom to display publicly the goods they buy, which is often impossible in their own countries. In the words of a reporter writing in *Folha de São Paulo*, "Why does the Brazilian love Miami? 'It is the safest city of Brazil,' jokes Solange Santos, of Chris Brooks. 'Here people parade freely with their cars, jewelry, Rolex, without guilt nor fear.'"[23]

The stories about Miami in our sample of news articles also show Miami as a place of glamour. Colombian newspaper stories, in particular, feature news about Latin American celebrities and showbiz in Miami. Celebrities define the status of Miami, from sports to music and TV. Media outlets report weddings, dating, breakups, vacations, and drug scandals in Miami. The boom in the production of telenovelas turned Miami into "a Hollywood of Latin telenovela."[24] Furthermore, the city is home to the Latino Grammys, new album releases, music tours, and performances. As *La Nación* put it, "Every artist dreams of recording in Miami."[25]

Art is a word that commonly emerges in the analysis of Argentine, Brazilian, and Colombian newspapers. We examined in detail a subsample of articles and op-eds and identified topics such as Art Basel and Wynwood, as well as other relatively recent artistic attractions. The visibility of the art scene in narratives written about Miami demonstrates the perceived sophistication of the city, which, in turn, affirms its status as a global city. We found the consistent message that Miami is making a concerted effort to be seen as a destination that offers more than beaches, shopping, and parties.

The resounding success of these artistic attractions receives significant attention in articles and op-eds about Miami. Enthusiasts call Miami the "capital of Latin American art" and declare that "Miami breathes art." This new image has created an unprecedented, flashy international profile for Miami. Visitors from all over the world and top art collectors in particular see Miami's Art Basel as the ultimate fair in the United States. As the billionaire Norman Braman noted, "I've been told that more private jets arrive here for Art Basel than fly to the Super Bowl."[26]

"BUY MORE, BETTER, AND CHEAPER"

Most of the conversation about Miami in Argentina, Brazil, and Colombia centers on consumption. Stories in the newspapers talk about ordinary people and the opportunities that Miami offers for consumption. The emphasis in our newspaper sample is on four aspects: prices, quality, variety, and brand. The image of the United States, when processed through Miami, emphasizes the attraction of the American culture of consumerism. When consumer culture is rendered in positive terms, its allure enhances positive opinions about the United States.

Colombian newspapers published numerous stories about the experience of ordinary tourists who make, "at the very least, one trip a year" to Miami to buy goods not only for themselves but also to resell back home.[27] Brazilian newspapers emphasized the variety of brands available in Miami's malls, and the fact that brand products are much cheaper in Miami than in Brazil. Many stories described the experience of Brazilian tourists going on a shopping spree, frequently stressing their desire to buy as many goods as possible. As a tourist from Salvador, Bahia, put it, "We came with three suitcases and will return with nine!"[28] Or, in the words of an employee in the Apple store in the Aventura Mall, "The Brazilian is the guy who asks for eight iPhones and five iPads."[29]

When the dollar is cheap, visitors have access to a dream of consumption through Miami ("Give me two," is a common phrase heard in Brazil, Argentina, and other countries). But even when the dollar is expensive, the relatively low U.S. prices for electronics and other products are advantageous for middle-class consumers.

Articles talked about shopping opportunities for different income levels, from the luxurious boutiques in Mary Brickell Village to the more affordable stores like Target, Ross, Marshalls, and factory outlets for major brands. We found numerous references to name brands in newspaper stories, particularly in regard to clothing and technology. Being brand conscious is central to the Miami experience across the three countries. Miami also provides prestige for Latin American brands. Articles highlighted the importance that Miami holds for the international expansion of Latin American products. For instance, Colombian brands such as Juan Valdez Café and Pan Pa'Ya have found a welcoming market in Miami. The allure of Miami helps strengthen a brand back home because the city is viewed as a paradigm of bling lifestyle, a desirable market, and a place that nurtures bold entrepreneurship in an environment that Latin Americans perceive as recognizable.

THE ALLURE OF A MIAMI ADDRESS

In the eyes of many Latin Americans, owning a second home in Miami represents a fundamental measure of success. And for many, Miami offers the kind of long-term stability that is difficult to find in Latin American countries.[30] However, not everyone is fleeing political turmoil, seeking protection from an economic slump, or depositing flight capital. Miami is also a market for optimism. Professionals, financiers, and entrepreneurs who want to enjoy their prosperity, often newly earned, strive to own property in an aspirational destination.

When the conditions are favorable, Miami's seduction grows as a place that provides safety and attractive prices. "Nowadays, Miami is transforming into Manhattan. Every day there is more investment, more construction, more museums, and more luxury restaurants. Nowadays everyone wants an apartment in Miami," noted *La Nación* in 2014.[31] Having a Miami address is a sign of success and a symbol of social standing.

In the early 2010s, affluent Brazilians were flocking to Miami in search of opportunities in the real estate market. As a commentator summarized the mood at the time, "Where will those with savings put their money in these times of low interest rates for loans and credit cards? In consumption?

In Chinese products? Or in Miami?"[32] When Brazilians wished to buy real estate abroad, most of them looked to buy in Miami:

> The Miami of shopping is also now the second home for Brazilians with money. The Mickey Mouse hat lost its space in the suitcase, and the Brazilians now buy houses, open businesses, and use the city as a platform to invest in the USA with the money earned at home.[33]

Miami is a place to be seen, a site for exposure. This is a consistent narrative in the hundreds of articles, columns, and editorials that we analyzed and in the stories told by our informants. The opportunity to buy a piece of a dream in the form of a condo or home in Miami conjures, for many Latin Americans, an image of style, prestige, and security that uniquely blends the United States and Latin America.

LAND OF OBSCENE CAPITALISM

There is a view of Miami that is in stark contrast to its perception as a land of opportunity in which happiness can be reached through consumption. From this alternative perspective, Miami is a paradigm of the harmful and pernicious side of capitalism. The city embodies the main problems of an unfettered market economy: excess, corruption, and fraud. It is seen as a hub of hemispheric corruption—a key theme in Latin American politics and society—and as a safe haven for outlaws, including those who violate the law while holding public office.

Argentine newspapers told stories involving Miami about tax evasion, secret accounts, flight capital, undeclared property assets, political corruption, money laundering, and recalcitrant behavior by politicians and businessmen. In Colombia, stories in our sample of articles tended to focus on drug trafficking, arms trafficking, and money laundering cases involving drug lords, guerrilla leaders, and politically connected paramilitary leaders. Corrupt government officials, fugitive millionaires, and infamous *narcos* are denounced as living in luxurious apartment buildings beyond the reach of the justice system. Even evangelical pastors relocate to Miami to enjoy the wealth acquired in Colombia doing "God's business."[34] Brazilian newspapers wrote about public officials and businessmen engaged in tax evasion and money laundering, and about Miami as the preferred destination among politicians for extravagant vacations, shopping, and sometimes activities related to secret financial transactions.[35]

A darker, very different side of Miami is expressed by the population of undocumented immigrants from Latin American countries. This is the flipside of success: clerks in small stores, domestic workers, gardeners, dishwashers, waiters, truck drivers, construction workers, strippers, prostitutes, hairdressers, and the tens of thousands who live the harsh reality of abuse and constant fear of deportation. There is a constant narrative across Argentina, Brazil, and Colombia of those who live in the dark without documentation, the plight of the thousands who emigrated in times of economic crisis and returned home, the lack of solidarity between legal and undocumented residents from the same country, the economic and emotional troubles in a cutthroat environment, and ghastly stories of deportation.

The reverse side of the wealth and glamour of Miami is an expression not uncommon for global cities. As Sassen explained, the growth of economic and social inequality, as well as the rapid expansion of an informal economy, are characteristics of global cities, where new affluent classes and low-income populations providing services for those classes share a common urban space.[36] The bifurcation seen in Miami, where vast economic and social differences are stark, is a defining element of the global urban environment. Globalization generates extreme wealth but at the same time deepens the clash between the human habitat and profit-making functions of the city.

Perhaps one of the most intriguing images of Miami, the "Magic City," is as a place that represents the falsehood of American ideals, the boorishness of American culture, and the pernicious and dangerous influence of the United States around the world. The city is portrayed by critics both as an expression of the deceit of the American dream and as a construct that runs against core values that intellectuals and progressives in Latin America hold dear: equality, solidarity, and sovereignty. Miami represents the downgrading of Latin America, the misguided belief in the goodness of the United States, and the hollowness of excessive consumption.

A CITY OF EXCESSES

Left-wing political leaders often use Miami as a rhetorical tool to dismiss the protests of the middle and upper-middle classes against public policies in their countries. "They want to be like Miami," is a common phrase used by politicians in countries like Argentina. Miami is evoked as shorthand for antipatriotic, superficial, and venal behavior. An opinion writer in Brazil, Cora Rónai, reflects on Miami as a city that generates ambivalent feelings, sometimes even embarrassment and antipathy:

> It is difficult to love a city that boasts of its own excesses, in which the main touristic activity is to go shopping. It is difficult to love a city in which all the corrupt politicians from Latin America buy mansions with profits from "wrongdoing." . . . It is difficult to love this city that serves as shelter to some of the most unpleasant characters in the news.[37]

Miami's conspicuous consumption is often posited as the antithesis of culture. Op-eds on travel and tourism presented a negative view of the city as a superficial, commodified place, well-suited for the new rich but vulgar at the core. When the former president of Argentina, Cristina Fernández de Kirchner, talked about the wave of Argentines buying condos in Miami, she said that she would prefer to have a second home in Paris.[38] Miami is also seen as a dangerous model for Latin America, one that betrays the core identity and values of the region. In the words of a Colombian journalist, "We need to challenge the face of Miami in Latin America and choose our own."[39]

This conception stands in contradiction to our earlier argument about Miami as a site in which biculturalism emerged as an alternative adaptive project to full assimilation to American culture. The fact that Miami represents a paradigmatic model of "acculturation in reverse" can be seen as *an affirmation* of Latin American identity. Furthermore, the case for Miami shows how language works as a variable in economic development by facilitating business connections. Spanish, which played a fundamental role in Miami's emergence as a financial and commercial center, is not stigmatized in this city, in contrast to other U.S. cities with large Latin populations such as Los Angeles. As noted by Guillermo Grenier, a professor at Florida International University, "In Los Angeles, when you hear Spanish, it is often the language that the waiters or the cutters doing your lawn speak in the background. In Miami, the people who own the restaurants and the lawn are the ones who speak Spanish."[40]

The alternative perspective of Miami as a land of excess and abuse represents an anti-Americanism grounded in the rejection of the values of free-market capitalism.[41] It also speaks to another theme that has profoundly shaped the image of Miami in Latin America: the city's role as a place of ideological contestation in the Americas.

BEDROCK OF ANTI-LEFT IDEOLOGY

Satan,

Fidel is now yours.

Give him what he deserves.

Don't let him rest in peace.

—A placard seen in Miami during the celebrations following the announcement of Fidel Castro's death, *USA Hispanic Press*

A great man has left us. Fidel has died. Long live Cuba!

Long live Latin America!

—Rafael Correa, president of Ecuador, quoted in *Al Jazeera*

The death of Fidel Castro was received—as expected—very differently in Miami and in most of Latin America. Miamians celebrated in the streets, banging pots and pans, dancing, and cheering. People waved the Cuban flag while singing the Cuban national anthem as they filled the streets of Little Havana. The restaurant Versailles was the center of the jubilation. The exile community celebrated with passion all night long.[42] Tomás Regalado, mayor of Miami and a Cuban American himself, hailed "the death of a dictator." He said, "The same way that Hitler's death was celebrated, we celebrate the death of someone who did great harm to four generations of Cubans."[43] In a similar vein, Marco Rubio, Republican senator for Florida and would-be presidential candidate, stated, "History will not absolve Fidel Castro; it will remember him as an evil, murderous dictator who inflicted misery and suffering on his own people."[44]

In stark contrast, Latin American heads of state and political leaders quickly moved to express their grief and recognition of Castro's significance.

Evo Morales, president of Bolivia, tweeted, "In the name of the Bolivian people, I express condolences and solidarity to Fidel's family, the government, and the Cuban people for the loss of a historic giant. Our admiration and respect goes out to Fidel, the leader that taught us to fight for the sovereignty of the state and the dignity of the peoples of the world."[45] Venezuelan president Nicolás Maduro reacted similarly, saying, "Sixty years since the departure of the Granma from Mexico, Fidel leaves us for the immortality of those who fight their entire lives. . . . Until victory, always."[46]

The presidents of Ecuador, Bolivia, and Venezuela were not the only ones who showed respect for the Cuban revolutionary leader. Mexican president Enrique Peña Nieto tweeted, "I mourn the death of Fidel Castro Ruz, leader of the Cuban Revolution and emblematic icon of the 20th Century. Fidel Castro was a friend of Mexico, and promoted a bilateral relationship based in respect, dialogue, and solidarity."[47] Several centrist and conservative leaders—from Colombian president Juan Manuel Santos to Brazilian president Michel Temer—acknowledged Castro's legend, and what it meant for their countries and the region as a whole.

This historical moment offers a perfect illustration of the role that Miami occupies in the ideological wars of Latin America. During the Cold War, many of the key players in Latin America's anti-Communist movement convened in Miami to plot against revolutionary forces in the region. After the Cold War, Miami continued to serve as a hub for those who oppose left-wing governments and politics in Latin America. There is no other city in the western hemisphere where one can find, in the same urban space, monuments honoring Anastasio Somoza's Nicaraguan National Guard and the 2506 Brigade, which made an unsuccessful attempt to overthrow Fidel Castro's regime during the Bay of Pigs invasion in 1961. Nearly three decades after the Cold War, Miami was the place where President Donald Trump announced a new policy on Cuba, denouncing his predecessor's "terrible and misguided" reconciliation with the government in Havana.[48]

MIAMI'S COLD WAR

During the Cold War, Miami played an important part in the anti-Communist crusade in Latin America and the Caribbean. The war against communism brought together a powerful transnational coalition that included authoritarian regimes, anti-Communist organizations, Central American paramilitary leaders, and Cuban exile groups, among others. The diffusion of ideas, the construction of networks, and the circulation of resources created a transnational movement of considerable influence in the 1970s and early 1980s.[49]

Miami was a hub for the activities of military and civilian actors advancing the global struggle against communism. The presence of a powerful and highly mobilized Cuban exile community was critical in this process, but the role of Miami in the Cold War went beyond the Cubans. From the point of view of the Left, Miami represented Washington's decision, following the Cuban Revolution, to advance a policy that sought to achieve stability through repression and the deployment of state terror. According to this perspective, the establishment of democracy in Latin America in the 1980s and 1990s was not an outcome of U.S. foreign policy but rather the result of opposition to that policy.

During the 1980s, after the 1979 collapse of the Somoza regime in Nicaragua, Cuban-exile organizations provided assistance to anti-Sandinista forces. Miami-based Cubans facilitated connections between the exiled Nicaraguan opposition and organizations committed to rolling back the advance of communism in Central America. The Cuban exiles viewed the anti-Sandinista struggle as a bridge to the liberation of their own country from the Castro regime. Cuban-exile organizations engaged in military training in South Florida, arms-trafficking operations, and coordination with other counterrevolutionary forces in Central and South American countries. Reportedly, Cuban exiles in Miami also collaborated with the Southern Cone military regimes in the hemispheric repressive enterprise known as Operation Condor.[50]

Successive waves of civilians, political dissidents, and former government leaders found refuge in Miami while their countries were being taken over or threatened by left-wing governments or Marxist insurgents. Central and South Americans converged in the city throughout the Cold War. This flow of people transformed Miami into Latin America's most important outpost of anti-Left ideology. The development structured the image of Miami in Latin America, provoking support and endorsement from center and right-wing groups while drawing fierce opposition from forces on the Left.

As noted in chapter 1, Miami is a new global city built, to a large extent, on the ruins of many failed political projects in Latin America. Specifically, the history of the Cuban Revolution, and much of the history in other countries, cannot be written without Miami. Politics and economics reinforce each other in the space of this city. The Cuban exile leadership lined up firmly behind the U.S. government in the international confrontation against communism; on the other hand, Cuban exiles' strong affinity to American capitalism bolstered financial and commercial activities encouraging a sustained flow of domestic and foreign investment to South Florida. Anticommunism and U.S.-style capitalism converged in Miami's unique experiment, which led to its shift from a provincial place to an economically successful global city.

RIGHT-WING CONSPIRACIES

The end of the Cold War did not diminish Miami's role as a central point of resistance to left-wing governments in Latin America. A recent example is Venezuela's twenty-first-century Bolivarian Revolution. The Venezuelan government of Nicolás Maduro often refers to Miami as part of a "conspiracy axis" against Venezuela: "From Madrid, the right; from Bogotá, the far right; and from Miami, the far, far right," Maduro said. "Together they have formed an axis to conspire against our homeland, and every day they spout drivel about Venezuela."[51] The left-leaning press in Latin America regularly denounces conspiracies bred in Miami, the intolerance of exiles, and the anti-Venezuelan actions of political opponents, businessmen, and journalists. Sympathetic media outlets help the Venezuelan government amplify the "shaming" of opposition leaders who invest or vacation in Miami, unabashedly displaying their wealth.

In the same ideological vein, the transition to neoliberalism experienced throughout most of Latin America in the post–Cold War era was deemed possible because state-sponsored violence in a number of countries in the region succeeded in preventing the rise of reformists, shattering social movements with the potential to sustain such reforms over the long haul.[52] One way or another, Miami is perceived as always connected to those Latin Americans driving, advocating or supporting an antipopulist agenda.

A relevant example is the resistance to the proposed Free Trade Area of the Americas (FTAA), a hemispheric initiative launched at the first Summit of the Americas in Miami in December 1994. The anti-FTAA movement gained remarkable momentum, culminating in the fourth such summit that took place in Mar del Plata, Argentina, in November 2005. Leftist presidents Lula da Silva of Brazil, Néstor Kirchner of Argentina, Evo Morales of Bolivia, and Hugo Chávez of Venezuela reacted against what they called "economic recipes that caused so much harm to Latin American countries."[53] One newspaper heralded, "The Miami spirit died in the IV Summit."[54]

For more than half a century, the city has been seen as a center of conspiracies against revolution, reform, or progressive governments in Latin America. This role has been intertwined with an image of Miami as the hemisphere's underworld, namely, a hub of illegal activities, corruption, and safe haven for "most wanted" Latin Americans—politicians, businessmen, military officers, and others.[55]

No other U.S. city comes close to this unique ideological profile. Miami is seen as simultaneously a dependable refuge for those defending democracy and personal freedoms in the hemisphere and a base of operations for those committed to extinguishing efforts to advance equality and social solidarity. As such, the city has acquired a unique position in Latin America's ideological divide.

BETWEEN CONSUMPTION AND IDEOLOGY

Miami occupies a singular identity in the region's imagination. It is a "dream city" that promises access to goods, leisure, and social status to the middle and upper classes in Latin America. It is also ubiquitous in the region through the media, particularly television, with an expansive reach to audiences. As the famous Don Francisco, host of *Sábado Gigante*, put it in the late 1990s, "Madison Square Garden and Radio City Music Hall may be more important to you Americans, but the big dreams of Latin artists are here, because whatever they do in Miami has impact in their homelands."[56]

Throughout Latin America, Miami is not just a city. It is a powerful brand. "Destinations aren't about geography, they're about psychology, they're about a feeling," in the words of Bill Talbert, president and CEO of the Greater Miami Convention and Visitors Bureau. "Get your brand and stay on it. . . . We sell one word, whether it's our music on hold, our cufflinks or our Braille business cards. It's one word: Miami, Miami, Miami."[57]

The city has strengthened a reputation for sophistication among Latin American elites that it did not have in earlier years. Miami is now drawing comparisons with Paris or London, with an emphasis on its world-class architecture, art, and restaurants. The city ranks sixth among the world's most important cities to ultra-high-net-worth individuals (UHNWI). Wealthy Russians have discovered the glamour of Miami, and according to Knight Frank's "Wealth Report," the city is now firmly on the radar of Chinese UHNWIs who are attracted to it because of its cultural diversity, quality of life, and enticing property prices.[58] The city has managed to project an image that has wide appeal—from those who dream of buying top brands at low prices to those who want an exclusive unit in the Sunny Isles' Porsche Design Tower, with a private sky garage.

Still, the other side of Miami is also firmly established in the Latin American mind: a hemispheric paradigm of inequality, political intolerance, and the excesses of capitalism. For the Left, Miami is the cradle of antirevolutionary and antireformist movements. It represents the "totality of capitalism and empire"—the convergence of right-wing ideology, financial crimes, drug trafficking, covert intelligence, and paramilitary operations.[59] Thus, the story of Miami's rise is seen as intertwined with the expansion of state violence in the Americas, the destruction of popular movements, and the triumph of neoliberalism.

CONCLUSION

The view of Miami from Latin America is not only fragmented, but incomplete. Most visitors to the city never travel to places like Miami Gardens or even know of its existence: for them, Miami encompasses the downtown and Brickell districts, South Beach, and Coral Gables. Still, two dimensions emerge very clearly, which concurs with our analysis in the first two chapters. First, Miami is perceived as an economic entrepôt with all the best conditions to do business between North America, Latin America and the

Caribbean, and Europe. Second, the city is a place of refuge. Political tremors in Latin America and the Caribbean consistently trigger flows of people and money to South Florida. For many Latin Americans, it is not only a site to find sanctuary from a hostile political environment but also a place to invest and save securely and in one's own language. This aspect plays a fundamental role in shaping Latin American views of the city.

But Miami is not only an outlier. It is a relevant case for understanding how global changes reconstitute the urban space through migrations, relocations, and demographic developments.

Miami is an emblematic global city aspiring to the top tier. It is also where, in both a symbolic and a practical sense, the resilient entrepreneurship of Latin Americans meets their long-standing inability to achieve a common vision of economic, social, and political stability. As the city's image and identity transform, the only constant is its unbreakable bond with the hemisphere below.

8 The Ethnic Mosaic and the Power Elite

In the late 1950s, Miami experienced three trends that
came together to create a "tipping point": the advent of air-
conditioning, the invention of jet propulsion, and the
arrival of Cubans. The three had nothing to do with each
other, but their convergence made the city what it is today.

—Alberto Ibargüen, president, Knight Foundation,
conversation with Alejandro Portes, April 2017

According to Ibargüen, air-conditioning allowed Miami to become a year-round city rather than a winter village; jet propulsion brought it within two to three hours from New York City, Boston, Bogotá, and Mexico City; Cubans turned the city inside out, reorienting it to the rest of the hemisphere and then the world. Remnants of the "winter village" that Miami had been still exist. Arguably, among the quaintest are the mechanical bridges that dot major transportation avenues across Biscayne Bay and the Miami River.

These bridges open on demand or at regular intervals to allow boat traffic to pass. Built for an era when cars and buses were scarce and yachts and sailboats even scarcer, they have become choke points in the city's present transportation crisis. Of these bridges, none is more visible than the one across the Miami River linking Biscayne Boulevard and Brickell Avenue. Built at the confluence of river and bay and adorned by an impressive statue of a Tequesta warrior, the original tribe inhabiting the place, the bridge has become a regular scene of confrontation between marine and street life. It is the most direct link between the booming downtown and the financial Brickell District, yet its frequent openings to give way to intense river traffic snarls automobiles and buses at peak times of the day.

Cross that bridge when you can, and you will find yourself in a jungle of high-rises inhabited by banks from all over the world and, farther afield, luxury condominium towers, ritzy restaurants and nightclubs, and an enchanting Bayfront promenade. The owners of the apartments, the patrons of the restaurants, and the joggers by the Bay are invariably white—native Anglo, European, or Cuban—the top echelon of Miami's income distribution. The servers in the restaurants and nightclubs, however, come in a wide variety of colors.

Return to downtown and cross the river again, this time going west on Flagler Street, and in just four blocks you are in a different world. The word *fritanga*—meaning Nicaraguan restaurant—is everywhere, as are all kinds of businesses advertising in Spanish. The people in the streets are uniformly dark Latins—Nicaraguan, Honduran, and other Central American migrants. St. John Bosco Parish, the "cathedral of exiles" that we encountered in chapter 1, is still there, its newly built, splendid church presiding over its uniformly poor, Spanish-speaking community.

The spatial character of urban phenomena cannot be better illustrated than in these contrasting images located just a few hundred meters apart. They are, however, only the first steps into the complex ethnic mosaic of this city. For the time being, we complete this initial pilgrimage in front of the small monument honoring the Nicaraguan National Guard. It was built by its former members, defeated in the Sandinista Revolution in their country. Located inside El Yambo Fritanga and Restaurant, the monument reads: "Honor and glory to the officers and soldiers that died in some place of Nicaragua defending the national decorum against international communism."[1] (See pl. 25.)

THE ETHNIC MOSAIC

The national and ethnic origins of the present population of Miami are too diverse to cover in their entirety, but apart from the most prominent players—Cubans, American Jews, and the remaining Anglos—there are other nationalities and ethnicities that play a significant role, demographically and socially. Of these, none is more important than the African American population that has been in and with the city since its beginnings.

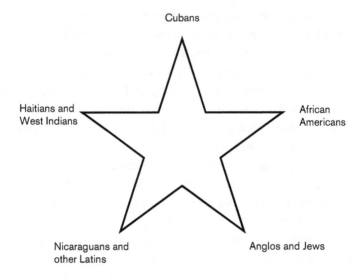

Figure 1. Miami's Ethnic Mosaic.

Miami's ethnic mosaic can be portrayed as a five-pointed star (fig. 1) in which Cuban and American Anglos and Jews occupy the best-known angles but in which the other three weigh significantly in the present mix.

African Americans

The story of how Henry Flagler marched his "Bahamian artillery" to the election that made Miami a city in 1896 is well known, as is the story of the subsequent relegation of these Bahamians and other blacks to Overtown and then Liberty City in the days of segregation.[2] More important for our purposes is what has taken place during the past twenty-five years. African Americans have maintained a stable demographic presence in the metropolitan area, representing 19 percent of the county's population, but this sizable presence has not translated into comparable political and economic power. By most accounts, African Americans are still at the bottom of the ethnic hierarchy both politically and economically, having been surpassed by more recent immigrant groups, including those of the same racial origins. Their median household income is significantly below the county average of $41,400, while they are overrepresented in the population that receives food stamps (25.5 percent countywide) and Supplemental Security Income (7.0 percent).[3]

The African American population is concentrated in certain areas of the city of Miami and in the municipalities of Florida City, Opa-Locka, and Miami Gardens. In Miami, Overtown—close to the central district—has been a traditional black residential area. It is now heavily decayed. It is also the locus of the area's opioid crisis. In 2016, a staggering 279 people died in Miami of fentanyl and other artificial drug overdoses. The majority of overdosed dead or dying addicts were found in Overtown streets.[4] The location of the area right next to downtown makes it ripe for redevelopment, a process that has been given impetus by David Beckham's planned soccer stadium in its midst.

Much of the black population displaced from Overtown by the construction of Interstate 95 originally went to live in Liberty City, an area hemmed in between the interstate on the east and Latin Hialeah on the west. It is also one of the poorest areas of the city, marked by the typical features of urban ghettos elsewhere: a sparse business presence—except for small food stores, pawn shops, and fast-food restaurants—a proliferation of storefront churches, and streets without people. We already introduced Liberty City and its core, Liberty Square, when discussing the street crime scene. The number and frequency of street shootings around Liberty Square finally prompted the authorities into action. Massive redevelopment of Liberty Square, the oldest public housing project in the area, is now planned with contributions from the county, the federal government, and the Related Group, a private development firm responsible for much of the growth downtown.[5]

Just north of Liberty City is the municipality of Opa-Locka, discussed in chapter 2. Together with Florida City in the far south of the county, Opa-Locka features the lowest median family income ($25,000); 40 percent of the population currently lives below the poverty line.[6] As in Liberty City, the physical appearance of Opa-Locka is that of a ghetto—cheap restaurants and food stores operated by Chinese or Latin owners, laundromats, an unkempt public park, and empty streets. The glorious arabesque City Hall, built by Glenn Curtiss, lies in ruins. Chances of its restoration appear slim, as the municipal government has been repeatedly rocked by corruption scandals. These range from major instances of fraud in the municipal budget to bribery related to things as minimal as turning on municipal water for the few businesses left in the area. The FBI has repeatedly raided Opa-Locka City Hall, and the last state-appointed emergency administrator, Merrit Stierheim, resigned in despair. At present, hopes center on the county taking over the bankrupt city government.[7]

Just north of Opa-Locka and reaching the Broward County line lies Miami Gardens. This is where many middle-class African American families escaping Overtown and Liberty City have settled. They have been joined there by large numbers of West Indian and Haitian immigrants. As noted in chapter 2, the city's population is three-fourths black, and, at 112,200 inhabitants, it is the largest predominantly black city in Florida.[8] Miami Gardens is not only black inhabited but black governed. Although street crime is high, local government under Mayor Oliver Gilbert III has done a good job of attracting businesses and middle-class residents to the area.

Miami Gardens does not feature areas of concentrated wealth, as in Coral Gables or Brickell Avenue, but it does not have the desolate streets of Liberty City or Opa-Locka either. Its median household income is almost at par with the county average ($42,040), and over half of the businesses in the city are black owned. The Gardens' main claim to fame is its sponsorship of the Orange Bowl, a nationwide televised event, presided over with panache by Mayor Gilbert and his assistants.[9] The rest of the year, the city is anchored by the major institutions that call it home: two universities and the Dolphins football stadium.

Black leaders interviewed during the course of our study converged on three basic reasons for the general lack of progress of blacks and their near-complete absence from the circle of power in Miami. The first is the lack of a symbolic reference point, the second is welfare, and the third is institutionalized discrimination. Absence of a national reference point means that, unlike Haitians and other black immigrants, African Americans do not have a country of origin in which to anchor their sense of self-worth and their ambitions. As a prominent black attorney put it, "Haitians, West Indians, and even Bahamians have left countries behind; they have a flag that they can wrap around their shoulders. Not so with American blacks, they are just American—citizens of a country that confines them to a permanent second-rate status."[10]

With regard to the destructive effects of welfare on black families, a longtime, prominent community leader in Liberty City said:

> I deal with houses in Liberty City where no one has ever worked. It is not that jobs are not there; people are just not motivated to take them. Whites said to black Americans, "You are entitled to special compensation because of the ways we treated you." That creates the welfare dependency pattern. Black Cubans and black Haitians are not entitled to it; they are not citizens, so they have to work like everybody else.[11]

Institutional discrimination is reflected in the general view of African Americans by city leaders, even leaders of other immigrants groups of color, as a "problem" to be solved or neutralized rather than as a human resource. For these leaders, the general quiescence and increasing apolitical character of the black American community is actually an asset to be preserved rather than an issue to be overcome. The complete absence of black Americans from Miami's power elite extends even to the leadership of progressive Miami Gardens. The city could as well be over the county line for all the downtown movers and shakers care. As one of our informants told us, "Take the Orange Bowl. It is advertised nationally as 'the game from Miami,' not from the Gardens. Nobody knows where Miami Gardens is. That is why the mayor, Gilbert Oliver, is a 'flamboyant figure.' He has to be in order to make his presence felt."[12]

In the 1980s, repeated riots in Liberty City and frequent confrontations between Cubans and African Americans over a number of issues were features of Miami life and culture. The city was "on edge" at the time, not only because of the political struggle between Anglo and Cuban elites, but also because of the mobilization of black Americans to confront the threat of double subordination—being shunted aside not only by a traditional Southern elite but also by a newly arrived "foreign" minority. What right did the Cubans have to elbow their way in, in such a manner? A black businessman and leader of the Miami Chamber of Commerce at the time put the matter starkly:

> There's the fear that they are taking over; there's still the concern that this is America and that a lot of the older Cubans do and say things that are the opposite of what America stands for. Some of the things those people say and do turn me off. It turns me off to see these small-minded zealots tell me

what to think. . . . They just got here! We were here before. I don't think they understand the system.[13]

Twenty-five years later, it was all over. Race riots were a thing of the past; black areas of town were politically inert. An African American attorney clarified what has taken place:

> The major change in Miami in the last quarter of a century is that it has become a Spanish-dominated city. Hispanicity is now its core and has become institutionalized. For other groups in this city, it is not just resignation or despair; it is the acceptance of how things are now.[14]

The response of the black middle class was to move to the extreme north of the county, turning Miami Gardens into its political center. Wealthier blacks became dispersed throughout the metropolitan area, exercising their new right to live wherever they wished. Though small in numbers, black elite families can be found in the most exclusive neighborhoods—Aventura, Miami Beach, even Fisher Island. At the opposite end, the black working poor and, in increasing numbers, the nonworking poor have been left to their own devices, confined to the traditional slum areas of Overtown, Liberty City, and Opa-Locka. Their situation, especially in relation to the fast economic growth taking place elsewhere in the metropolis, is dire. For the longtime Liberty City community activist already cited:

> The situation now is worse than thirty years ago. In 1980, the motivation for the riots was, "they don't let me be what I want to be." Today, "they do let me in, but the problem is I don't want to." There is no ambition, no motivation among young blacks to achieve any more.[15]

Haitians

Archbishop of Miami Thomas Wenski made his name as a young priest by championing the cause of a downtrodden and largely forgotten group. Haitians, "the refugees that nobody wants," as Alex Stepick called them, had been arriving in Miami since the 1970s.[16] Those caught at sea by the Coast Guard were promptly returned, but others found their way in. In 1980, a large influx of Haitians managed to enter by hitching their fortunes to the Mariel exodus from Cuba. Advocates for the Haitians pointed out the patent injustice that while refugees from Cuba were promptly admitted into the United States, those from Haiti were summarily turned back. In the end, the federal government relented, but it refused to grant refugee status to either group. Instead, they were labeled as "entrants, status pending."[17]

Destitute and heavily discriminated against because of their color, Haitians settled in one of the poorest areas of Miami, adjacent to Liberty City. The place was originally called Lemon City, but with the appearance of brightly colored Caribbean small shops and restaurants, it was rebaptized Little Haiti. Still no one went there; even African Americans kept their distance from the new arrivals. It was then that Father Wenski made his appearance. He got the Archdiocese of Miami to let him occupy an abandoned convent nearby and turn it into a community center. With Haitian labor, he repaired the church and garden and rebuilt the convent. Notre Dame d'Haiti was born, becoming the spiritual home of the downtrodden refugees. Before community leaders could emerge to take up their cause, Father Wenski was the voice that spoke for the Haitians. Sunday Mass at Notre Dame d'Haiti was something to behold—men and women dressed in their finest and ritual prayers recited and sung with rhythmic claps and a Caribbean beat.[18]

Gradually, the community improved, as Haitians borrowed a page from what Cubans had done on the other side of town and started operating a number of small businesses. Little Haiti patterned itself deliberately after Little Havana, although it fell short of its model. The causes were directly traceable to the two groups' contrasting modes of incorporation. Early Cuban refugee waves were uniformly white; they brought a great deal of education and business expertise; and they were warmly received by the U.S. government and public as allies in the global struggle against communism. The U.S. Congress enacted the Cuban Adjustment Access Act in the 1970s, granting legal access and refugee status to all Cuban escapees from communism. The Small Business Administration and other federal agencies put in place a panoply of programs to support Cuban enterprises in Miami and the revalidation of professional titles from the island.[19]

None of this happened for the Haitians, whose reception by the government and society at large was quite negative. Haitian efforts at business development were thwarted by lack of capital and pervasive discrimination. The colorful Haitian Caribbean Marketplace was built in the heart of the community, hoping to attract tourists from downtown. (See pl. 22.) No one came. White tourists made no distinction between Little Haiti and nearby Liberty City; both were seen as equally threatening black areas. In a few years, the Caribbean Marketplace had to close its doors.[20]

Relations between the two major Miami black communities were, at best, tense. African Americans did not regard the arrival of Haitian refugees as a benefit to themselves. Speakers of a foreign tongue and carriers of a vibrant but different culture, they were regarded at best as strangers and at worst as competitors for housing, jobs, and social services. Instances of solidarity and common mobilization by both black communities did happen, but they were, by and large, exceptional. On their part, Haitians manifested a distinct reticence to assimilate to African American culture and identity. Carriers of a rich national tradition themselves, they did not see any gain in casting their lot with the most downtrodden group in the local ethnic mosaic. Tensions between American blacks and black Haitians were reflected in repeated clashes at Edison Senior High, the school that youths from both communities attended.[21]

Fast forward to the present. Changes during the past two decades have been rather dramatic. Haitian entrepreneurs and civic leaders eventually succeeded in creating their own enclave. While it still could not match the Cubans', it acquired its own political and economic identity. Notre Dame d'Haiti is still there, and the Caribbean Marketplace has reopened its doors, but the core of the community has moved north, to the city of North Miami. Resettlement of the former refugees there has totally transformed local politics and civic life. North Miami's mayor is now Smith Joseph, born in Saint-Louis du Nord, Haiti. A drive around the city preceding the last municipal election revealed a large number of posters of candidates for mayor and city commissioner, invariably Haitian. The local high school, North Miami Senior High, has become "the" Haitian educational center, offering classes in French and Haitian Creole. The increasing political visibility of the Haitian community propelled one of its own, Jean Monestime, to a seat as county commissioner and to a prominent position on the county board.[22]

Resettlement of Haitian families in North Miami and out of Little Haiti has been due, in part, to the sudden popularity of the latter. The Wynwood area, now experiencing explosive growth fueled by its art scene, is directly south of Little Haiti. Land and buildings have been snapped up in Wynwood, so artists, gallery owners, and developers have started looking north. The formerly forlorn Lemon City is now in the local growth machine's cross-hairs as the next frontier for expensive condominium towers and malls. Ironically, this new development has triggered a defensive reaction among Haitian community activists to maintain their old community. It may have been poor and isolated, but it was theirs. In the words of Marlene Bastien, community leader and likely city commissioner candidate in the next election:

> Through their efforts and determination, Haitians were able to lift this area to the level of a cosmopolitan neighborhood that is now desirable to others. . . . [T]he Caribbean Marketplace has reopened, but there are developers already interested in buying it. In the 1980s, there were lots of protests and mobilizations in defense of Haitian refugees in this area. That historical memory is worth preserving.[23]

When a community shifts from struggling for survival to defending its historical memory of success, things have surely improved. Haitians are still not part of the power elite in the metropolis, nor are they part of its growth machine, but they have established a solid and visible presence as full members of its ethnic mosaic.

Nicaraguans

Latin American dreams of power often end up in Miami dust. Two Cuban presidents are buried in the Woodlawn Cemetery fronted by Calle Ocho. They were joined there by the latest Nicaraguan dictator, Anastasio Somoza. He had only two years to enjoy his plush Miami Beach mansion before he died. His overthrow by the Sandinista Revolution in 1979 was the prelude to a near-repeat performance of the Cuban drama two decades earlier. Like the Cuban upper classes had done following the arrival of communism to power, the Nicaraguan elites promptly moved their property and themselves to Miami. The middle classes followed in the early to mid-1980s, creating a visible presence in the westernmost suburb, Sweetwater. Small Nicaraguan businesses started to proliferate in that city, imitating, in all particulars, what had happened earlier in Little Havana.[24]

The local middle school was duly renamed for the great Nicaraguan poet Rubén Darío, and busts of Darío proliferated in the emerging Nicaraguan enclave. The population was there to fuel this development, as hundreds of thousands of Nicaraguan refugees moved to Miami during the late 1980s. As with Cubans before, all sorts of ethnic organizations proliferated. The decade saw the emergence of the Miami-Managua Lions Club, the Nicaraguan-American Bankers Association, the Association of Nicaraguan Architects and Engineers of Florida, the Nicaraguan Medical Association, *La Estrella de Nicaragua* newspaper, and many others. Los Ranchos restaurant, a direct import from Managua, became an instant hit, spawning five branches throughout the metropolitan area.[25] All signs were there for a repeat performance of what Cubans had done and the rise of a second powerful Latin group in Miami.

It did not happen, however, and the causes of that outcome are instructive. They had to do less with the education and motivation of the new exiles than with the circumstances surrounding their arrival. As seen before, Cubans had been received with open arms in the wake of Castro's Revolution by the federal government and American society at large. Circumstances two decades later were quite different. Embarked in an all-out effort to prevent another Communist regime in its backyard, the Reagan administration did not see the arrival and settlement of Nicaraguan refugees in the United States as helpful. Instead, it sought to keep discontent with the Sandinista regime bottled up in Nicaragua and encouraged escapees to join the U.S.-backed Contra forces in Honduras rather than settle in Miami.[26]

While leaders of the Contra movement were given refugee status in the United States and their Miami headquarters were supported by the CIA, the attempt by rank-and-file Nicaraguans to join the exodus was decisively resisted. Thousands of would-be asylees were deported by the Immigration and Naturalization Service (INS), and those granted asylum were not provided with any resettlement assistance. In the late 1980s, the INS mounted a major operation at the Texas border aimed at summarily adjudicating asylum requests by arriving Nicaraguans and immediately sending back those whose requests were rejected.[27]

This negative context of reception played havoc with the refugees' effort to consolidate their community in Miami. Except for the earlier elite waves and those directly involved in the Contra war, Nicaraguans arriving in the late 1980s were treated no better than undocumented immigrants, denied asylum and confined to economic penury. Their minds occupied by obtaining a work permit, escaping the INS if denied, and surviving in the informal economy, the new refugees were in no condition to build a viable economic enclave. Unlike the Cubans, they lacked the legal security and external assistance that had proven so decisive in the latter's success.

The single card in the Nicaraguans' favor was precisely their reception by the local Cuban community. By the late 1980s, Cubans had consolidated their own enterprises and occupied prominent positions in the local political structure. They saw the Nicaraguans as brothers in arms, suffering under another Communist regime supported by the Castro government and seeking, like themselves, refuge and assistance to rebuild their lives. Thus, as the federal government tried to stop the exodus and make life difficult for those arriving, the local government in Miami took exactly the opposite stance.[28]

Witnessing the "inhuman" conditions suffered by Nicaraguan refugees in a private homeless shelter, the Cuban city manager of Miami at the time, Cesar Odio, ordered it closed and made arrangements to move the refugees to Bobby Maduro Stadium, a facility built by wealthy Cubans in the 1950s and the spring training site of the Baltimore Orioles. Odio assured the refugees that they would receive the same consideration given to Cuban Mariel entrants. His action mobilized squads of city rescue workers: welders fenced off the entrance to the baseball field, carpenters built partitions, cots were placed along the stands in neat rows. The auxiliary Cuban bishop of Miami, Agustín Román, paid a visit; doctors from the Pasteur Clinic—run and staffed by Cuban American physicians—set up an examination room under a stairway.[29]

Underneath the stadium seats, two former Cuban political prisoners, Alfredo Menocal and Antonio Candales, manned a green telephone that rang incessantly. As City of Miami employees, they were trying to find jobs for the new refugees. A hotel representative inquired about the availability of Nicaraguan maids. A construction foreman asked about day laborers. Some callers, ignorant of the stadium's newest tenants, wanted to know when the Baltimore Orioles would be having batting practice. Two days after Odio's original declaration, the Cuban American manager of Miami-Dade County, Joaquín Aviño, unveiled a plan to build a temporary trailer camp to house new arrivals. A week later, Odio flew to Washington, DC, to persuade INS commissioner, Alan Nelson, to reverse the policy of denying work permits to newly arrived Nicaraguans. Despite the pleas of the Florida senators at the time to "regain control of our borders," Nelson granted Odio's request. Upon return to Miami, Odio went directly to the stadium, where he was cheered and had bestowed on him the title "father of the Nicaraguan refugees."[30]

Arriving in Miami and seeing how their spring training camp had been transformed, the Orioles promptly made arrangements to move to Sarasota. Never mind. What happened in Bobby Maduro Stadium was symbolic of what took place in the community at large. To a person, Cubans lined up behind the new refugees, committing their considerable economic and political resources in the effort to protect and resettle them. That effort culminated in the passage by the U.S. Congress of the Nicaraguan Adjustment and Central American Relief Act (NACARA) in 1997, which granted the new refugees legal resident status and the right to work in the United States. NACARA was initiated and steered through Congress primarily by the Cuban American delegation from Miami. Congressman Lincoln Díaz-Balart, a Cuban American, wrote the bill.[31]

Cuban support played a decisive role in facilitating resettlement of the large population of Nicaraguan refugees in Miami, but it was insufficient to bring it to a position of political prominence or consolidate a strong economic presence. In addition to federal reluctance to commit resources to the new refugees, a second key development conspired against consolidation of their own enclave. The victory of the Contras and return of democracy to Nicaragua promptly created a return flow of political leaders, entrepreneurs, and professionals. The incoming Nicaraguan administration under newly elected president, Violeta Chamorro, lobbied heavily for the return of the former exiles and appointed many of them to prominent positions.[32]

This development short-circuited the consolidation of a strong Nicaraguan community in Miami. Existing ethnic organizations shriveled or disappeared. A dense traffic of people and goods arose between Miami and Managua, with multiple flights per day. With Nicaraguan democracy restored, the U.S. government strongly encouraged the former refugees to go back, and the Cuban community saw no reason to continue supporting them. Thereafter, Nicaraguans still living in South Florida were no different from other economic migrants; only their protected status under the enduring NACARA legislation gave them an edge.

The Nicaraguan resettlement experience brings into relief the importance of contexts of exit, as well as contexts of reception, in the incorporation of immigrants and refugees in the United States. Unlike Cubans, the Nicaraguan exodus lacked finality, being interrupted by changing political circumstances at home. Ironically, the triumph of the Contra war spelled the end of a viable Nicaraguan enclave in Miami. Even the return of the Sandinistas to power via electoral politics a few years later did not reignite the exodus. By then, the die was cast.[33]

The Nicaraguan and Nicaraguan American population of Miami is still quite sizable, numbering about 150,000 in 2015. Politically and economically, it is nearly invisible. Nicaraguans have repaid the solid assistance received from Cuban leaders by supporting their initiatives and their power. Cuban candidates have consistently counted on the Nicaraguan vote in local elections. In recent years, many former Nicaraguan refugees have left their fledgling community in Sweetwater to settle in East Little Havana. While Rubén Darío Middle School is still there and the Divine Providence Church on Flagler and 102nd Avenue is still regarded as the "cathedral of Nicaraguans," much of this population has opted to leave the far west of the metropolitan area and reoccupy places of former Cuban concentration.[34] Unlike Cubans and even Haitians who have imprinted Miami with many symbols of their presence and culture, there are few such icons in areas where Nicaraguans concentrate. The little memorial to fallen members of the defunct National Guard at El Yambo restaurant and scattered busts of Rubén Darío here and there are all that exist at present.

Other Groups

Miami's ethnic mosaic comprises many groups that if not as sizable or as settled as those previously discussed are nevertheless becoming increasingly important. Miami's Latin population is now more than half non-Cuban. Aside from Nicaraguans, the fastest rising nationality is Venezuelan. Escaping the disastrous Bolivarian regime in their country, Venezuelans are concentrated in the city of Doral. They have come to resemble the first Cuban and Nicaraguan arrivals, with former elites and an increasing number of professionals migrating to Miami.[35]

Doral is an affluent municipality close to the international airport. The concentration of Venezuelans there reflects both the elite character of this population and its earnest hope that their country does not follow, in the end, the example of Cuba. Hence, Venezuelans in Miami are not yet considered political refugees "proper." Many travel back to their country to visit family members, attend to their businesses there, and take needed resources. Close proximity to MIA is thus a valuable feature of their new place of settlement.

As in the case of Nicaraguans, Venezuelans' movement into Miami lacks finality. Yet while in the Nicaraguan case the exodus was interrupted by the onetime defeat of Sandinistas at the polls, in the case of Venezuelans it is defined by political uncertainty and instability back home. Eligible voters in Doral were able to elect a Venezuelan mayor of the city, Luigi Boria, but he was subsequently defeated by a Cuban American candidate. Despite considerable economic resources, the lack of finality in their settlement pattern has so far prevented the consolidation of a strong Venezuelan presence in Miami.[36]

Other sizable South American immigrant populations include Argentines, Brazilians, and Colombians. These groups are made up primarily of upper- and middle-class businesspeople and professionals. As in the case of Venezuelans, many are former members of the elite in their respective countries escaping bouts of political instability or threatened by populist takeovers. As noted in chapter 1, Miami has been the beneficiary of political instability among its Latin neighbors to the south. This pattern repeats itself with notable regularity.

Once in Miami, South American immigrants have dispersed throughout the metropolitan area, failing to create a visible presence anywhere. There is no identifiable "Little Bogotá" or "Little Rio" that would reflect the presence of these groups. For most of its members, settlement in Miami is also regarded as tentative. They retain houses in their respective countries, divide their time between these countries and South Florida, and often remain more concerned with politics back home than in their adopted city. As in the case of Venezuelans, lack of permanent settlement decisively weakens their political presence, despite sizable numbers.[37] While South American immigrants often complain about the Cubans' firm hold on political and economic power, the underlying reason is that earlier Cuban exiles and their children are the only Latin group that made a durable decision to adopt Miami as "their" city.

Jamaicans and other West Indians make up another sizable immigrant group in South Florida, but, unlike Haitians, these black groups have not created a distinct presence either in Miami-Dade or in Broward County (Fort Lauderdale) to the north. Migration from Jamaica and other West Indian nations is mostly nonpolitical, triggered instead by economic motives. Although ethnographic reports point to the desire of many West Indians to differentiate themselves from black Americans, in reality they end up settling in middle-class suburban black areas and not creating a distinct political or economic profile.[38] As a longtime observer of this community notes, its basic motto is "Don't make waves":

> There are over 350,000 Jamaicans and other West Indians in Dade and Broward Counties, but you would not know it. There is not a single West Indian mayor or any other senior elected official in either county. They are content with letting others rule in their place. However, they also try to keep their distance from American blacks.[39]

North of Miami Beach and close to the Broward line is the municipality of Sunny Isles. In recent years, it has experienced a growing concentration of Russians and other Eastern Europeans, accompanied by the emergence of Russian restaurants and ethnic shops. Russian waiters and bartenders have started to make their presence felt in restaurants and nightclubs in Sunny Isles and its neighboring cities. For the most part, this emerging concentration is due to the purchase of luxury apartments by wealthy Russians.[40] Climate and the desire to take their money out of their unpredictable country have fueled this new inflow in a pattern that resembles the behavior of South American elites. Unlike the latter, however, Russians have concentrated in a single spot, and the presence of so many well-heeled Russian families in Sunny Isles has attracted a secondary inflow of other migrants seeking to provide these families with a range of culturally defined services. Hence, the white and blond population that one sees frequenting bars and shops in the northern beaches of Miami are not the Anglos of yesteryear but mostly Eastern Europeans. Signs in the Cyrillic alphabet fronting a number of restaurants and other businesses complete the transformation.

THE CIRCLE OF POWER

> The Non-group, and especially Alvah Chapman, did rule Miami until the 1980s. Now, no one does.
> —Former mayor of Miami, interview, April 2016

> No one really rules Miami now; it is a fragmented global city. Mayor [Carlos A.] Giménez is the most powerful man in the county, but he is constrained by the rules. . . . However, right now, 90 percent of the political power in Miami-Dade is in the hands of Cubans.
> —Former president of a major local university, interview, February 2016

The themes of social and political fragmentation, along with the political hegemony of Cubans, were repeated time and again in the course of our interviews with leaders and members of the community. In the end, the Miami power structure may be conceptualized as a circle with a number of participants along its circumference but no one at the center (fig. 2). Power holders alternatively cooperate and compete with one another, but in the absence of a core, decisive action on major issues is often postponed. The current fate of the SMART project, designed to solve the metropolitan traffic crisis, serves as an example. The current plan is presented in map 4. Months since its creation, little has been accomplished on the ground. Mayor Giménez and his diligent traffic director, Alice Bravo, are committed to it, but they are constrained at every turn by competing interests and contradictory rules. Most worrisome, the six SMART corridors do not readily connect with one another, leaving open the possibility of six disjointed two-way commutes rather than a truly integrated public transport system. Meanwhile, trolleys proliferate in different municipalities and ridership on the existing metro system—buses, Metrorail, and

Figure 2. The Circle of Power.

Metromover—continues to decline. Left to itself, SMART may turn out to be anything but.[41]

The circle of power in metropolitan Miami is crisscrossed by two major ethnic affiliations: Cubans and Jews. The concentration and political hegemony exercised by Jews in Miami Beach in the past lingers. Unlike transients from other places, major Jewish entrepreneurs have a long presence in the area, culturally extended and solidified by a network of synagogues. Jewish wealth practically monopolized large-scale philanthropy in Miami until recent years, as illustrated by the following large civic projects: the Adrienne Arsht Performing Arts Center, the Ziff Opera House, and the Frost Museum of Science. A Jewish businessman, Norman Braman, a longtime Miamian, led the successful recall referendum that removed county mayor Carlos Alvarez from office. Despite this confrontation, relations between Jewish and Cuban entrepreneurs are generally cordial, the two groups intermarrying frequently. According to a

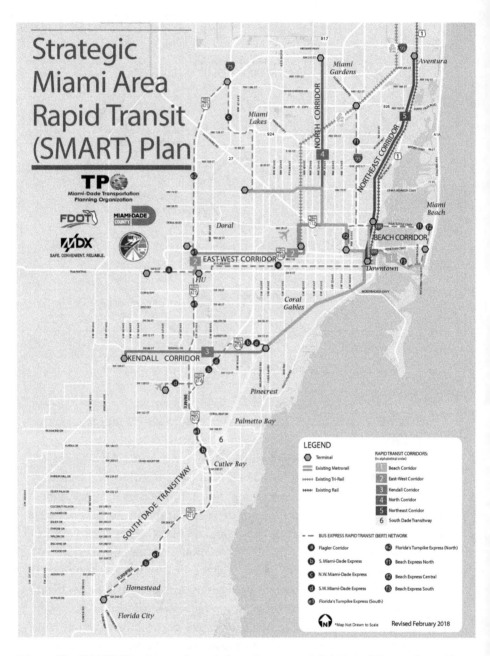

Map 4. The SMART Plan. Lines 1 through 6 are the proposed SMART public transit corridors. Contributed by the Miami-Dade TPO, April 2018.

well-placed informant, "Cubans run the politics in Miami; Jews largely run the economy."[42]

This remark was made with pre-1980 exiles and their children in mind. As discussed in chapter 6, the Cuban community is deeply divided between this group and post-1980 arrivals, including refugees who arrived as recently as 2016. The latter group is probably more numerous, but, despite its demographic weight, it is nearly invisible politically. As in the case of Nicaraguans, the more recent refugee flow from Cuba is marked by its lack of permanence. Concerned about relatives in Cuba, sending a continuous flow of remittances to them, and traveling back frequently to the island, these migrants remain uncertain as to where their loyalties and long-term life prospects lie. The Cubans who rule Miami politically are the old-timers and their children. Like local Jews, they have no doubt where their loyalties lie. Despite much talk about anomie, transience, and fragmentation, these groups hold the city together, each marked by internal solidarity and a moral compass that transcends short-run interests.

The Moral Community

> The death of Jorge Mas Canosa symbolized the end of an era.
> It marked the end of the "intransigent exile" committed to
> return at all costs to Cuba. It also marked the time when the
> Mesa Redonda and the Non-group came together, symboliz-
> ing the end of a decades-old confrontation and the rise of
> Cubans to power.
> —Miami civic leader, interview, April 2016

The ideology of intransigent anticommunism had imprinted the Cuban exile community of Miami since the early 1960s and, not incidentally, underlined the networks of solidarity that gave rise to its economic enclave.[43] With these networks consolidated and Cuban enterprises in full bloom by the late 1990s, it was time to turn a page. What our informant above meant is that the death of Mas Canosa, president of the Cuban-American National Foundation and the most prominent leader of the intransigent era, marked the end of that stage. While the Cuban exile community continued to oppose the Castro regime at every turn, it now did so at a distance—in international meetings and Washington policy circles—while leaving direct confrontation to dissidents inside Cuba. The community turned its attention inward, to its adopted city. The new focus on Miami did not mean, however, the end of the networks that had buttressed the remarkable economic and political rise of early exiles and their children. A series of institutions—cultural, religious, and civic—ensured that the old moral community remained alive in some form.

A number of these entities, imported from prerevolutionary Cuba, also ensure that patterns of close-knit solidarity within the Cuban community continue. One of the most significant is the network of bilingual private schools created by early exiles to educate their children and now schooling the Cuban third generation. Of these, none is more important than Belen Prep. El Colegio de Belen was a renowned Jesuit-run school in Cuba, attended by children of the elite. Among its most prominent graduates was Fidel Castro himself. Once in power, however, he expelled the Jesuits, who joined the Cuban exodus in Miami. Regrouping there, the Jesuits proceeded to reestablish their school, first in modest church premises downtown and then on its own campus on the western outskirts of the city.[44]

There exists now a "Belen Family" of friends, alumni, and supporters of the school. Even prominent Cuban Americans who did not attend Belen visit it regularly. Congresswoman Ileana Ros-Lehtinen was a frequent presence. The commencement address for the graduating class of 2017 was delivered by Senator Marco Rubio. Guillermo García-Tuñón, S.J., is the genial current principal of Belen Prep. Known affectionately as "Father Willy," he is a common sight at ceremonies and events of the Miami elite and is regularly asked to deliver the invocation and the required blessings.[45]

CITY ON THE EDGE

The special envoy for water affairs of the Netherlands leaned against the railing between the newly raised sidewalk in Miami Beach's Sunset Harbor and the old one well below. He snapped a picture, nodded approvingly to the assistant city engineer, and said, "This is the way to do it," and then immediately, "It's not enough."[46] Lurking beneath the ethnic mosaic, the power circle, and all the complexities and dynamics of a rising global place is the real possibility that it will all be drowned by the ocean. No one in South Florida likes to talk about it, but the Dutch envoy did not mince words: "Miami is at the edge. This is a risky place."[47]

The chair of Miami's Sea Level Rising Committee, Wayne Pathman, has repeatedly warned Metro commissioners of the dire consequences that will follow if present danger signs are ignored. Sea-level rises will have a "chilling impact" on the economy, according to Pathman, including sky-rocketing insurance rates.[48] Meanwhile, construction cranes continue to populate, even crowd, the city's skyline. Traveling north on I-95 from downtown in April 2017, we counted no fewer than thirty-six cranes, many erecting new luxury towers right by the water.[49]

The counterpoint between the rising sea level and the local growth machine's resolve to continue expanding the built environment represents one of the most dramatic aspects of the contemporary scene in South Florida. Citizens, developers, and authorities live mostly in the present, concerned with issues of crime, rising housing prices, and traffic conges-tion. All of these pale by comparison, however, to the impending danger. Miami may be the newest and also the shortest-lived global city. That pos-sibility and the struggle to resist it represent the defining features of the city's future. The amazing mood of optimism in face of the obvious threat is made evident not only by the feverish pace of construction, but by the prices that the new luxury houses and condominiums can command. As late as June 2017, a major local real estate company bought a full newspa-per page to advertise its new properties. Under the head, "This Year Make Finding a New Home Your Personal Goal," it listed apartments at Bellini Williams Island in Aventura "starting at 1.4 million"; in Coral Gables Waterway, "from 1.3 million"; and in Pinecrest, "at 2.19 million and above."[50] The key issues running counter to this optimism at present and the threat confronting the city's future are examined in detail next.

Driving into the Flood

TRAFFIC AND CLIMATE CHANGE

> The harder and less predictable urban transportation
> becomes, the more attractive private cars remain—
> and the more congested roads are.
>
> —Michael Lewis, "High Fives for the High Sign in Rare
> Nine-Way Tri-Rail Deal"

Driving the approximately eighteen miles between North Miami and the Coral Gables campus of the University of Miami takes approximately half an hour on Sundays or at 5:00 A.M. on weekdays. During the workweek, it takes an hour at midday and close to three hours at 5:00 P.M. Any automobile trip of any length in Miami-Dade County must be planned carefully, lest you arrive hopelessly late and with frayed nerves. Moreover, the automobile is the only viable means of transport to most parts of the county; public transit is either nonexistent or hopelessly slow.

Traffic congestion is choking the city. The root cause of the problem is easy enough to identify: sustained population growth and endless highrise construction in the condominium canyons of Miami Beach, downtown Miami, and other areas have taken place around the same streets and highways that were there thirty years ago. Collins Avenue, along which most of Miami Beach development has taken place, is still four lanes wide. It is now one-way north of 62nd Street, but this hardly alleviates congestion during most working hours. Biscayne Boulevard, which is also U.S. 1, has been the principal artery in and out of downtown Miami for decades. It is now clogged most of the time and becomes a literal parking lot after a Miami Heat game in the adjacent American

Airlines Arena or when concertgoers leave the Adrienne Arsht Performing Arts Center.[1]

The only rapid transit system worth the name is Metro Rail, running on elevated tracks from Dadeland in the south to downtown Miami, with a line going west to Miami International Airport. There is also a Metro Mover that transports people at no charge through points downtown and to the Brickell financial district. Otherwise, there is nothing. No rapid transit connects Miami with Miami Beach, and west of the airport or north of downtown there is no such system. To reach the Beach or the municipalities north and west of the urban core, you need to either drive or take your chances on the unreliable bus system.

Buses are the only means of public transportation that cover the entire county, but ridership has been declining steadily. Comparing 2008 to 2016, the county government tallied over 12 million fewer bus rides, a steep 15 percent plunge.[2] In contrast, use of Metro Rail and Metro Mover has held steady or even improved. The problem with buses is not only that they are slow and rarely on time, but there is stigma attached to them. Middle-class people see buses as the means of transportation used by the old, the disabled, and the poor—not themselves. Downtrodden racial groups are disproportionally found on buses, which again encourages others to jump into their cars. Lila, one young woman, declared to the interviewer in a recent study, "I felt like I was too good for the bus."[3] That is surely the kiss of death.

To counteract this trend, several municipalities—including Miami, Miami Beach, and Coral Gables—have resorted to trollies. Trollies are actually disguised buses, cutely designed to resemble old trams. They have been a success. That they charge nothing helps, but the key element is the absence of social stigma. Trolleys are touristy and nice and are used by both locals and visitors. "People like me"—middle-class men and women—willingly ride the various trolley routes. The problem, however, is that those routes are confined mostly to individual municipalities. The longest is a new line from downtown Miami to Coral Gables, a joint project of the two cities.[4]

Traffic congestion has become *the* major immediate problem in Miami, and the urgency to alleviate it is heard daily and at all levels of government and citizen groups. The active, vice-mayor of Miami-Dade, Alice Bravo, in charge of public transportation, is seen almost daily in the media announcing new measures. These range from buying new, faster, and cleaner electric buses to attempts to synchronize and centrally monitor traffic lights across the county.[5] So far, nothing seems to have worked. The principal north-south artery, U.S. 1, has reached the point of saturation, being congested at all working hours and well into the night. Desperate drivers take to secondary streets, speeding through residential neighborhoods. Ensuing protests by alarmed neighbors then lead City and Metro officials to take new measures. These include attempts to "calm" traffic by closing streets and erecting new traffic circles or other barriers. More irate than ever, drivers are thrown back onto U.S. 1 as the only alternative.[6]

Mercifully, U.S. 1 runs parallel to the Metro Rail south of downtown, so that those willing to leave their cars behind can take the train, at least as far as Dadeland, a distance of approximately ten miles. South of Dadeland and all the way to the southernmost city of Homestead, there is only a bus line running on a dedicated highway lane. West of the airport is the same story, so large suburban communities such as Westchester are reachable only by car or by the slow and stigmatized buses. Remarkably, not even Florida International University, a vast institution next to the Florida Turnpike, has access to rapid transit.[7]

The underlying reasons for the traffic emergency in Miami-Dade align closely with the political history of the city. The current county mayor, Carlos Giménez, expressed his frustration about the emergency in these terms: "We in this community have not been willing to take the first steps and to keep on going. If we had taken bold steps twenty-five or thirty years ago, we would have that system by now."[8]

Twenty-five or thirty years ago, the city was on edge, immersed in the power plays of competing ethnic blocs, as described in chapters 1 and 2. Neither the retreating Anglo establishment nor the ascending Cuban elites had time to think about traffic. For members of Chapman's Non-Group, transportation by car on the seemingly ample boulevards of the day and by bus for the less fortunate was just fine. As elected Cuban officials took over during the late 1980s and 1990s, they also did not see the problem. Their sole urban experience had been in Havana—a city that did not have a metro system and that also relied on buses and cars. In comparison to the narrow streets and alleyways of Old Havana, the wide-open avenues of Miami seemed ample enough to accommodate traffic for years to come.

As the Cubans ceded power to a more amorphous and more decentral-ized leadership structure in the 2000s, the problem compounded. Traffic flows and public transit are metropolitan-wide issues, but no one seemed to be in charge of them. Instead, individual power players—from private developers in the local growth machine to hotel chains to sports entrepre-neurs—pursued their own interests, oblivious of the broader effects. Traffic was someone else's problem. Individual municipalities did the same, building short-distance trolley routes within their limits. Hialeah and Miami Beach both have them, but it would be a difficult enterprise to move from one of these cities to the other without an automobile.

The lack of suitable public transportation and the traffic emergency in Miami thus mirror the evolution of its political order. Neither old-line Anglo leaders nor their Cuban successors had the vision to understand what was coming. The problem may be viewed, however, from another angle: Miami is a victim of its own success. No one in the late 1980s expected Miami to grow as it did. Gloomy predictions at the time envi-sioned it would become a "Banana Republic" or a "Paradise Lost." For rea-sons described at length in earlier chapters, this majority-minority metropolis actually worked, acquiring a global profile and displacing its numerous competitors as the center of north-south finance and trade in the Americas. But this success had unanticipated consequences.[9]

In the wake of Miami's momentous transformation, going from here to there was almost an afterthought. No one anticipated that the brilliantly laid out boulevards and bridges of an earlier era would be paralyzed by growth, posing a systematic threat to the city's future. It has taken time to come to this realization, but the reaction so far consists more of talk than action. Endless measures and plans have been proposed, but as the may-or's anguished comment above indicates, nothing effective is yet in place. Putting some electric buses in the streets or "calming" irate drivers by erecting traffic circles can only go so far. Further, proposed ideas like reversible lanes in rapidly growing municipalities like Doral have been bogged down in traffic studies that show conflicting conclusions while traffic continues to plague drivers.

In 2016, the Miami-Dade Metropolitan Planning Organization unani-mously adopted a plan to introduce rapid transit. The SMART plan, shown in map 4 (chap. 8), includes the following six "corridors":

1. Beach corridor between Miami Beach and Miami.

2. East-West corridor, along State Route 836 (the Dolphin Expressway).

3. Kendall corridor, from Dadeland to S.W. 162nd Avenue (also running east-west).

4. North corridor, from downtown Miami along N.W. 27th Avenue to Miami Gardens (N.W. 215th St.).

5. Northeast corridor, from downtown to the city of Aventura, along the Florida East Coast (FEC) railroad tracks, paralleling Biscayne Boulevard.

6. South corridor, from Dadeland to Homestead and Florida City, along U.S. 1.[10]

This impressive plan was approved by the Metropolitan Board Transit Solutions Committee and its governing board. Major hurdles remain in its implementation. First, no one has yet decided how rapid transit will be implemented along each of these corridors. For example, there is already a dedicated bus line in the South corridor, but Homestead and Florida City are urgently lobbying for light rail. Second, no priorities were established by the Metropolitan Board, with the predictable result that cities along each corridor jostled to be first. One commentator likened the situation to crabs in a basket: when one is about to reach the top, the others pull it down.[11]

This tug-of-war again reflects the atomization of the city and the absence of strong will at the top. The situation was partially overcome by the intervention of the private Miami-Dade Chamber of Commerce. That intervention led to the decision to start with the South corridor first and proceed with others as studies permitted.[12] The South corridor, running to rural areas of the county, is arguably the least crucial to resolving the present emergency. Still, the others are marred by uncertainty. Mayor Giménez himself declared that the county needs to begin environmental studies as they take time to complete. Meanwhile, transportation director Alice Bravo commented, "We don't have one area of density, and areas of rapid employment growth are also difficult to pinpoint."[13]

Clearly, it will be some time before a regular line crisscrosses Biscayne Bay between Miami and Miami Beach, or light rail is in operation to the western suburbs, paralleling the Dolphin Expressway. It is worth repeating that Miami's traffic conundrum reflects both the city's youth and its spectacular growth. It has been difficult to shake off the image of a relaxed winter resort and assume that of a global city. The Brickell bankers and the builders and developers of the growth machine have long embraced the latter image, but the citizenry and, in particular, its government has been rather slow to catch up.

A final example of uncertainty and lack of direction came in early 2016 with the proposal by the Miami Downtown Development Authority to cut the number of car lanes on Biscayne Boulevard from eight to four in order to make way for a pedestrian promenade, tentatively baptized Biscayne Green. Biscayne Boulevard (U.S. 1) is the main artery through the downtown area, surrounded by high-rises. It is also the scene of frequent gridlock, as discussed above.[14]

While commendable in its intent, the proposal for Biscayne Green is remarkably impractical, as it would make an emergency situation even worse. Pedestrian walks are nice things to have once you have met and resolved the challenge of public transit. At present, it would simply compound that challenge since no alternative to cars and buses has yet been devised. The proposal to reduce the number of lanes on Biscayne Boulevard in the midst of a traffic crisis reflects again the lack of an overarching decision center and of a clear set of priorities.

AN OCTOPUS IN THE PARKING LOT

On November 20, 2016, the local section of the *Miami Herald* carried a remarkable story. A resident of a Miami Beach condominium on his way to the basement garage was confronted with the unexpected sight of an octopus occupying his parking spot (fig. 3). The basement garage floods regularly at high tide, but until that day no marine fauna had been spotted in it. Apparently, the animal had nestled in one of the building's drainage pipes. Originally built to carry stormwater into the sea, they are now partially submerged and perform the opposite role. According to a biology professor at the University of Miami, the sight of the octopus is only the first of many to come. The Atlantic, teeming with marine life, is making its presence increasingly felt in city streets and basements. For the author of

Figure 3. Octopus in Parking Garage. Photo by Assia Fresegna.

the *Herald* article, the octopus in the parking lot is the functional equivalent of the proverbial canary in the coal mine.

A SINKING GLOBAL CITY

The higher-ups in Miami and in state government do not like to talk about it. What is happening is almost inconceivable. The fact is, however, that, indifferent to interethnic struggles, political compromises, banking strategies, and traffic congestion, the sea is slowly reclaiming the peninsula and, most urgently, its southern part. The endless debates and delays with regard to Miami's traffic gridlock may be related, at least unconsciously on the part of authorities, to the anticipation of what is coming. For what good is it to build a multibillion-dollar rapid transit system when a few decades from now it may be underwater? Traffic jams will surely disappear along Biscayne Boulevard and Collins Avenue when, instead of eight- or four-lane traffic corridors, they become canals.

The evidence that sea levels are rising, and fast, is undeniable. For the past few years, the daily high-water mark in the Miami area has been rising at the rate of almost an inch a year, almost ten times the rate of average global sea rise. The region has been designated "ground zero when it comes to sea-level rise" and "the poster child for the impacts of climate change." Talking about the latter on Earth Day, 2014, President Obama declared, "Nowhere is it going to have a bigger impact than here in South Florida."[15]

According to the Inter-Governmental Panel on Climate Change, sea levels could rise by more than 3 feet by the end of this century. The U.S. Army Corps of Engineers projects that they could rise by as much as 5 feet; and the National Oceanic and Atmospheric Administration (NOAA) predicts up to 6½ feet. Others predict as much as 15 to 20 feet in an unknown period.[16] According to maps released by NOAA, a large portion of what is today Miami-Dade would be underwater with a 3-foot rise in the ocean and by 7 feet, there would be little left. (See maps 5, 6, and 7.)

With the average elevation of the region scarcely over 4 feet above sea level, just a 2-foot elevation would put 25,000 houses underwater, flood $14 billion worth of property, and submerge 134 miles of road, according to estimates recently published by the *Miami Herald*.[17] In several parts of the metropolitan area, it is already happening. Shorecrest in the northeast section of Miami floods regularly. On the corner of 79th Street and 10th Avenue, people regularly awake to a lake of seawater in the street at knee level. These events are still exceptional but increasing. By 2045, the Union of Concerned Scientists projects that large parts of the city will be flooded daily and even twice in a day.[18]

You can readily see the evidence by walking in high tide through many parts of South Miami Beach. The city has resorted to elevating many streets by a foot or more, but those that are not fill with seawater to the extent of stopping traffic. Through ingenuous engineering devices, other low-lying parts of the globe have managed to fend off the sea and permit human habitation. The Netherlands is well known for these remarkable feats of human imagination. If this is possible in Holland, why not in Miami? The problem here is geology. The city is built on limestone that rose from the ocean during the last ice age. Limestone is a highly porous rock. Building a dike on limestone is like putting a wall on top of a tunnel; the water will simply go underground. In low-lying areas like the Shorecrest neighbor-

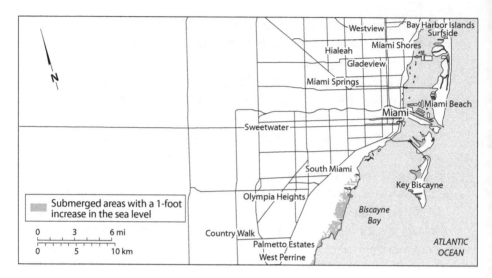

Map 5. Miami-Dade County 1-Foot Sea Rise. Note: Dark gray indicates submerged or regularly flooded areas.

hood in Miami, the floodwaters do not come from Biscayne Bay directly but from the ground. They simply percolate up from the limestone.[19]

At Miami Beach, an enterprising city engineer has toyed with the idea of injecting some kind of resin in the subsoil to insulate the rock layer. This would be the equivalent of caulking the entire region. Barring this, builders could be required to lay a waterproof shield below the foundations of houses and buildings to stop the salt water from inundating them. Such solutions will not work because floodwaters blocked at some points would find their way to others and because waterproofing will only last a few years.[20]

Faced with such realities, Miami Beach has already invested $100 million in a system of gigantic pumps to drain floodwater and dump it into Biscayne Bay. Of course, this just transfers the problem from one place to another because rising bay waters then go on to flood low-lying areas on the mainland. In a more promising vein, Eric Carpenter, public works director of Miami Beach, argues that "the only tried and true solution to combating rising sea level is to raise with it."[21] Thus, he proposes to elevate the entire city infrastructure—roads, buildings, and parks—by two, three,

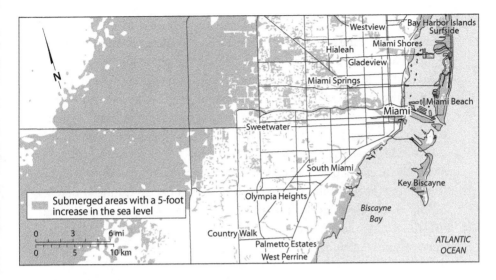

Map 6. Miami-Dade County 5-Foot Sea Rise.

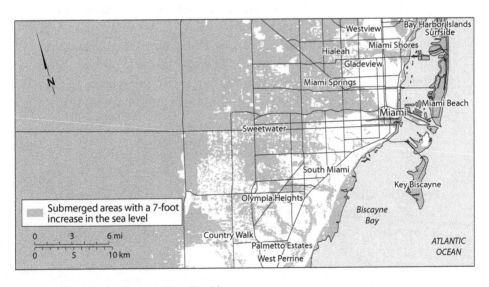

Map 7. Miami-Dade County 7-Foot Sea Rise.

or even four feet during the next half century. Private construction would follow suit, building on elevated ground and retrofitting existing buildings so that living space starts five or more feet above where it is today.[22]

All told, Miami Beach has developed a plan to invest $500 million during the next five years to add to its system of giant pumps, to elevate streets, and to put in place new building regulations. For many experts, this is just money down the drain: pumps will be flooded by rising ocean waters, which will also catch up with elevated streets and buildings.[23] Hence the ocean and the beach that gave Miami its raison d'être are now threatening its destruction. It would the height of tragedy indeed that, as the city managed to master the economic mysteries of globalization and turn them to its advantage, other natural forces unleashed by the same process—those of climate change—bring about its demise.

COPING WITH THE FLOOD

Traffic congestion and gridlock are major problems in the immediate future, but rising sea levels represent an existential threat. How they are handled will largely determine the long-term fate of this metropolis. Aside from the limestone underneath, the area is bound by the Atlantic Ocean to the east, Florida Bay to the south, and the Everglades to the west. There is nowhere to run. The following are the four solutions proposed so far to this looming threat: denial, technology, infrastructure above the sea, and exodus.

Denial

Despite the scientific evidence, some people still insist that there is no threat. The denier in chief is the current governor of Florida, Rick Scott. He has even forbidden state employees to use the term "climate change":

> "We were told not to use the words 'climate change,' 'global warming,' or 'sustainability,'" said Christopher Byrd, an attorney with the Florida Department of Environmental Protection in Tallahassee from 2008 to 2013. "That message was communicated to me and my colleagues by our superiors in the Office of the General Counsel."[24]

This unwritten policy went into effect after Governor Scott took office in 2011. Scott has repeatedly said that he does not believe that climate change is caused by human activity, scientific evidence to the contrary. According to Byrd, after Scott took office, "Deputy General Counsel Larry Morgan gave us 'a warning to beware of the words global warming, climate change, and sea-level rise and advised us not to use those words in particular.'"[25]

Governor Scott's stance may also be labeled the "Charlie Brown solution": when a serious problem arises, you wait and ponder; you don't try to solve it but hope it goes away. Perhaps the rise in sea levels will sink some unfortunate island elsewhere and leave Florida alone. Perhaps, somehow, the pumps will work. Not naming the problem to see if it disappears is only one form of the denial stance. Another may be referred to as benign neglect: admitting that a problem exists but not giving it much importance. The $6.8 billion budget for Miami-Dade County for 2016 contained only one passing reference to climate change. The budget compensated for past spending cuts on libraries, workers' salaries, parks, and public safety but contained not a line about climate change and sea-level rise.[26]

Mayor Giménez, a conservative Republican, has not publicly questioned global warming and sea-level rises. As late as 2016, he seemed to think that they were less important than parks, libraries, and traffic. The phrase "sea-level rise" appeared only once in his 2016 plan, on page 265 of volume 3. Even then, it was on a list of "unfunded capital projects." Protecting coastal parks in Miami-Dade would cost an estimated $175 million, but those funds did not appear in Giménez's budget.[27] Maggie Fernandez of the local League of Women Voters put it as follows: "In this three-volume budget, there is one mention of sea-level rise. This has to be a joke given that we're ground zero for climate change."[28]

Not all local officials have adopted a complacent stance. Aside from the activist mayor of Miami Beach, discussed below, others—including conservative leaders—have sounded the alarm. In a joint op-ed in the *Miami Herald* the former Republican mayors of Miami and Coral Gables, Tomás Regalado and James Cason, called upon GOP presidential candidates on the eve of their 2016 debate at the University of Miami to address the issue of climate change:

To date, all of this year's Republican presidential candidates either have rejected global warming outright or dismissed any solutions. . . . It's a looming crisis that we must deal with and soon. . . . By the end of the century, four to six feet of flooding would make this region unrecognizable. . . . These are the facts. We shouldn't waste time debating them.[29]

They went on to join a bipartisan group of 21 mayors in Florida to urge organizers to include questions about climate change in all debates.[30] Local government leaders, water lapping over local roads and sidewalks, know that political prevarication is suicide. In this context, the chair of the Department of Geological Sciences at the University of Miami and an expert on the subject, Professor Harold R. Wanless, issued two lapidary statements: "Much of the region has less than a half century to go," and, referring to Governor Scott's prevarications, "It's beyond ludicrous to deny using the term climate change. It's criminal at this point."[31] The arrival of another climate change denier to the U.S. presidency in January 2017 has reinforced Scott's position and added weight to the stubborn deniers of scientific evidence. The office of denier in chief has moved from Tallahassee to Washington, DC.

The Science Fix

An alternative to denial is to turn to science and scientific innovations. This amounts to the hopeful wish that just as humanity has been able to put men on the moon and make all communications instantaneous, it will also be able to contain a rising sea. The Netherlands and other low-lying areas of the world are already doing it, so what about a waterproof resin to caulk the entire limestone underbelly of Miami?

Miami Beach's former mayor, Philip Levine, was first in the line of danger, and he became an ardent advocate of the scientific fix. The battle with the elements has already been joined at the Beach. This is what Levine had to say about it: "When you're doing this, there's no textbook, there's no 'How to Protect Your City from Sea Level Rise,' go to Chapter 4. So the city would have to write its own. We have a team that's going to get it done."[32] In reply to a critical comment that the giant pumps installed by the city represent just a band-aid in the short to medium term, Levine replied:

I believe in human innovation. If thirty or forty years ago, I'd told you that you were going to be able to communicate with your friends by looking at your watch or with an iPhone you would think that I was out of my mind. . . . Thirty or forty years from now, we're going to have innovative solutions to fight against sea-level rise that we cannot even imagine today.[33]

Levine is not the only science optimist. Between his musings about a resin to caulk the subsoil, chief city engineer Bruce Mowry posited, "If we can put a man on the moon, then we can figure out a way to keep Miami Beach dry."[34] Belief in science or science fiction has taken a peculiar form. At the initiative of the Rockefeller Foundation, both Miami and Miami Beach, as well as Miami-Dade County, have created "Resiliency Offices" and appointed spirited functionaries to head them. They are not scientists, properly speaking, but designated specialists employed to keep the citizenry's spirits high. Thus, Jim Murley, chief resiliency officer of Miami-Dade County in 2016, said:

In the next three to five years, the city will concentrate on updating its storm water infrastructure to help floodwaters drain faster. . . . [W]e want to design and construct a sewer and water system that is resilient to six feet of sea-level rise and a Category 5 hurricane.[35]

And his then counterpart in Miami Beach, Susy Torriente: "This is not just about pumps and raising streets. This is about how can we start to look at all the operations of the city through the lens of resiliency."[36]

Conjuring science by bureaucratic appointment is certainly an innovation, but none of the resiliency offices or officers has come up with a viable solution to withstand a six-foot rise in sea levels. At that point, according to the NOAA maps, there will be little left to defend. According to Professor Wanless, these offices are politically and economically motivated—an expedient to calm the fears of home owners and prospective investors. The ironies of fighting the consequences of climate change with the technology at hand are already apparent. The giant pumps bought by Miami Beach to drain seawater off its streets and deposit it in Biscayne Bay will likely contribute to flooding of the low-lying areas of the mainland. The stormwater system in low-lying areas, built half a century ago and designed to carry floodwater into the bay, now brings bay water into the streets.

If Miami is in the process of modernizing its sewers and stormwater system, where will the floodwater be sent? If it is deposited in the bay, it will simply raise the bay's level; if it is sent west, it would compromise the freshwater reserves in the Everglades, already endangered by rising salt water seeping from below. The situation poses a major challenge for science and for those who place their faith in it. As the South Florida Water Management District's chief engineer puts it, "You can't build levees on the coast and stop the water. It would just come underground."[37]

Nevertheless, the optimists dismiss these problems as just so many challenges to be overcome. John Sawizlak, global director of resiliency for the engineering firm AECOM, thinks that Miami could even replace Amsterdam as the true leader in the fight against the seas: "Don't go to Amsterdam to see how to prevent from being cut off by the sea. Come to Miami to see how to live with water."[38]

Waterworld

Eric Carpenter may, in the end, be right. The solution, according to the Miami Beach engineer, is to raise the entire city—streets, buildings, parks—moving apace with rising sea levels.[39] Now picture what this would entail. The Beach, as we know it, would disappear, swallowed by the ocean. With seawater now lapping at them, condominium high-rises would have to be protected by massive concrete walls and its foundations insulated by some form of Mowry's newly invented resin. To ease the pressure, first and second floors would have to be sacrificed, letting seawater occupy city streets and thus convert them into canals. To communicate across buildings and with commercial areas, bridges would have to be built across the canals and automobiles replaced by boats and gondolas.

In short, a waterworld akin, in its best renditions, to Amsterdam or Venice. Miami, as it exists today, would disappear, to be substituted by a series of islands defended from submersion by the available technology and connected by water. Ironically, the city's traffic problems—at least in their present form—would disappear. Congested Collins Avenue, Bird Road, and U.S. 1 would become waterways, with water taxis and gondolas taking people to their destinations. Traffic jams of the future would take place against a marine backdrop. A related idea has been put forth by

Isaac Stein, a former University of Miami student who now works for an urban planning and landscaping firm. His solution? Make Miami Beach "floodable" with the creation of new bays and shorelines, along with new boardwalks and flood-adapted buildings.[40]

It would be difficult to envision the entire metropolitan area transformed and defended in this manner. A Venice-like Miami would be much smaller than the present city. There is no high ground to occupy. Hemmed in between the Atlantic Ocean and the Everglades, the city has nowhere to move. Unless technology somehow manages the miracle of raising new land from waterlogged swamp and defending it from an encroaching sea, there would be no alternative to a much smaller city on stilts. Even this reduced alternative seems unlikely. The heat transferred from atmospheric warming is already in the oceans and will continue melting the polar caps for the foreseeable future.[41] Thus, every rise of elevation of the city, achieved at great cost, will only last for a few years, requiring another massive investment in the short to medium term.

Exodus

If the worst happens, the city would have to be evacuated and the place returned to nature. It would not be the same swampland as it was at the turn of the twentieth century; there would be no land at all. In short, South Florida would cease to exist. Stages leading to this dismal outcome would not involve solely physical forces but economic and social ones as well. If Wanless is right, at some point insurers will cease writing policies for businesses and home owners and bankers would stop advancing mortgages for new high-rises and private homes. The real estate market would collapse and, with it, the economic ability of the county and city governments to confront the threat of a rising ocean.

Miami has seen economic collapse before. After the massive hurricane of 1926, the real estate market went under. And by the late 1920s you could not give away land that had fetched high prices just a few years before.[42] The difference is that the 1926 hurricane did not wipe out the land and, eventually, both the city and its property values recovered. The present situation is different. Short of a major scientific or technological breakthrough, the property collapse brought about by the rising sea would prove irreversible. Having lost their homes and businesses and finding no incentive to rebuild, people would simply abandon the place. Thus, the exodus might happen even before the ocean finally obliterates the land. The mayor of South Miami, Philip K. Stoddard, is a scientist himself and a professor at Florida International University. He is under no illusions about the long-term fate of the region: "Ultimately, we give up and leave. This is how the story ends."[43]

No one wants to think about this outcome even as the Atlantic makes its presence increasingly felt in many neighborhoods. Compounding the problem is the political fragmentation of the metropolitan area and the absence of decisive leadership at the top. As we have noted in earlier chapters, citing knowledgeable informants, "no one rules Miami at present." This state of affairs, which in other circumstances could be praised as the triumph of democracy over small-town politics, may now turn out to be a fatal handicap.

A longtime observer of the local scene concurs:

What [all the problems facing the city] have in common is we need a small, unified leadership planning for them before a shot is fired. . . . Once we did. Five leaders led by Alvah Chapman, publisher of the *Miami Herald*, . . . called all the shots in Miami. What they wanted, everyone did. It was not democratic, but it worked.[44]

Perhaps it is too early to welcome the return of Southern-style elite rule, as implemented by Chapman and the Non-group. But it will be absolutely necessary for elected leaders and those in the private sector to come together in a common, decisive effort before it is too late. "Resiliency" municipal offices are nice to have, but they will not suffice given the magnitude of the threat. In addition to getting rid of climate-change-denying leaders, such as the current president of the United States and the current governor of Florida, it will be necessary to muster the best scientific and technological knowledge available in order to confront the threat or find the best ways to adapt to it.

A Venice-like Miami is not entirely inconceivable, provided that the necessary physical and economic planning is put in place long before the looming threat becomes unstoppable. A scientific miracle such as is hoped for by Miami Beach's former mayor and his chief engineer looks increasingly improbable, but perhaps vigorous planning and innovative measures can save what we can from an impending disaster.

We wish to conclude this book on a positive note. Perhaps the optimism of Levine and the serious stance of the former mayors of Miami and Coral Gables will carry the day. The social and economic energies released by the city's ascension to global status are tremendous. It is still possible that a new, cohesive ruling coalition will emerge and that new technologies may confront or at least retard the effect of rising seas. In this battle for its very existence, Miami has little time to waste.

Postscript

> In the early years of the twenty-first century, New York City
> lost its soul. . . . [I]t's a continuous process of living
> and working, a gradual buildup of everyday experience,
> the expectation that neighbors and buildings that are here
> today will be here tomorrow. A city loses its soul when this
> continuity is broken.[1]
>
> —Sharon Zukin, *Naked City*

In her highly readable account of the social and cultural transformation of
New York, Sharon Zukin takes us through the stages that transformed a
gritty, dirty, and gray city into one peopled by shiny skyscrapers and clean
but empty parks. Hers is a cri de coeur echoing the profound dislike by at
least a certain class of New Yorkers of what has happened to their town.
Zukin follows in the footsteps of Jane Jacobs's classic *Death and Life of
Great American Cities* in deploring the demise of the urban scene created
by descendants of European immigrants and populated by myriad small
businesses catering to the locals—an Italian cheese shop here, a Jewish
tailor shop there, a Chinese restaurant in the other block next to a Polish
jewelry store.[2]

For Jacobs, these and many other sparks of social life risk being extin-
guished by the monolithic office towers, large public housing projects,
intrusive highways, and monumental cultural centers that brought along
"a great blight of dullness," all the while reducing residents to passive
pawns. Zukin leads us into the increasingly desperate pilgrimage of those
deploring these changes in search of "authenticity."[3] Urban authenticity is
found in generally declining, shabby street corners and neighborhoods,
not yet touched by the greed of developers and the arrogance of planners.

Authenticity is marked by continuity with what went on before, a legacy with which to confront the dullness of the modernist world, "when every new building looks like the same big glass box, old redbrick buildings and cobblestone streets gain cultural distinction."[4]

Unfortunately, the quest for authenticity in urban life often ends up destroying what it finds. When a street or neighborhood is identified as hip or distinct, artists, literati, and academics come to shop and perhaps settle there. Alerted by the buzz, corporate managers do not take long to cash in. The first Starbucks makes its appearance, followed by a Subway, and an H&M clothing store housed in an old loft. Rental prices increase, and if the trend continues the urban growth machine soon tears down old warehouses to build high-price apartment towers marketed to those thirsty to imbibe the local flavor. By the time these new gentrifiers move in, old-timers have long left, and the charm with which they endowed the place gives way to another place of predictable, bland, and safe upper-middle-class consumption.[5]

The search for authenticity is not unique among New Yorkers but extends as well to educated urbanites in other old cities. Zukin cites approvingly a London novelist moving into an as yet untouched corner of his city: "I came to Hackney because it is full of weird places and eccentric people and has a grubby glamour to it that has not yet been stamped out and flattened into the same cloned corporate hell-hole as the rest of Britain."[6]

"AUTHENTICITY" IN MIAMI

Zukin's quest and that of his motivated soulmates in cities of the U.S. Northeast and across the Atlantic would be remarkably out of place in Miami. There are no old neighborhoods to find and move into for the sake of nostalgia and distaste for the corporate "hell-hole." It is perhaps this absence that motivated the Dutch geographer Jan Nijman to make "transience" the core of his analysis of Miami life, a notion with which we have wrestled throughout this book. There are no historical and decaying neighborhoods that one can walk through, as Sampson did in his memorable tour of Chicago (chap. 5).

"Old" neighborhoods in Miami are, for the most part, themselves reproductions of places elsewhere—aging theme parks that with time begin to
acquire some patina of reality. This is as true of established and flourishing Coral Gables as decrepit and decayed Opa-Locka. The postmodern
consumerist culture and bling lifestyle that Latin Americans, as seen in
chapter 7, simultaneously decry and celebrate are superimposed on the
physical facade of sleek new high-rises, super-luxury hotels, and vast malls
where reproductions of monuments and buildings in London, Paris, and
New York itself are common. Like Las Vegas, much of Miami has made
the *absence* of local history a virtue, turning itself into a postmodern replica of events and architecture elsewhere. But Miami is more complex
than Las Vegas. Tucked here and there one finds versions and inklings of
the authenticity so central to inhabitants of older cities to the north. It
may be worthwhile, as an introduction to a summary of the main themes
of this study, to dwell briefly on three of these experiences. We revisit
places discussed in previous chapters as they reveal unsuspected facets
under the new lens of authenticity.

South Beach

As seen in chapter 2, the fifteen or so blocks south of Lincoln Road in
Miami Beach have become one of the world centers of vibrant nightlife,
displays of fashion, and rowdy consumerism. It is the de rigueur destination for first-time tourists and well-heeled smart people in search of
action. It was not always that way. Before the great hurricane of 1926, the
area was a poor cousin to its neighborly developments to the north—featuring Spanish tile and wrought iron in spades and owned by the
Firestones, the Deerings, and other millionaires of the day. Yet after the
devastating storm and the Great Depression that followed you could not
give land away in Miami.[7]

Desperate about the situation, the Lummus brothers—developers of
South Beach—decided to break away from the anti-Semitic code under
which property deeds had been written in the city until then. In their view,
a well-heeled New York Jewish buyer was better than no buyer at all. This
decision triggered a mass flow of northeastern and midwestern Jews to
South Florida in subsequent years. For these hardworking immigrants

from czarist Russia and Eastern Europe, the warm beaches and azure ocean waters were a welcome reward for their many years of toil up north. They bought property in droves, turning Miami Beach into the most Jewish city, on a per capita basis, in the country.[8]

Unlike previous wealthy inhabitants of the place, Russian Jews had no particular taste for wrought iron, nor could they afford it. Instead they settled for a more modest and practical style of architecture better suited to their mental image of a seaside resort, an American Odessa. Art Deco was their choice, featured in the hotels with rounded corners and marine oval windows, all painted in pastel colors. South of Lincoln Road, Art Deco was king, and hotels and apartment houses in that area became almost uniformly populated by aging retired Jews.[9]

In due time, the buildings began to decay in tandem with their occupants, and by 1960, those Art Deco hotels were ready for the bulldozer and replacement by shiny new towers. The city government simply waited for the process to play itself out, as more and more of the aging population died. Miami Beach, and South Beach in particular, hit bottom in the early 1980s as newly arrived Mariel Cubans, many just released from Cuban jails, started preying on the remaining Jews and turned the area into a decayed but lively drug scene. These were the years of *Miami Vice*, shot in the increasingly deserted South Beach streets. Demolition of the area seemed inevitable, but at that moment and unexpectedly the desire for "authenticity" arrived.[10]

A coalition of local conservationists, with Barbara Capitman at its lead, argued that South Beach's Art Deco district was unique in the country and ought to be preserved. Attracted by the quaint architecture and also the low rents, gay couples, local artists, and bohemians of all types moved in. They also actively supported the preservation campaign. This coalition eventually won, earning for the area a National Historic Place designation in the mid-1980s. Art Deco hotels fronting the ocean—the Cardozo, the Colony, the Marlin, the Clevelander, the Betsy, and many others, thus gained a new lease on life. Hip Europeans, including Gianni Versace, bought mansions next to them. Rapidly, South Beach sprang back to life.[11]

Conservationists had won, and the local growth machine eager to tear down those old hotels lost but not for long. If it could not get rid of the Art Deco district, it could certainly exploit its new chic. The "authenticity" of old Jews basking in the Florida sun and the low-price kosher restaurants never came back. Instead, the area was transformed into the endless procession of glitzy nightclubs and bars and expensive tourist restaurants that we see today. The Cardozo, the Clevelander, and the Betsy are still there, but staying in one of their elegantly refurbished suites has become an increasingly expensive proposition.

Wynwood

The area adjacent to the black ghetto of Overtown, Wynwood, had been occupied for decades by poor Puerto Rican migrants. By the 1990s, however, most of them had left and the area had turned into a collection of warehouses and cheap wholesale shoestores operated by Koreans. Very little to rescue there. As presciently recognized by its New York developer, Tony Goldman, Wynwood's "authenticity" did not come from its former residents but from the graffiti artists covering the warehouse walls, initially poor young ghetto kids. Instead of having them chased away by police, Goldman invited them and their successors to practice their art on his walls. As discussed in chapter 4, the new fashion caught on. Soon Korean warehouse owners were paying to have their walls decorated, and subsequently reputable painters from northern cities were "renting" wall space so that their art would be featured in Wynwood.[12]

As it always happens when a rundown area is rediscovered, the initial settlers were poor artists, bohemians, and a few brave gallery owners. As the place caught on, chic restaurants and bars started to bloom, followed by reputable art dealers and boutiques. Wynwood became a mecca not only for local artists and literati but also for tourists from all over the world. Inevitably, property capitalists came in and began wholesale purchases of land and buildings in the neighborhood. The more tourists who came to sample the rundown flavor of the place, the faster the rents rose. As always, the process culminated with the construction of new high-rise condominiums for those eager to bask in the local atmosphere and able to afford it. As the construction equipment moved in, artists, writers, and gallery owners now unable to afford the rents moved out.[13] The "authenticity" of the graffiti walls gave way to a new make-believe world of glitter and consumerism, not too different from what had already taken place in South Beach.

Little Havana

North of Wynwood is Little Haiti, which, as seen earlier, is next in line in the gentrification path as artists, galleries, and bohemians move there in search of cheaper rents. Little Haiti is old Lemon City, colonized and brought to life by Haitian refugees in the 1980s. Nostalgia for those days is prompting some of these former refugees, now established members of the middle class, to try to defend the area against the "great blight of dullness" that Jacobs deplored. Their chances for success are poor, however. Few Haitians sit on corporate boards or are members of the local power circle, and those who have influence do not appear to be interested in the area. The Caribbean Market (see pl. 22) seems destined to follow the Art Deco hotels in South Beach and the walls of Wynwood—a touch of color and local lore in the midst of faceless condominium towers.

Little Havana stands a better chance. Authenticity here consists of the modest houses, corner stores, and little restaurants in the area where Cuban refugees settled at the start of their sojourn in America. There is nothing particularly graceful about these streets, but Caribbean rhythms, the aroma of Cuban coffee, and the occasional old man puffing on his cigar are features of the place. Located directly west of the Brickell bank district, Little Havana appears ripe for development. Standing in the way is a coalition of local preservationists, backed by the circumstance that many Cuban Americans now in power grew up in Little Havana.[14]

The place is only about half a century old, but it comes closest to the nostalgic neighborhoods that Zukin describes in globalized New York. Now that three generations of Cubans have grown up in Miami, affluent children of the earlier refugee generation like to return to their old haunts for a lunch of roast pork, rice, and beans, a street corner *cafecito*, or a cigar purchased from a tobacco roller at a local store. While few Cubans live there, it is the sentimental heart of the community. Given its political power, it is unlikely that it will suffer the fate of Wynwood or Little Haiti.[15]

But if the growth machine cannot put Little Havana under the bulldozer, it can do the second-best thing, as was done in South Beach: convert it into a glitzy tourist attraction. Already two-decker tour buses roll regularly onto Calle Ocho, the Ball and Chain and Cuba Ocho nightclubs do a brisk business selling overpriced mojitos to visitors from Ohio and

Indiana, and old-timers playing at Domino Park and minding their own business find themselves ceaselessly photographed by the same tourists. "I am going to get myself some Cubans," says the camera-armed Minnesotan as he descends from the tour bus. The few Cubans who remain in the area can only grin and bear its transformation from historic drama into tourist attraction. Local club and restaurant prices have risen accordingly.

RETURNING TO THEORY

The search for authenticity that is the core of Jacobs's and Zukin's books is nothing but a present-day version of the age-old confrontation between alternative definitions of the city as a site for human habitation and as an engine for capital accumulation. That contradiction, discussed in chapter 2, is also faithfully projected in urban space. In New York, it is the contrast between the relentless march of the skyscraper corporate front line and the remnants of old-time ethnic neighborhoods still left standing. In Miami, where there are few authentic places to rescue, the spatial character of urban phenomena is best observed in the contrast between downtown, Brickell Avenue, and South Beach and the endless expanses of working-class and poor neighborhoods west and north of the metropolitan area.

New York is the iconic global city, but Miami keeps approaching it, and its quest to achieve globality is reflected both in its impressive skyline and in the growing economic and social gap between the classes. Neither city has resolved the problem of how to better allocate resources among its inhabitants, and indeed the character of both as loci for high-end capital accumulation is best shown in the flight of the elites into the protected comfort of downtown luxury apartments or remote gated communities. The counterpoint between community and transience is linked directly to the class structure of the city and to its ethnic mosaic, described in chapter 8.

The transience that has impressed so many observers of Miami is certainly exemplified by the absentee condominium owners, foreign investors, and short-time revelers in South Beach and other nightlife places. By their very nature, global entrepreneurs and executives are not local. Below them, however, there are middle-class and working-class communities that live in the area year-round and that over time have been creating their own sense of place. Hialeah and Miami Gardens to the north are on that course, as are the more affluent cities of Coral Gables and Pinecrest to the south.

Equally important, the city's moral core is anchored by certain groups that have lived in the area for several generations. These include the Cuban refugees of the 1960s and 1970s and their descendants and the established Jewish entrepreneurial community. These are the communities that have prevented Miami from descending to the level of Las Vegas—a twenty-four-hour entertainment circus. It is the Cubans who today defend Little Havana as their own claim to authenticity. While South Beach has been thoroughly transformed by local property capital, a network of synagogues and philanthropic and civic associations keeps the Jewish community active and visible. Hence, underneath a lifestyle of dissipation and consumerist culture, there is attachment to place, as demonstrated in the aftermath of Hurricane Andrew (see Prescript) and in the recent preparations for Irma.

While Miami is quite different from American cities up north, the concepts that have anchored our understanding of cities for decades and, more recently, of the rise of global cities apply here. Miami is certainly one of them, though not fully consolidated and certainly troubled. Of these troubles, none is more important than the sea.

IRMA . . . ALMOST

The existential threat posed by the heating and rising oceans almost became reality in fall 2017. Irma, a category 5 hurricane as powerful as Andrew but far larger, came bearing down on the city. By extraordinary luck, it deviated west by a few degrees, but it could have happened. The magnitude of destruction would have been far greater than during the Big Wind of 1992. It can happen again. The number of hurricanes in the Atlantic in 2017 is a reflection of a heating ocean, as scientists had predicted. More important, there is no going back: whatever efforts at climate remediation are put in place, it is probably too late to turn the tide.

The enormous physical vulnerability of the area—hemmed in between ocean and swamp and built on porous limestone—is compounded by its social vulnerability. The atomized character of the power structure makes it difficult for anyone to lead the city in a major emergency. Cities and the metropolitan government keep appointing "resiliency" officers to calm the public, while property capitalists keep building in Miami Beach and next to Biscayne Bay. Of the alternative approaches to the major threat faced by Miami, reviewed in the last chapter, these individuals and entities resolutely adhere to the one that that denies that anything serious is happening or to the one that puts blind faith in the power of science to save the place. But, in the end, as Mayor Stoddard has prophesied, "we may all have to leave."[16]

IN SYNTHESIS

For many people throughout Latin America and the Caribbean, Miami has been a refuge in the face of national turmoil—from the Cuban Revolution to the Chávez regime in Venezuela. The relative liberality of U.S. immigration policy, combined with crises abroad, triggered wave after wave of migration to Miami, including three generations of Cubans and many others from different parts of Latin America and the Caribbean. As such, the city grew to be an extension of Latin America.

Miami redefines Americanness: In Miami, ethnic minorities have become the majority, and most of the population originated in Latin America and the Caribbean. This is a city that has experienced an exceptional change from a power structure dominated by an Anglo elite to a political order governed by Cuban émigrés and their offspring. The process of acculturation in reverse transformed city politics in a way that is not found in other cities in the United States.

This is an American city where language functions as an economic development variable, easing business transactions and helping cement the city's financial stature. Spanish (as well as Portuguese and Haitian Creole) and transnational networks have made Miami a unique, and successful, economic experiment.

While Miami's Latin American core reshapes how we think about the U.S. economy, it also leans heavily on U.S. rules and norms. The "Miami Experiment"—an ethnic mosaic resulting from incessant waves of immigrants—has worked because of the foundation provided by the U.S. rule of law regime. High levels of crime may still exist, but the city offers a level of legal and political stability unheard of in Latin America. This underscores the strong economic connection with Latin America and allows Miami to be a center of commerce and aspirational goals for Latin Americans, particularly as a site for consumption.

Miami is a new global city with a remarkable capacity to rebound from local economic decay, national economic crises, and, so far, natural disasters. It is a city whose diversity sets the tone for the new America. But at the same time it is a fragile metropolis because of the intersection of three features: inequality and social disparity, weak social cohesion, and political fragmentation. While possessing a moral core anchored in its old ethnic communities, Miami today is as much defined by the absence of vision and strong leadership at the top as by the continuous work of a growth machine that keeps building, regardless. The existential threat confronting the city is as much physical as it is social.

The story with which this book began—northern escapees from the cold and grime and southern ones from political turmoil, all of them in search of salvation in the sun—frames a history of rapid growth confronted at present by an enormous threat. Miami has been a safe haven in the face of turmoil, but it is now a treacherous frontier facing climate change. The flipside of Miami's allure is that it leaves a lingering question in our minds: Will nature eventually shut down the city's growth machine? Whatever happens, the events that have defined the evolution of this city mark a unique chapter in the history of modern urbanization.

Notes

PRESCRIPT

1. Helen Muir, *Miami, U.S.A.* (Miami, FL: Pickering Press, 1990), 149–50.
2. Sean Rowe, "Hugo's Homeboys," *New Times*, September 2–8, 1992, 13–14.
3. "The Worst Wind," *New Times*, September 2–8, 1992 (special issue).
4. This common pattern has been noted by specialists in the field in the past; see Frederick L. Bates and Walter G. Peacock, "Disasters and Social Change," in *The Sociology of Disasters*, ed. R.R. Dynes and C. Pelanda (Gorizia, Italy: Franco Angeli Press, 1987), 291–330.
5. These articles consistently focused on the theme that people who barely spoke to each other before came together to share what little they had in the days after the hurricane. One such article announced in its headline: "At Long Last, Neighbors: The Storm That Tore South Dade Apart Has Brought Many of Its People Together" (Curtis Morgan, *Miami Herald*, September 5, 1992, 1–2F).
6. David Satterfield, "We Will Rebuild Hits $11 Million," *Miami Herald*, September 19, 1992, 1A, 20A.
7. Lisandro Pérez, "Hurricane Has Severely Tilted Community Demographics," *Miami Herald*, September 27, 1992, 4M.
8. "The Worst Wind."
9. Satterfield, "We Will Rebuild Hits $11 Million."

CHAPTER ONE. INTRODUCTION

1. Portes and Stepick, *City on the Edge.*
2. Pirenne, *Medieval Cities.*
3. Ibid.
4. Castells, *The City and the Grassroots.*
5. Sassen, *The Global City;* Zhou, *New York's Chinatown.*
6. Portes and Stepick, *City on the Edge,* 8.
7. Ibid., 17.
8. We use the term "Latin" instead of "Latino/a" to refer to people of Latin American descent. While the latter term is commonly used in academic and public discourse in the United States, we believe that "Latin" is more appropriate for our study. The category "Latino/a" understood as a pan-ethnic group identity is problematic in an urban center such as Miami, where the variety of backgrounds and experiences tends to favor national-origin identity.
9. Didion, *Miami,* 51.
10. Portes and Stepick, *City on the Edge,* 14–15.
11. Ibid., 14.
12. Ibid., 15.
13. Eckstein, *Back from the Future.*
14. Botifoll, "How Miami's New Image Was Created."
15. Portes and Stepick, *City on the Edge,* chap. 2.
16. Aranda, Hughes, and Sabogal, *Making a Life in Multiethnic Miami,* chap. 5; Portes and Shafer, "Revisiting the Enclave Hypothesis," 157–90.
17. Aranda, Hughes, and Sabogal, *Making a Life in Multiethnic Miami,* 171.
18. Handlin, *Boston's Immigrants;* Banfield and Wilson, *City Politics;* Suttles, *The Social Order of the Slum;* Wilson, *The Truly Disadvantaged;* Robert Sampson, *Great American City.*
19. Eckstein, *Back from the Future;* Portell-Vila, *Nueva historia de la República de Cuba;* Suarez, *Cuba.*
20. Suarez, *Cuba;* Eckstein, *The Immigrant Divide;* Portes and Stepick, *City on the Edge,* chaps. 5, 6.
21. Eckstein, *The Immigrant Divide;* Nijman, *Miami: Mistress of the Americas;* Portes and Stepick, *City on the Edge,* chap. 6.
22. Didion, *Miami;* Nijman, *Miami: Mistress of the Americas.*
23. Portes and Stepick, *City on the Edge,* chap. 2.
24. Allman, *Miami, City of the Future,* 393, 398.
25. U.S. Census Bureau, *American Community Survey, 3-Year Estimates, Miami-Dade County,* 2011.
26. Field interview, Miami, March 2015.
27. Field interview, Miami, January 2017.
28. "Marlins Park," Wikipedia.

29. Hanks and Vazquez, "David Beckham Group Buys Private Land Needed for Miami Soccer Stadium."

30. "Jorge M. Pérez. Art Museum of Miami-Dade County," Wikipedia.

31. "Miami-Dade Approves $49 Million Bailout of Frost Science."

32. Allman, *Miami, City of the Future*, 393.

33. For a detailed description of the economic and cultural evolution of the Italian city-states of the late medieval and early modern period, see Arrighi, *The Long Twentieth Century*.

34. Nijman, *Miami: Mistress of the Americas*.

35. Field interview, Coral Gables, February 2015.

36. Field interview, Miami, March 2015.

37. Field interview, Miami, April 2015.

38. Field interview, Miami, March 2015.

39. Field interview, Miami, March 2015.

40. Miami-Dade County, Department of Economic Resources, "Economic and Demographic Profile, 2014."

41. Field interview, Miami, February 2016.

42. Field interview, Miami Beach, February 2016.

43. Venezuelans escaping the Bolivarian Revolution and now consolidating their hold in the municipality of Doral in northwestern Dade County represent the latest episode in this now-familiar dynamic.

CHAPTER TWO. THE DEMOGRAPHY AND ECOLOGY OF THE CITY

1. Lamarche, "Property Development and the Economic Foundation of the Urban Question," 85–118.

2. Ibid.

3. Ibid.

4. Ibid.; Castells, *The City and the Grassroots*.

5. Lamarche, "Property Development"; Lojkine, "Contributions to a Marxist Theory of Capitalist Urbanization," 119–46.

6. Logan and Molotch, *Urban Fortunes*.

7. Sassen, *The Global City*.

8. Ibid.

9. Ibid.; Massey, *Categorically Unequal*.

10. Sassen, *The Global City*; Castells and Portes, "World Underneath," 11–37.

11. Miami-Dade County, "Miami-Dade County Profile," 2015, 4, 6, 15; U.S. Census Bureau, *American Community Survey, Miami-Dade County*, 2015.

12. U.S. Census Bureau, *American Community Survey*, 2015.

13. Miami-Dade County, "Miami-Dade County Profile," 2015.

14. Ibid., 4, 14.

15. Portes and Stepick, *City on the Edge*, chap. 6; Nijman, *Miami: Mistress of the Americas*, chap. 4; Kanter, *World Class*.

16. Portes and Stepick, *City on the Edge*, chap. 8; Nijman, *Miami: Mistress of the Americas*, chap. 4.

17. Bragg, "Alliance Fights a Plan to Develop a Florida Getaway Born of Racism," 26; "Virginia Key," Wikipedia.

18. Bragg, "Alliance Fights a Plan."

19. "Virginia Key."

20. Bragg, "Alliance Fights a Plan."

21. Portes and Stepick, *City on the Edge*, chap. 5; Rieff, *Going to Miami*.

22. Roth, "A Half-Century Serving Migrants," 1.

23. Ibid.

24. Many members of the Miami growth machine are themselves Latin and revere the area as their spiritual home. That gives Little Havana exceptional staying power relative to other centrally located neighborhoods. Instead of being scheduled for demolition to give way to yet another wave of high-rises, Little Havana has been preserved, so far, as a place for periodic pilgrimages and celebrations and, increasingly, a tourist destination.

25. Portes and Stepick, *City on the Edge*, chap. 4; Redford, *Billion Dollar Sandbar*, chaps. 4, 5; George, "Colored Town," 432-37; Sofen, *The Miami Metropolitan Experiment*.

26. George, "Colored Town"; Allman, *Miami*; Portes and Stepick, *City on the Edge*, 76-80.

27. U.S. Census Bureau, *American Community Survey*, 2014.

28. Field interview, City of Miami official, February 19, 2016.

29. Redford, *Billion Dollar Sandbar*, chap. 4; Rieff, *Going to Miami*, 6.

30. Redford, *Billion Dollar Sandbar*, chaps. 5-8; Portes and Stepick, *City on the Edge*, chap. 4.

31. Redford, *Billion Dollar Sandbar*, chaps. 5-8; Rieff, *Going to Miami*, 10-11.

32. Redford, *Billion Dollar Sandbar*, 95.

33. This park is located off Alton Road on the west (Bay) side of Miami Beach.

34. U.S. Census Bureau, *American Community Survey*, 2014.

35. Ibid.; Portes and Stepick, *City on the Edge*, 84-85.

36. Nijman, *Miami: Mistress of the Americas*, chap. 6.

37. Sofen, *The Miami Metropolitan Experiment*, 13; Rieff, *Going to Miami*, 10-11.

38. Portes and Stepick, *City on the Edge*, 74-75.

39. Ibid.; Allman, *Miami*, 21-23.

40. Redford, *Billion Dollar Sandbar*, 148; Portes and Stepick, *City on the Edge*, 75.

41. Field interview with Cuban entrepreneur, Coconut Grove, January 2016; *Political Cortadito*, "Coral Gables: Raul Valdes-Fauli Plans Comeback as Mayor," 1.

42. U.S. Census Bureau, *American Community Survey, Miami-Dade County*, 2014.

43. Nijman, *Miami: Mistress of the Americas*, 175; interview with James Cason, former mayor, Coral Gables, January 2017.

44. U.S. Census, *American Community Survey, Miami-Dade County*, 2014.

45. "Hialeah, Florida," Wikipedia.

46. Ibid.; Rieff, *Going to Miami*; Allman, *Miami*, 223–24.

47. Portes and Stepick, *City on the Edge*, chap. 5; Portes and Fernandez-Kelly, "No Margin for Error," 12–36; Pérez, "Cuban Miami."

48. Fernandez-Kelly and Konczal, "Murdering the Alphabet"; Fernandez-Kelly and Garcia, "Informalization at the Core."

49. Portes and Puhrmann, "A Bifurcated Enclave"; Eckstein, *The Immigrant Divide*.

50. "Hialeah Park Race Track," Wikipedia.

51. Fernandez-Kelly and García, "Informalization at the Core"; fieldwork by authors, Hialeah, February 2014 and February 2016.

52. "Opa-Locka, Florida," Wikipedia, accessed February 16, 2016; fieldwork by authors, Opa-Locka, March 2016; Allman, *Miami*, 196–99.

53. "Opa-Locka, Florida"; fieldwork by authors, Opa-Locka, March 2016.

54. U.S. Census Bureau, *American Community Survey, Miami-Dade County*, 2014.

55. Ibid.; "Miami Gardens, Florida," Wikipedia.

56. Allman, *Miami*, 196–99; Salah and Weaver, "Opa-Locka: State to Take over Troubled City's Finances."

57. Robbins, "A Way to Unwind Marine Stadium, Seaport Deeds."

58. Smiley, "10,000-Foot Injection Well Could Change How Miami Flushes."

59. Robbins, "A Way to Unwind."

CHAPTER THREE. BETWEEN TRANSIENCE
AND ATTACHMENT

1. Field interview with foundation president, Miami, February 2015.

2. Field interview with business leader, Miami, December 2014.

3. Field interview with member of a community organization, Miami, January 2017.

4. Raymond, Brown, and Weber, "The Measurement of Place Attachment"; Altman and Low, *Place Attachment*; Aranda, Hughes, and Sabogal, *Making a Life in Multiethnic Miami*.

5. Kasarda and Janowitz, "Community Attachment in Mass Society," 329.

6. Aranda, Hughes, and Sabogal, *Making a Life in Multiethnic Miami;* Gerson, Stueve, and Fischer, "Attachment to Place"; Harris et al., "Relocation and Privacy Regulation"; Tartaglia, "Different Predictors of Quality of Life in Urban Environments"; Mesch and Manor, "Social Ties, Environmental Perception, and Local Attachment."

7. Anton and Lawrence, "Home Is Where the Heart Is"; Fried, "Continuities and Discontinuities of Place."

8. Casakin, Hernández, and Ruiz, "Place Attachment and Place Identity in Israeli Cities."

9. Deibert, "Making Sense of Miami"; Krueger, "The Cuban-American Generation Gap."

10. Anton and Lawrence, "Home Is Where the Heart Is," 452.

11. Zukin, *Naked City;* Zukin, Kasinitz, and Chen, *Global Cities, Local Streets.*

12. Nijman, *Miami, Mistress of the Americas,* vi.

13. Ibid., 135.

14. Cuban Research Institute, *Cuba Poll,* 9.

15. Weiss, "New Group Offers Young Cuban-Americans Free Trips to Cuba."

16. Krueger, "The Cuban-American Generation Gap"; LiPuma and Koelble, "Cultures of Circulation and the Urban Imaginary."

17. There has been a proliferation of art museums in Miami, which raises questions about their long-term viability. As the *New York Times* noted, "Here, hardly a season goes by without the announcement of yet another new art museum or expansion—all fueled by the homegrown excitement and international attention surrounding the Art Basel Miami Beach fair each December." Sokol, "When It Comes to Contemporary Art, Miami Wants More, More, More."

18. Aranda, Hughes, and Sabogal, *Making a Life in Multiethnic Miami,* 292.

19. Portes and Fernandez-Kelly, *The State and the Grassroots,* 7–8.

20. Levitt, DeWind, and Vertovec, "Transnational Migration"; Levitt and Glick Schiller, "Conceptualizing Simultaneity"; Wimmer and Glick Schiller, "Methodological Nationalism and the Study of Migration"; Levitt, "Transnational Migrants"; Portes, Haller, and Guarnizo, "Transnational Entrepreneurs."

21. Portes and Fernandez-Kelly, *The State and the Grassroots,* 6–8.

22. Saxenian, "Brain Circulation," 30.

23. Saxenian, "Silicon Valley's New Immigrant Entrepreneurs," 54. See also Saxenian, "Local and Global Networks of Immigrant Professionals in Silicon Valley" and *The New Argonauts.*

24. Gallup and Knight Foundation, *Why People Love Where They Live and Why It Matters,* 5–6.

25. Ibid. Gallup interviewed about 1,000 residents (adults age 18 or older) in Miami-Dade County. The survey's main goal was to obtain people's views of their community. Particularly relevant for our research interests were questions that

asked them "how good or bad they perceived the community to be on an attribute." See Gallup and Knight Foundation, "Data Report," especially pp. 1–5. In the discussion that follows, we utilize both the results reported by Gallup and findings based on our own analysis of the raw data. The statistical analysis is available from the authors.

26. Skocpol and Fiorina, *Civic Engagement in American Democracy*, 3–4.

27. Corporation for National and Community Service, "Volunteering and Civic Engagement in Miami, FL."

28. Miami Foundation, "Miami and Civic Participation."

29. Guest and Lee, "Sentiment and Evaluation as Ecological Variables"; Cuba and Hummon, "A Place to Call Home."

30. See, e.g., Aranda, Hughes, and Sabogal, *Making a Life in Multiethnic Miami;* Portes and Rumbaut, *Immigrant America*.

31. Yúdice, "Miami: Images of a Latinopolis."

32. Aranda, Hughes, and Sabogal, *Making a Life in Multiethnic Miami*, 116; U.S. Bureau of Labor Statistics, "Occupational Employment Statistics, 2015"; Miami-Dade County, Department of Regulatory and Economic Resources, "Income and Poverty in Miami-Dade County: 2013."

33. Sohmer, "Growing the Middle Class."

34. Florida and Pedigo, "Miami's Great Inflection," 28.

35. Metropolitan Center, "Miami Soul of the Community Indicator Study," 31.

36. Shahbazi, "Focus on South Florida: The Digital Divide."

37. Miami-Dade County, GreenPrint Project Team, "Housing"; Metropolitan Center, "Miami Soul of the Community Indicator Study," 47–50; *Miami Herald*, "Editorial: Affordable Housing for All."

38. Metropolitan Center, "Miami Soul of the Community Indicator Study," 44–45.

39. Portes, Fernandez-Kelly, and Light, "Life on the Edge," 5.

40. Ibid.

41. Cortright, "The Young and Restless and the Nation's Cities," City Observatory Report, October 2014.

42. Florida, *Who's Your City?*

43. Morelix et al., "The Kauffman Index: Startup Activity."

44. Florida and Pedigo, "Miami's Great Inflection," 14.

45. Brookings Institution, "The Geography of Foreign Students in U.S. Higher Education."

46. Florida and Pedigo, "Miami's Great Inflection," 20; Martin and Florida, "Insight—Rise Revisited."

47. Luis & Associates, "A Tale of Ten Cities."

48. Center for Information and Research on Civic Learning and Engagement, *The RAYSE Index*.

49. LiPuma and Koelble, "Cultures of Circulation and the Urban Imaginary."

50. Alesina and La Ferrara, "Ethnic Diversity and Economic Performance," 762.

51. Ibid.

52. García Canclini, *Imagined Globalization,* 140.

53. Ibid.

54. Portes and Fernandez-Kelly, *The State and the Grassroots.*

55. Field interview, Miami, January 2017.

56. Enrique Santos and Joe Ferrero, *Sweet Home Hialeah,* online video clip, YouTube, September 18, 2008.

57. "Sweet Home Hialeah . . . / Dominos, dice, and a lot of gossip / Corruption, fines, and accidents / Unemployment, scandals, and cellulite."

58. "Best of Miami: 'Sweet Home Hialeah,' by Enrique Santos and Joe Ferrero, *Miami New Times.*

59. *Sweet Home Hialeah,* "Spanglish Prescription," Blog post, August 17, 2010.

60. Field interview, Miami, January 2017.

61. Walker, "The Media's Role in Immigrant Adaptation."

62. Shumow and Pinto, "Spanish-Language Immigrant Media in Miami-Dade County, Florida."

63. Hughes et al., *Haitian Community Media in Miami.*

64. Walker, "The Media's Role in Immigrant Adaptation," 174.

65. Allison, "Hyper-Gentrification Comes to Miami"; Iannelli, "Little Haiti Will Gentrify Faster than Any South Florida Neighborhood in 2017"; Munzenrieder, "The Six Phases of a Gentrifying Neighborhood in Miami"; Robinson, "Miami Zoning Law Allows Wiping Out of Neighborhoods, Gentrification."

66. Bolstad, "High Ground Is Becoming Hot Property as Sea Level Rises"; Moulite, "Color of Climate."

67. "Cities for Tomorrow" conference, *New York Times,* New York, July 11, 2017.

68. Hannah-Jones, "From Bittersweet Childhoods to 'Moonlight.'"

CHAPTER FOUR. THE ECONOMIC SURGE

1. Smiley, "Police Investigate New Spate of Liberty Square Shootings."

2. Interview with Tomás Regalado, former mayor of Miami, February 2016.

3. Fernandez-Kelly and Konczal, "Murdering the Alphabet."

4. Field visits to area, April 2015 and February 2016; Miami-Dade County, "Economic and Demographic Profile, 2014"; Miami-Dade County, "Analysis of Current Economic Trends—First Quarter of 2015."

5. Interview with Mayor Regalado, February 2016.

6. Field visits to Wynwood, April 2005 and February 2016; Field interview, Miami, February 2016.

7. Nijman, *Miami: Mistress of the Americas,* 71.

8. Allman, *Miami;* Portes and Stepick, *City on the Edge,* chap. 4.

9. Miami-Dade County, "Miami-Dade County Profiles—American Community Survey, 2015"; South Florida Regional Planning Council, *Comprehensive Economic Development Strategy, 2012-2017.*

10. Nijman, *Miami: Mistress of the Americas,* 72; Portes and Stepick, *City on the Edge,* chaps. 4, 5.

11. Rieff, *Going to Miami;* Portes and Stepick, *City on the Edge,* chaps. 5, 6.

12. Portes and Stepick, *City on the Edge,* chap. 5; Portes, "The Social Origins of the Cuban Enclave Economy of Miami."

13. Nijman, *Miami: Mistress of the Americas,* 73-74. Field interview with former FIU president, February 2016.

14. Nijman, *Miami: Mistress of the Americas,* 85.

15. Ibid., 82.

16. Rieff, *Going to Miami;* Didion, *Miami;* Nijman, *Miami: Mistress of the Americas,* 84.

17. Nijman, *Miami: Mistress of the Americas,* 82-83.

18. Ibid., 87.

19. Interview with former mayor Regalado; Interview with former Miami mayor Manuel ("Manny") Diaz, April 2015.

20. Allmann, *Miami,* 30, 55-56; "Paradise Lost?," *Time,* November 23, 1981, 22-32.

21. U.S. Bureau of Economic Analysis, "Miami-Dade County, 2014"; Miami-Dade County, "Economic and Demographic Profile, 2014," 3; South Florida Regional Planning Council, *Comprehensive Economic Development Strategy,* 22. The discrepancy in figures is due to the inclusion by the Planning Council of figures for adjacent Broward and Monroe Counties, in addition to Miami-Dade.

22. Data kindly provided for this study by former Miami mayor Manuel Diaz, interviewed March 18, 2015.

23. "Port Asian Service, Volume Rise 11%," *Miami Today;* Miami-Dade County, "Economic and Demographic Profile, 2014"; Miami-Dade County, Department of Regulatory and Economic Resources, 2015, 5.

24. Miami-Dade Metropolitan Planning Organization, "Miami-Dade County Compendium of Transportation: Facts and Trends Report."

25. Ibid., 4.

26. Ibid., 24.

27. Ibid., 6-7, 16; "Flying Goldmine," *Miami Today,* April 20, 2017, 2.

28. Miami-Dade Metropolitan Planning Organization, 19-20, 34; Miami-Dade Chamber of Commerce, "Transit Projects and Infrastructure to Support an Increasingly Global Population," Report.

29. Miami-Dade Chamber of Commerce, "Transit Projects."

30. Miami-Dade County, "Analysis of Current Economic Trends—First Quarter of 2015." Nijman, *Miami: Mistress of the Americas,* 106-7.

31. Miami-Dade County, "Economic and Demographic Profile, 2014," 15–16; Miami-Dade County, "Analysis of Current Economic Trends, 2015," 7–8.

32. Miami Association of Realtors, "Brazil Is Top Foreign Country Searching for South Florida Real Estate."

33. Miami-Dade County, "Analysis of Current Economic Trends, 2015," 8–9, appendix.

34. Miami-Dade Chamber of Commerce, "Top Business Projects for 2015 and Beyond."

35. Kerbel and Westlund, *Leading the Way*, 10; Nijman, *Miami: Mistress of the Americas*, 80.

36. Kerbel and Westlund, *Leading the Way*, 9–10.

37. Florida, Department of Financial Services, "Report, 2015"; Nijman, *Miami: Mistress of the Americas*, 80.

38. Kerbel and Westlund, *Leading the Way*, 13–14.

39. Ibid., 15.

40. Florida, Department of Financial Services, "Report, 2015." Kerbel and Westlund, *Leading the Way*, 22, 24.

41. Portes and Stepick, *City on the Edge*, 161.

42. Ibid., chaps. 5, 6.

43. Nijman, *Miami: Mistress of the Americas*, 84, 89–90.

44. Kerbel and Westlund, *Leading the Way*, 22–26.

45. Florida, Department of Financial Services, "Report, 2015."

46. Kerbel and Westlund, *Leading the Way*, 9–12.

47. Interview with Maurice Ferré, former mayor of Miami, April 2016; Portes and Stepick, *City on the Edge*, chap. 6.

CHAPTER FIVE. CRIME AND VICTIMIZATION
IN MIAMI

1. Sampson, *Great American City*, chap. 1.

2. Ibid., 11.

3. Park, *The City;* Park, *Human Communities*.

4. Merton, "Social Structure and Anomie," 175–214.

5. Ibid.

6. Ibid.

7. Sampson, *Great American City*, chap. 6; Martinez and Lee, "On Immigration and Crime"; Thomas and Znaniecki, *The Polish Peasant in Europe and America*, vol. 4.

8. Gambetta, *The Sicilian Mafia;* Handlin, *Boston's Immigrants*.

9. Sung, *The Story of the Chinese in America;* Nee and de Bary Nee, *Longtime Californ';* Zhou, *New York's Chinatown*.

10. Oscar Lewis, "The Culture of Poverty."

11. Ibid.

12. Moynihan, "The Negro Family," chap. 5.

13. Sampson, *Great American City*, 99.

14. Telles and Ortiz, *Generations of Exclusion;* Stepick and Portes, "Flight into Despair"; Mills, *The Puerto Rican Journey.*

15. Rabin, "Gunfire Chatters Months of Calm at Complex Where Young King Carter was Killed."

16. Rabin, "Father Loses 2nd Son in Ambush; All 4 of His Children Shot This Month."

17. Burch, "After a 6-Year-Old Dies, a Miami Family Works to Keep Children Safe."

18. Ovalle, "3 Miami-Dade Teens Formally Charged in Killing of 6-Year-Old King Carter."

19. Rabin, "Father Loses 2nd Son in Ambush."

20. Moynihan, "The Negro Family"; Sampson, *Great American City,* chaps. 1, 6.

21. Portes and Haller, "The Informal Economy."

22. Ibid.; Portes, *Economic Sociology,* chap. 7.

23. Fernandez-Kelly and Garcia, "Informalization at the Core"; Fernandez-Kelly and Konczal, "Murdering the Alphabet'"; Pérez, "Cuban Miami."

24. Munzenrieder, "Opa-Locka Hialeah Flea Market Raided."

25. Ibid.

26. "Larceny," "Burglary," legal-dictionary.thefreedictionary.com/.

27. Florida, Department of Law Enforcement, "Crime in Florida, 2015 Florida Uniform Crime Report."

28. Ibid.

29. Ibid.

30. Ibid.

31. Weaver, "Medicare Fraud Rampant in South Florida," 4–50.

32. Weaver, "FBI Agents Bust Miami Medicare Ring While Some Suspects Flee to Cuba."

33. Ovalle, "22 Face Charges in Miami Drug Money Laundering Ring Involving 'El Chapo' Cartel."

34. Weaver, "Medicare Fraud"; Fernandez-Kelly and Konczal, "'Murdering the Alphabet'"; Portes and Puhrmann, "A Bifurcated Enclave."

35. Fernandez-Kelly and Konczal, "'Murdering the Alphabet'"; Pérez, "Cuban Miami"; Portes and Stepick, *City on the Edge.*

36. Nehamas, "How Secret Offshore Money Helps Fuel Miami's Real Estate Boom."

37. Al-Jamea and Rizvi, "Before He Went on Lam, Italian Fugitive Used Miami Firms to Set up Offshore."

38. Veblen, *The Theory of the Leisure Class.*

39. Nijman, *Miami: Mistress of the Americas;* Field interviews, Miami, March 2015 and January 2016.

CHAPTER SIX. A BIFURCATED ENCLAVE

1. Grenier and Stepick, *Miami Now!;* Pedraza-Bailey, "Cuba's Exiles," 3–34; Portes, Clark, and Lopez, "Six Years Later."

2. Camayd-Freixas, "Crisis in Miami"; Portes and Stepick, *City on the Edge,* chaps. 1, 2, 6.

3. Portes and Stepick, *City on the Edge,* 22.

4. Ibid., 22, 29.

5. Ibid., 30–32; Nijman, *Miami: Mistress of the Americas.*

6. Portes and Stepick, *City on the Edge,* 34–36.

7. Ibid., 36.

8. Ibid., 32.

9. Stepick et al., *This Land Is Our Land;* Portes and Shafer, "Revisiting the Enclave Hypothesis."

10. Stepick et al., *This Land Is Our Land;* Pérez, "Cuban Miami"; Portes and Shafer, "Revisiting the Enclave Hypothesis."

11. See table 4 and comments below.

12. Tamayo, "Politicians Call for Revision of Cuban Adjustment Act."

13. Eckstein, *The Immigrant Divide.*

14. Padilla, "Miami: El mundo en blanco y negro," 5.

15. Portes, "The Cuban-American Political Machine."

16. Eckstein, *The Immigrant Divide.*

17. Portes, "The Cuban-American Political Machine"; Chardy and Tamayo, "A Sudden Surge in Cuban Migrants."

18. The "wet foot, dry foot" policy was negotiated by the Clinton administration and Cuban authorities in the wake of the so-called Rafters Crisis of 1994. Under the new policy, Cubans caught at sea by the U.S. Coast Guard would be returned to the island, while those who reached U.S. territory, either by sea or by crossing a land border, would continue to be accepted. This policy encouraged a continuous clandestine flow of migrants escaping Cuba by boat and, with the new facilities to obtain a passport and leave the island legally, prompted others to travel to third countries seeking to reach the United States by crossing the land border with Mexico. See Wikipedia, "Wet Foot, Dry Foot Policy"; Barrios, "People First."

19. See Barrios, "People First"; Whitefield, "Obama Ending 'Wet Foot, Dry Foot' Cuban Immigration Policy"; Gomez, "Obama to End 'Wet Foot, Dry Foot.'"

20. Portes and Shafer, "Revisiting the Enclave Hypothesis."

21. Ibid.

22. For a description of this study and its sample, see Portes and Rumbaut, *Legacies;* Portes, Fernandez-Kelly, and Haller, "Segmented Assimilation on the Ground."

23. It is possible that part of this difference may reflect underreporting of income by post-Mariel Cubans working in the informal economy. As seen in chapter 5, there is significant, albeit unquantified, evidence of involvement of recent Cuban arrivals in informal activities and fraudulent schemes against the Medicare system. Income from such activities would naturally go unreported. Participation in such activities by recent arrivals also denotes the stark differences in patterns of social and economic adaptation relative to the older Cuban exile community.

24. Telles and Ortiz, *Generations of Exclusion;* Hirschman and Falcon, "The Educational Attainment of Religio-Ethnic Groups in the United States."

CHAPTER SEVEN. MIAMI THROUGH LATIN
AMERICAN EYES

1. Chiozza, *Anti-Americanism and the American World Order*, 27; Katzenstein and Keohane, *Anti-Americanisms in World Politics*, 3, 12.

2. Katzenstein and Keohane, *Anti-Americanisms in World Politics*, 10.

3. Chiozza, *Anti-Americanism and the American World Order*, 126.

4. Azpuru and Boniface, "Individual-level Determinants of Anti-Americanism in Contemporary Latin America"; Baker and Cupery, "Anti-Americanism in Latin America."

5. Katzenstein and Keohane, *Anti-Americanisms in World Politics*, 15; Chiozza, *Anti-Americanism and the American World Order*, 127.

6. Piñeiro, "Miami."

7. U.S. Department of Commerce, Office of Travel and Tourism Industries, *Survey of International Air Travelers: U.S Travel and Tourism Statistics*, various years.

8. The airport is the principal point of entry to Miami, receiving 96 percent of all those arriving in the city. See Miami-Dade Aviation Department, *Gateway to Miami, to Florida, and to the Americas*, 2015; Miami-Dade Aviation Department, Cities Served by Region Non-Stop, 2016; Enterprise Florida Gateway, *Florida: Gateway to Latin American and the Caribbean.*

9. "Florida: Gateway to the Americas."

10. Marti Garro, "Del shopping a los negocios."

11. *América Economía*, "Mejores ciudades para hacer negocios,"

12. Baker and Cupery, "Anti-Americanism in Latin America," 118; Enterprise Florida Gateway, *Florida: Gateway to Latin American and the Caribbean.*

13. Nehamaso, "La corrupción en América Latina alimentó el boom inversor de Miami"; Yun, Hale, and Cororaton, "2015 Profile of International Home Buyers in Miami Association of Realtors Business Areas"; Jackson, "Miami Real Estate Market Embraces Brazilians"; Fagundes, "Brasil aquece venda de imóveis em Miami."

14. Chiozza, *Anti-Americanism and the American World Order*, 128; Iglesias Illia, *Miami*, 20; "Miasma americano," *O Globo*, January 31, 2006.

15. Veblen, *The Theory of the Leisure Class;* Postrel, "Inconspicuous Consumption"; Chaudhuri and Majumdar, "Of Diamonds and Desires"; Podoshen, Li, and Zhang, "Materialism and Conspicuous Consumption in China."

16. See Lamarche, "Property Development and the Economic Foundation of the Urban Question"; Logan and Molotch, *Urban Fortunes.*

17. Kim, Lloyd, and Cervellon, "Narrative-Transportation Storylines in Luxury Brand Advertising."

18. Florida, "Big Cities Are the Future of Global Consumption."

19. Dorfmann, "New Wealth Seeks a 'Home.'"

20. Sassen, *The Global City.*

21. We selected newspapers based on the following criteria: (1) mainstream print outlets with large circulation in the respective country, broad geographic readership across the nation, and extensive thematic sections; (2) reasonable variation in terms of the newspaper's political orientation, including conservative and liberal publications displaying a wide range of opinions; and (3) electronic access to search and read all the print news articles published in the past decade.

22. Aparicio, "Adiós Miami."

23. *Folha de São Paulo*, "Brasileiro investe em segunda casa no exterior."

24. *Folha de São Paulo*, "Miami se transforma em Hollywood das novelas Latinas"; Rohter, "Miami, the Hollywood of Latin America."

25. Apicella, "Cualquier artista sueña con grabar en Miami."

26. Duggan, "Could Miami Be the Next Art Mecca?"

27. *El Tiempo*, "Consejos para comprar en el exterior en tiempos de dólar caro."

28. *O Globo*, "Compras."

29. Sampaio, "EUA a granel."

30. Vetere, "Negocio inmobiliario con acento argentino en Miami."

31. Ibid.

32. Cantanhêde, "Poupar ou consumir?"

33. Fagundes, "Brasil aquece venda de imóveis em Miami."

34. Bonilla, "El negocio de Dios."

35. According to *O Globo*, more than half of the members in the lower house of the Brazilian Congress traveled to Miami in 2009 using congressional air tick-

ets; see *O Globo*, "Miami é destino preferido dos diputados, diz site." As Eduardo Cunha, former speaker of the lower house, said in reference to Miami, "Everyone is here"; see *O Globo*, "Está todo mundo aqui." In 2016, Cunha was accused of taking millions in bribes from Petrobras, the state oil company, and was expelled from Congress; see *BBC*, "Eduardo Cunha: Former Brazil Congress Speaker Arrested."

36. Sassen, *The Global City*.

37. *O Globo*, "Uma noite em Miami."

38. *Clarín*, "Cristina irónica con el récord inmobiliario de argentinos en Miami."

39. Betancur, "'La vida en las ciudades empeora.'"

40. As quoted in Fajardo, "How Miami Became the Capital of Affluent Latin America."

41. Azpuru and Boniface, "Individual-Level Determinants of Anti-Americanism in Contemporary Latin America."

42. Alvarez, "Miami's Cuban Exiles Celebrate Castro's Death"; Smith-Spark, "Crowds Flood Streets of Miami's Little Havana to Cheer Castro's Death"; Ovalle et al., "Cuban Exiles Pour onto Miami Streets to Celebrate Fidel Castro's Death."

43. *Miami Diario*, "Alcalde Tomás Regalado sobre Fidel Castro."

44. Wootson, "Marco Rubio: Fidel Castro's Death Changes Nothing in Cuba."

45. Evo Morales Ayma, "A nombre del pueblo boliviano expreso condolencias y solidaridad a familia, Gob. y pueblo cubano por la pérdida de un gigante de la historia," Tweet, November 26, 2016, 3:39; Evo Morales Ayma, "Nuestra admiración y respeto por Fidel, el líder que nos enseñó a luchar por la soberanía del Estado y la dignidad de los pueblos del mundo," Tweet, November 26, 2016, 3:40.

46. Nicolás Maduro, "A 60 años de la partida del Granma de México parte Fidel hacia la Inmortalidad de los que luchan toda la Vida . . . Hasta la Victoria Siempre . . .," Tweet, November 26, 2016, 01:58.

47. Enrique Peña Nieto, "Lamento el fallecimiento de Fidel Castro Ruz, líder de la Revolución cubana y referente emblemático del siglo XX," Tweet, November 25, 2016, 22:20; Enrique Peña Nieto, "Fidel Castro fue un amigo de México, promotor de una relación bilateral basada en el respeto, el diálogo y la solidaridad," Tweet, November 25, 2016, 22:22.

48. Wagner and DeYoung, "Trump announces revisions to parts of Obama's Cuba policy."

49. Armony, "Transnationalizing the Dirty War."

50. Armony, *Argentina, the United States, and the Anti-Communist Crusade in Central America, 1977–1984*, 157–60.

51. *El Espectador*, "Maduro afirma un eje Madrid-Bogotá-Miami de conspiración contra Venezuela."

52. Grandin, *The Last Colonial Massacre;* see also Grandin, "An Interview with Greg Grandin."

53. *Página/12,* "K, antineoliberal."

54. *ABC Paraguay,* "El 'espíritu de Miami' desfallece en la IV Cumbre de Presidentes."

55. Recently, for the role of Miami in the so-called Panama Papers, see Nehamas and Gurney, "Panama Papers."

56. Rohter, "Miami, the Hollywood of Latin America" (Don Francisco's quotation); Yúdice, "Miami: Images of a Latinopolis"; Mato, "La industria de la telenovela."

57. Oates, "Interview: Miami Tourism CEO Explains the Essence of Destination Branding."

58. Knight Frank, "The Wealth Report," 2015.

59. Grandin, "The Panama Papers Are Only the Beginning."

CHAPTER EIGHT. THE ETHNIC MOSAIC AND
THE POWER ELITE

1. Field trip, April 2017.

2. Portes and Stepick, *City on the Edge,* chap. 8; Allman, *Miami: City of the Future,* 120–24.

3. U.S. Census Bureau, "Miami-Dade County," 2016.

4. Ovalle, "Amid Miami's Opioid Crisis, Addicts Get New Clean Needles."

5. Field interview, Liberty City, March 7, 2017.

6. U.S. Census Bureau, "Opa Locka: Breakdown of Families in Poverty."

7. Weaver, Sallah, and Lepri, "FBI Agents Blow Lid off Opa-Locka City Corruption Probe"; Weaver, "Stierheim Bows Out: Says City May Be Beyond Saving."

8. U.S. Census Bureau, Miami-Dade County, 2016; "Miami Gardens," Wikipedia.

9. "Miami Gardens," Wikipedia. Field interview, Miami, February 2017.

10. Field interview, Miami, February 2017.

11. Field interview, Liberty City, March 2017.

12. Field interview, Miami, February 2017.

13. Field interview, Miami, February 1987.

14. Field interview, Miami, February 2017.

15. Field interview, Liberty City, March 2017.

16. Stepick, "The Refugees Nobody Wants; Haitians in Miami."

17. Stepick and Portes, "Flight into Despair."

18. Portes and Stepick, *City on the Edge,* chap. 8.

19. Ibid., chap. 6; Pérez, "Cuban Miami."

20. Portes and Stepick, *City on the Edge*, chap. 8; Stepick, "The Refugees Nobody Wants." For an image of the Marketplace, as it looks now, see pl. 22.

21. Stepick, "The Refugees Nobody Wants."

22. Field trip to Little Haiti, March 2017; Danseyar, "Jean Monestime Wants Details."

23. Field interview, Miami, March 2017.

24. Portes and Stepick, *City on the Edge*, chap. 7; Fernandez-Kelly and Curran, "Nicaraguans."

25. Rodríguez, "Navigating Uneven Development"; Field interview, Sweetwater, April 2017.

26. Portes and Stepick, *City on the Edge*, chap. 7.

27. Ibid.

28. Ibid.; Rodríguez, "Navigating Uneven Development"; Fernandez-Kelly and Curran, "Nicaraguans."

29. Portes and Stepick, *City on the Edge*, 163–66.

30. Ibid.

31. "The NACARA Act," Wikipedia; Interview with Nicaraguan newpaper editor, Miami, April 2017.

32. Rodríguez, "Navigating Uneven Development."

33. Ibid.; Fernandez-Kelly and Curran, "Nicaraguans."

34. Field trip, Miami, April 2017; Interview with Nicaraguan newspaper editor, April 2017.

35. Interview with former mayor of Doral, January 2017.

36. Interview with former mayor of Miami, April 2016; and with editor of local newspaper, March 2017. See also Aranda, Hughes, and Sabogal, *Making a Life in Metropolitan Miami*.

37. Aranda, Hughes, and Sabogal, *Making a Life in Metropolitan Miami*; Interview with former mayor of Miami, April, 2016.

38. Portes and Stepick, *City on the Edge*, chap. 8; Kasinitz, Battle, and Miyares, "Fade to Black?"

39. Field interview, Miami, February 2017.

40. Trump Towers is situated in Sunny Isles and from the start became one of the principal Russian acquisition sites in this area.

41. For critical views of the SMART plan, see Lewis, "How Smart Is SMART Plan When Transit Use Is Falling"; Ferré, "Will Fixed-Rail Decongest Miami-Dade Roadways?"

42. Field interview, Miami, February 2016.

43. Portes and Stepick, *City on the Edge*, chap. 6; Nijman, *Miami: Mistress of the Americas*.

44. See also Portes and Stepick, *City on the Edge*, chap. 5; Pérez, "Cuban Miami."

45. Field interview, Belen Prep School, April 2017; and Miami, February 2016.

46. Viglucci, "He Kept the Netherlands Dry; Now He Aims to Defend Miami and the World from Rising Seas."

47. Ibid.

48. Robbins, "Miami Kicks in More Money for Battling Sea Level Issues."

49. Field trip by senior author and his team, April 2017.

50. Two-page ad by EWM Realty, a Berkshire Hathaway affiliate, *Miami Today*, June 1, 2017, 20–21.

CHAPTER NINE. DRIVING INTO THE FLOOD

1. Lewis, "Bad as Downtown Traffic Is, Planners Try to Make It Worse," 6.

2. *Miami Today*, "Transit Use Still Falling," 1; Lewis, "To Persuade Gus to Hop Back on the Bus, Upscale Its Image," 6.

3. Lewis, "To Persuade Gus."

4. Robbins, "Three-Year-Old Miami Trolley's Users Rise 4% Year over Year," 7; Robbins, "New Trolley Routes Draw Big Numbers," 1.

5. Danseyar, "Four of 30 County Electric Buses Set to Go Out for Proposals Soon," 3; Danseyar, "New Plan in Testing to Synchronize Traffic Lights," 1.

6. Robbins, "City Moves Fast to Slow U.S. 1 Traffic Entering Neighborhoods," 3; Robbins, "City, County to Meet on Out-of-Sync U.S. 1 Signals," 1.

7. Danseyar, "Partnership Aims to Create 3 Express Bus Lines along 836," 5.

8. Cited in Lackner, "Six Corridor Transportation Plan Awaits Funding."

9. Lewis, "Miami's Strong Economy Broadens"; Interview with Maurice Ferré, former Miami mayor, April 8, 2016.

10. Lackner, "Six Corridor Transportation Plan Awaits Funding."

11. Lewis, "Don't Just Plan to Plan the Planning of Transit—Get It Rolling," 6.

12. Robbins, "South Dade Transit Plan Priority Aim," 1.

13. Cited in Lackner, "Six Corridor Transportation Plan Awaits Funding."

14. Lewis, "Bad as Downtown Traffic Is."

15. Kolbert, "The Siege of Miami," 8.

16. Gillis, "Flooding of Coast Caused by Global Warming Has Already Begun," 9; Reid, "South Florida Climate Change Efforts Move toward Action Stage"; Kolbert, "The Siege of Miami."

17. Wilson, "Staying Afloat amid Climate Change."

18. Delgadillo, "The Realities of Sea-Level Rise in Miami's Low-Income Communities"; Kolbert, "The Siege of Miami."

19. Kolbert, "The Siege of Miami;" Delgadillo, "The Realities of Sea-Level Rise."

20. Kolbert, "The Siege of Miami."

21. Malone, "An Idea to Mitigate Rising Seas."

22. Kolbert, "The Siege of Miami"; Interview with Harold Wanless, November 2016.

23. Interview with Harold Wanless, November 2016.

24. Korten, "In Florida, Officials Ban Term 'Climate Change,'" 2.

25. Ibid., 4.

26. Hanks and Vazquez, "Climate Change Dominates Miami-Dade Budget Hearing," 1–4.

27. Ibid., 2.

28. Ibid.

29. Regalado and Cason, "In Miami-Dade, GOP Candidates Must Address Climate Change in Debate," 1.

30. Ibid.; Grimm, "South Florida Mayors Face Reality of Rising Seas and Climate Change," 1–8.

31. Cited in Korten, "In Florida," 7; Interview with Harold Wanless; Kolbert, "The Siege," 3.

32. Kolbert, "The Siege," 7.

33. Ibid.

34. Ibid., 19.

35. Cited in Delgadillo, "The Realities of Sea-Level Rise," 33.

36. Ibid., 7.

37. Cited in Kolbert, "The Siege," 16.

38. Cited in Bojnansky, "Miami Beach Property Values May Fall as Sea Levels Rise," 2.

39. Malone, "An Idea."

40. Cited in Bojnansky, "Miami Beach Property," 2.

41. Harold Wanless, "The Coming Reality of Sea-Level Rise."

42. Portes and Stepick, *City on the Edge*, chap. 3.

43. Cited in Gillis, "Flooding of Coast," 6. Similar trenchant conclusions concerning Miami's future have been reached by a recent analyst of global climate change. See Goodell, *The Water Will Come*, chaps. 5, 11.

44. Lewis, "Get a Leaders' Council Ready, We Can't Dodge Bullets Forever," 6.

POSTSCRIPT

1. Zukin, *Naked City*, 1, 6.

2. Jacobs, *The Death and Life of Great American Cities*.

3. Ibid., cited in Zukin, *Naked City*, 220.

4. Zukin, *Naked City*, 14.

5. Ibid. See also Gans, *The Urban Villagers*.

6. Kunzru, "Market Forces," *Guardian*, cited in Zukin, *Naked City*, 19.

7. Redford, *Billion Dollar Sandbar,* chap. 4.

8. Portes and Stepick, *City on the Edge,* 73.

9. Redford, *Billion Dollar Sandbar,* 95; Portes and Stepick, *City on the Edge,* chap. 4.

10. Rieff, *Going to Miami.*

11. Portes and Stepick, *City on the Edge,* chap. 4.

12. Garcia, "The Walls of Wynwood."

13. Ibid.; see in particular chaps. 2, 7.

14. Nijman, *Miami: Mistress of the Americas;* Aranda, Hughes, and Sabogal, *Making a Life in Metropolitan Miami.*

15. Field interviews in Miami, January 2016 and April 2017. See also Stepick et al., *This Land Is Our Land.*

16. For a brave attempt to put an optimistic slant on the climate crisis, see Oppenheimer, "Will Miami Disappear under the Rising Sea?"

References

ABC Paraguay. "El 'espíritu de Miami' desfallece en la IV Cumbre de Presidentes." November 7, 2005. www.abc.com.py/edicion-impresa /internacionales/el-espiritu-de-miami-desfallece-en-la-iv-cumbre-de-presidentes-867308.html.

Alesina, Alberto, and Eliana La Ferrara. "Ethnic Diversity and Economic Performance." *Journal of Economic Literature* 43, no. 3 (2005): 762–800.

Al Jazeera. "Fidel Castro's Death—World Reactions." November 26, 2016. www.aljazeera.com/news/2016/11/fidel-castro-death-world-reactions-161126095542185.html.

Allison, Melissa. "Hyper-Gentrification Comes to Miami." *Zillow Porchlight,* September 3, 2015. www.zillow.com/blog/hyper-gentrification-miami-182713/.

Allman, T. D. *Miami: City of the Future.* Gainesville: University of Florida Press, 2013.

———. "Miami: City of the Future." *Departures,* September 24, 2014. www .departures.com/travel/travel/miami-city-future?iid=sr-link1.

Altman, Irwin, and Setha Low, eds. *Place Attachment.* New York: Plenum, 1992.

Alvarez, Lizette. "Miami's Cuban Exiles Celebrate Castro's Death." *New York Times,* November 26, 2016. www.nytimes.com/2016/11/26/us/miami-cubans-fidel-castro.html.

América Economía. "Mejores ciudades para hacer negocios." March 10, 2016. www.americaeconomia.com/negocios-industrias/conozca-el-ranking-2016-de-las-mejores-ciudades-para-hacer-negocios-de-america-l.

Aparicio, Enrique. "Adiós Miami." *El Espectador,* January 30, 2016. www .elespectador.com/opinion/adios-miami.

Apicella, Mauro. "Cualquier artista sueña con grabar en Miami." *La Nación,* May 3, 2007. www.lanacion.com.ar/905176-cualquier-artista-suena-con-grabar-en-miami.

Aranda, Elizabeth, Sallie Hughes, and Elena Sabogal. *Making a Life in Multi-ethnic Miami: Immigration and the Rise of a Global City.* Boulder, CO: Lynne Rienner, 2014.

Armony, Ariel C. *Argentina, the United States, and the Anti-Communist Crusade in Central America, 1977–1984.* Athens: Ohio University Press, 1997.

———. "Transnationalizing the Dirty War: Argentina in Central America." In *In from the Cold: Latin America's New Encounter with the Cold War,* edited by Gilbert M. Joseph and Daniela Spenser, 134–68. Durham, NC: Duke University Press, 2008.

Arrighi, Giovanni. *The Long Twentieth Century: Money, Power, and the Origins of Our Time.* London: Verso Books, 1994.

Azpuru, Dinorah, and Dexter Boniface. "Individual-Level Determinants of Anti-Americanism in Contemporary Latin America." *Latin American Research Review* 50, no. 3 (2015): 111–34.

Baker, Andy, and David Cupery. "Anti-Americanism in Latin America: Economic Exchange, Foreign Policy Legacies, and Mass Attitudes toward the Colossus of the North." *Latin American Research Review* 48, no. 2 (2013): 106–30.

Banfield, Edward C., and James Q. Wilson. *City Politics.* Cambridge, MA: Harvard University Press, 1963.

Barrios, Jarrett. "People First: The Cuban Travel Ban, Wet Foot–Dry Foot and Why the Executive Branch Can and Should Begin Normalizing Cuba Policy." *Connecticut Public Interest Law Journal* 11, no. 1 (2011): 1–30.

Bates, Frederick L., and Walter G. Peacock. "Disasters and Social Change." In *The Sociology of Disasters,* edited by R. R. Dynes and C. Pelanda, 291–330. Gorizia, Italy: Franco-Angeli Press, 1987.

BBC. "Eduardo Cunha: Former Brazil Congress Speaker Arrested." October 19, 2006. www.bbc.com/news/world-latin-america-37709537.

Betancur, Laura A. "'La vida en las ciudades empeora': Experta en planeación." *El Tiempo,* September 9, 2014. www.eltiempo.com/archivo/documento /CMS-14504781.

Bojnansky, Erik. "Miami Beach Property Values May Fall as Sea Levels Rise." *The Real Deal,* April 7, 2016. www.therealdeal.com/miami/2016/04/07 /miami-beach-property-values-may-fall-as-sea-levels-rise-experts/.

Bolstad, Erika. "High Ground Is Becoming Hot Property as Sea Level Rises." *Scientific American,* May 1, 2017. www.scientificamerican.com/article /high-ground-is-becoming-hot-property-as-sea-level-rises/.

Bonilla, María Elvira. "El negocio de Dios." *El Espectador,* January 19, 2014. www.elespectador.com/opinion/el-negocio-de-dios-columna-469595.

Botifoll, Luis. "How Miami's New Image Was Created." *Occasional Papers* 1. Coral Gables: Institute of Inter-American Studies, University of Miami, 1985.

Bragg, Rick. "Alliance Fights a Plan to Develop a Florida Getaway Born of Racism." *New York Times,* March 28, 1999. www.nytimes.com/1999/03 /28/us/alliance-fights-a-plan-to-develop-a-florida-getaway-born-of-racism .html.

Brey, Elisa. Review of *Generations of Exclusion: Mexican Americans, Assimilation, and Race,* by Edward Telles and Vilma Ortiz. *Revista Internacional de Sociología* 69, no. 1 (2011): 271–75.

Brookings Institution. "The Geography of Foreign Students in U.S. Higher Education: Origins and Destinations." August 29, 2014. www.brookings .edu/interactives/the-geography-of-foreign-students-in-u-s-higher-education-origins-and-destinations/.

Burch, Audra D. S. "After a 6-Year-Old Dies, a Miami Family Works to Keep Children Safe." *Miami Herald,* March 19, 2016. www.miamiherald.com /news/local/community/miami-dade/article66969847.html.

Camayd-Freixas, Yohel. "Crisis in Miami: Community Context and Institutional Response in the Adaptation of Mariel Cubans and Undocumented Haitian Entrants in South Florida." Commissioned report. Boston Urban Research and Development, 1988.

Cantanhêde, Eliane. "Poupar ou consumir?" *Folha de São Paulo,* May 4, 2012. www1.folha.uol.com.br/fsp/opiniao/40783-poupar-ou-consumir .shtml.

Cappello, Juan Pablo. "Time to Bury 'Silicon Beach' in the Sand." *Miami Herald,* April 13, 2016. www.miamiherald.typepad.com/the-starting-gate/2016/04 /time-to-bury-silicon-beach-in-the-sand.html.

Casakin, Hernán, Bernardo Hernández, and Cristina Ruiz. "Place Attachment and Place Identity in Israeli Cities: The Influence of City Size." *Cities* 42, pt. b (2015): 224–30.

Castells, Manuel. *The City and the Grassroots.* Berkeley: University of California Press, 1983.

Center for Information and Research on Civil Learning and Engagement. *RAYSE Index.* www.civicyouth.org/rayse/.

Chardy, Alfonso, and Juan O. Tamayo. "A Sudden Surge in Cuban Migrants." *Miami Herald,* December 7, 2013.

Chaudhuri, Himadri Roy, and Sitanath Majumdar. "Of Diamonds and Desires: Understanding Conspicuous Consumption from a Contemporary Marketing Perspective." *Academy of Marketing Science Review* 11 (2006): 1–18.

Chiozza, Giacomo. *Anti-Americanism and the American World Order.* Baltimore: Johns Hopkins University Press, 2009.

Clarín (Argentina). "Cristina irónica con el récord inmobiliario de argentinos en Miami." July 16, 2013. www.clarin.com/politica/cristina-refirio-ironicamente-argentinos-miami_0_BkPe2mIsP7x.amp.html.

Clark, Terry N., ed. *The City as an Entertainment Machine.* New York: Lexington Books, 2011.

Corporation for National and Community Service. "Volunteering and Civic Engagement in Miami, FL." www.volunteeringinamerica.gov/FL/Miami.

Cortright, Joe. "The Young and Restless and the Nation's Cities," City Observatory Report, October 19, 2014. www.cityobservatory.org/wp-content/uploads/2014/10/YNR-Report-Final.pdf.

Cuba, Lee, and David Hummon. "A Place to Call Home: Identification with Dwelling, Community, and Region." *Sociological Quarterly* 34, no. 1 (1993): 111–31.

Cuban Research Institute. *Cuba Poll: How Cuban Americans in Miami View U.S. Policies toward Cuba.* Miami: Florida International University, 2014.

Dahlberg, Nancy. "Start-Up City: Miami Panelists Discuss Building Tech Hub." *Miami Herald,* February 13, 2013.

———. "Technology on the Money: Fintech Startups Take Root in South Florida." *Miami Herald,* April 17, 2016. www.miamiherald.com/news/business/technology/article72340332.html.

Danseyar, Susan. "Four of 30 County Electric Buses Set to Go out for Proposals Soon." *Miami Today,* August 4, 2016, 3.

———. "Jean Monestime Wants Details." *Miami Today,* May 11, 2017, 23.

———. "New Plan in Testing to Synchronize Traffic Lights." *Miami Today,* June 23, 2016, 1.

———. "Partnership Aims to Create 3 Express Bus Lines along 836." *Miami Today,* October 13, 2016, 5.

Dean, Josh. "A Wynwood Tech Incubator Is at the Heart of America's Newest Start-Up Scene." *Departures,* September 24, 2014. www.departures.com/art-culture/culture-watch/lab-miami.

Deibert, Michael. "Making Sense of Miami: What America's Refuge City Says about the US's Future." *Guardian,* July 2, 2015. www.theguardian.com/cities/2015/jul/02/miami-florida-cuba-multicultural-metropolis-diversity-hispanic-haiti.

Delgadillo, Natalie. "The Realities of Sea-Level Rise in Miami's Low-Income Communities." *CityLab,* October 23, 2016.

Didion, Joan. "Goodbye to All That." In *Slouching Towards Bethlehem*. New York: Farrar, Straus and Giroux, [1968] 2008.

———. *Miami*. New York: Random House, 1987.

Dorfmann, Jessica. "New Wealth Seeks a 'Home': The Rise of the Hedge City." *Harvard International Review*, April 15, 2015. www.hir.harvard.edu /article/?a=10888.

Duggan, Bob. "Could Miami Be the Next Art Mecca?" *Big Think*, n.d. www.bigthink.com/Picture-This/could-miami-be-the-next-art-mecca.

Eckstein, Susan. *Back from the Future: Cuba under Castro*. New York: Routledge, 2003.

———. *The Immigrant Divide: How Cuban Americans Changed the US and Their Homeland*. New York: Routledge, 2009.

Enterprise Florida Gateway. "Florida: Gateway to Latin American and the Caribbean." April 2015. www.enterpriseflorida.com/wp-content/uploads /florida-gateway-to-latin-america-and-the-caribbean-.pdf.

El Espectador. "Maduro afirma un eje Madrid-Bogotá-Miami de conspiración contra Venezuela." February 19, 2015. www.elespectador.com/noticias /elmundo/maduro-afirma-un-eje-madrid-bogota-miami-de-conspiracio-articulo-545129.

Fagundes, Álvaro. "Brasil aquece venda de imóveis em Miami." *Folha de São Paulo*, April 4, 2011. www1.folha.uol.com.br/fsp/mercado/me0404201101 .htm.

Fajardo, Luis. "How Miami Became the Capital of Affluent Latin America." *BBC Mundo*, May 16, 2016. www.bbc.com/news/world-us-canada-36281648.

Fernández Campbell, Alexia. "Why This European Incubator Targets Miami for Its Next Tech Hub." *Atlantic*, November 10, 2015. www.theatlantic.com /politics/archive/2015/11/why-this-european-incubator-targets-miami-for-its-next-tech-hub/433362/.

Fernandez-Kelly, Patricia, and Sara Curran. "Nicaraguans: Voices Lost, Voices Found." In *Ethnicities: Children of Immigrants in America*, edited by Rubén G. Rumbaut and Alejandro Portes, 127–55. New York: Russell Sage Foundation, 2001.

Fernandez-Kelly, Patricia, and Anna M. García. "Informalization at the Core: Hispanic Women, Homework, and the Advanced Capitalist State." In *The Informal Economy: Studies in Advanced and Less Developed Countries*, edited by Alejandro Portes, Manuel Castells, and Lauren A. Benton, 247–64. Baltimore: Johns Hopkins University Press, 1989.

Fernandez-Kelly, Patricia, and Lisa Konczal. "Murdering the Alphabet: Identity and Entrepreneurship among Second Generation Cubans, West Indians, and Central Americans." *Ethnic and Racial Studies* 28, no. 6 (2005): 1153–81.

Florida. Department of Financial Services. "Report, 2015." 2016.

———. Department of Law Enforcement. "Crime in Florida, 2015." *Florida Uniform Crime Report.* 2016.

"Florida: Gateway to the Americas." *Inbound Logistics,* June 15, 2004. www .inboundlogistics.com/cms/article/florida-gateway-to-the-americas/.

Florida, Richard. "Big Cities Are the Future of Global Consumption." *City Lab,* April 14, 2016. www.citylab.com/life/2016/04/big-cities-are-the-future-of-global-consumption/478128/.

———. *Cities and the Creative Class.* New York: Routledge, 2005.

———. *Who's Your City?* New York: Basic Books, 2008.

Florida, Richard, and Steven Pedigo. "Miami's Great Inflection: Toward Shared Prosperity as a Creative and Inclusive Global City." Report, Florida International University, Miami, 2016. www.creativeclass.com/_wp/wp-content /uploads/2016/06/FIU_Miamis_Great_Inflection_Web1.pdf.

Folha de São Paulo (Brazil). "Brasileiro investe em segunda casa no exterior." May 13, 2012. www1.folha.uol.com.br/fsp/imoveis/42462-brasileiro-investe-em-segunda-casa-no-exterior.shtml.

———. "Miami se transforma em Hollywood das novelas latinas." March 18, 2012. www1.folha.uol.com.br/fsp/ilustrada/31858-miami-se-transforma-em-hollywood-das-novelas-latinas.shtml.

Fried, Marc. "Continuities and Discontinuities of Place." *Journal of Environmental Psychology* 20, no. 3 (2000): 193–205.

Gallup and Knight Foundation. "Data Report." Soul of the Community Project. Miami, 2010.

———. *Why People Love Where They Live and Why It Matters: A Local Perspective.* Miami: Gallup and John S. and James L. Knight Foundation, 2010.

Gambetta, Diego. *The Sicilian Mafia: The Business of Private Protection.* Cambridge, MA: Harvard University Press, 1996.

Gans, Herbert J. *The Urban Villagers: Group and Class in the Life of Italian-Americans.* New York: Free Press of Glencoe, 1962.

Garcia, Alfred. "The Walls of Wynwood: Art and Change in a Global Neighborhood." PhD dissertation, Princeton University, 2017.

García Canclini, Néstor. *Imagined Globalization.* Durham, NC: Duke University Press, 2014.

George, Paul S. "Colored Town: Miami's Black Community, 1896–1930." *Florida Historical Quarterly* 56, no. 4 (1978): 432–47.

Gerson, Kathleen, Ann C. Stueve, and Claude S. Fischer. "Attachment to Place." In *Networks and Places,* edited by C. S. Fischer, 139–61. New York: Free Press, 1977.

Gillis, Justin. "Flooding of Coast Caused by Global Warming Has Already Begun." *New York Times,* September 3, 2016.

O Globo. "Compras." March 30, 2006.

———. "Está todo mundo aqui." January 5, 2013.

——. "Miami é destino preferido dos diputados, diz site." April 24, 2009.

——. "Miasma americano." January 31, 2006.

——. "Uma noite em Miami." November 21, 2013.

Goldstein, Andrew. "Collector Rosa de la Cruz on Making Miami an Intellectual Art Capital." *Artspace*, November 28, 2014. www.artspace.com/magazine /interviews_features/how_i_collect/collector-rosa-de-la-cruz-on-making-miami-an-intellectual-art-capital-52540.

Gomez, Alan. "Obama to End 'Wet Foot, Dry Foot.'" *USA Today*, January 12, 2017. www.usatoday.com/story/news/world/2017/01/12/obama-ends-wet-foot-dry-foot-policy-cubans/96505172/.

Goodell, Jeff. *The Water Will Come: Rising Seas, Sinking Cities, and the Remaking of the Civilized World*. New York: Little, Brown, 2017.

Grandin, Greg. "An Interview with Greg Grandin." 2004. www.press.uchicago .edu/Misc/Chicago/305724in.html.

——. *The Last Colonial Massacre: Latin America in the Cold War*. Chicago: University of Chicago Press, 2004.

——. "The Panama Papers Are Only the Beginning." *The Nation*, April 5, 2016. www.thenation.com/article/the-panama-papers-are-only-the-beginning/.

Grenier, Guillermo J., and Alex Stepick. *Miami Now! Immigration, Ethnicity, and Social Change*. Gainesville: University Press of Florida, 1992.

Grimm, Fred. "South Florida Mayors Face Reality of Rising Seas and Climate Change." *Miami Herald*, March 24, 2016, 1–8.

Guest, Avery M., and Barrett A. Lee. "Sentiment and Evaluation as Ecological Variables." *Sociological Perspectives* 26, no. 2 (1983): 159–84.

Handlin, Oscar. *Boston's Immigrants: A Study of Acculturation*. Cambridge, MA: Harvard University Press, 1941.

Hanks, Douglas. "This Mall Will Be So Ginormous That It Comes with Its Own Suburb." *Miami Herald*, June 29, 2016. www.miamiherald.com/news/local /community/miami-dade/article86722232.html.

Hanks, Douglas, and David Smiley. "David Beckham Group Buys Private Land Needed for Miami Soccer Stadium." *Miami Herald*, March 26, 2016.

Hanks, Douglas, and Michael Vazquez. "Climate Change Dominates Miami-Dade Budget Hearing." *Miami Herald*, September 3, 2015.

Hannah-Jones, Nikole. "From Bittersweet Childhoods to 'Moonlight.'" *New York Times*, January 3, 2017. www.nytimes.com/2017/01/04/movies/moonlight-barry-jenkins-tarell-alvin-mccraney-interview.html.

Hirschman, Charles, and Luis Falcon. "The Educational Attainment of Religio-Ethnic Groups in the United States." *Research in Sociology of Education and Socialization* 5 (1985): 83–120.

Hughes, Sallie, Yves Colon, Tsitsi Wakhisi, and Lilia Santiague. "Haitian Community Media in Miami: Transnational Audiences, Journalists and Radio Programmers." A Community Media Working Paper, 2012. www

.researchgate.net/publication/317958778_Haitian_Community_Media_
in_Miami_Transnational_Journalists_Audiences_and_Programmers.

Iannelli, Jerry. "Little Haiti Will Gentrify Faster than Any South Florida
Neighborhood in 2017." *Miami New Times,* January 6, 2017. www
.miaminewtimes.com/news/study-little-haiti-will-gentrify-faster-than-
any-south-florida-neighborhood-in-2017–9041375.

Iglesias Illia, Hernán. *Miami: Turistas, colonos y aventureros en
la última frontera de América Latina.* Buenos Aires: Editorial Planeta,
2010.

Jackson, Nancy Beth. "Miami Real Estate Market Embraces Brazilians."
New York Times, December 29, 2011. www.nytimes.com/2011/12/30
/greathomesanddestinations/30iht-remiami30.html.

Jacobs, Jane. *The Death and Life of Great American Cities.* New York: Vintage,
1961.

Johnson, Reed, Luciana Magalhaes, and Jeffrey Lewis. "Rich Brazilians, Wary
of Government, Look Abroad." *Wall Street Journal,* February 15, 2015.
www.wsj.com/articles/rich-brazilians-wary-of-government-look-abroad-
1423182280.

Kanter, Rosabeth Moss. *World Class: Thriving Locally in the Global Economy.*
New York: Simon & Schuster, 1995.

Kasarda, John D., and Morris Janowitz. "Community Attachment in Mass
Society." *American Sociological Review* 39, no. 3 (1974): 328–39.

Kasinitz, Philip, Juan Battle, and Inés Miyares. "Fade to Black? The Children of
West Indian Immigrants in South Florida." In *Ethnicities: Children of
Immigrants in America,* edited by Rubén G. Rumbaut and Alejandro Portes,
267–300. New York: Russell Sage Foundation, 2001.

Katzenstein, Peter J., and Robert O. Keohane. *Anti-Americanisms in World
Politics.* Ithaca, NY: Cornell University Press 2007.

Kerbel, Marcos A., and Richard Westlund. *Leading the Way: A Comprehensive
History of International Banking in Florida.* Miami: Florida International
Bankers Association, 2004.

Kim, Jae-Eun, Stephen Lloyd, and Marie-Cécile Cervellon. "Narrative-
Transportation Storylines in Luxury Brand Advertising: Motivating
Consumer Engagement." *Journal of Business Research* 69, no. 1 (2016):
304–13.

Knight Frank. "The Wealth Report." 2015. www.content.knightfrank.com
/research/83/documents/en/wealth-report-2015-2716.pdf.

Kolbert, Elizabeth. "The Siege of Miami." *New Yorker,* December 21, 2015.
www.questia.com/magazine/1P3–3916753921/the-siege-of-miami.

Korten, Tristram. "In Florida, Officials Ban Term 'Climate Change.'" *Miami
Herald,* March 8, 2015. www.miamiherald.com/news/state/florida
/article12983720.html.

Krueger, Alyson. "The Cuban-American Generation Gap." *New York Times*, August 16, 2016. www.nytimes.com/2016/08/18/fashion/cuban-american-parents-children-travel.html?_r=0.

Kunzru, Hari. "Market Forces." *Guardian*, December 6, 2005.

Lackner, Catherine. "Six Corridor Transportation Plan Awaits Funding, Timetable." *Miami Today*, April 28, 2016, 8.

Lamarche, François. "Property Development and the Economic Foundation of the Urban Question." In *Sociology: Critical Essays*, edited by C. V. Pickvance, 85–118. New York: St. Martin's Press, 1976.

Lansberg-Rodriguez, Daniel. "Venezuela's Government-Sponsored Anti-Semitism." *Foreign Policy*, August 15, 2014. www.foreignpolicy.com/2014/08/15/venezuelas-government-sponsored-anti-semitism/.

"Latin America Internet Usage Statistics." Internet World Stats. www.internetworldstats.com/stats10.htm.

Lewis, Michael. "Bad as Downtown Traffic Is, Planners Try to Make It Worse." *Miami Today*, February 19, 2015.

———. "Don't Just Plan to Plan the Planning of Transit—Get It Rolling." *Miami Today*, June 23, 2016.

———. "Get a Leaders' Council Ready, We Can't Dodge Bullets Forever." *Miami Today*, October 20, 2016.

———. "High Fives for the High Sign in Rare Nine-Way Tri-Rail Deal." *Miami Today*, June 6, 2016.

———. "How Smart Is SMART Plan When Transit Use Is Falling." *Miami Today*, May 4, 2017.

———. "Miami's Strong Economy Broadens from 'Two-Legged Stool.'" *Miami Today*, April 16, 2016.

———. "To Persuade Gus to Hop Back on the Bus, Upscale Its Image." *Miami Today*, January 12, 2016.

Lewis, Oscar. "The Culture of Poverty." In *Economic, Applied, and Development Anthropology*, 187–220. New York: Basic Books, 1966.

LiPuma, Edward, and Thomas Koelble. "Cultures of Circulation and the Urban Imaginary: Miami as Example and Exemplar." *Public Culture* 17, no. 1 (Winter 2005): 153–80.

Logan, John R., and Harvey L. Molotch. *Urban Fortunes: The Political Economy of Place*. Berkeley: University of California Press, 1987.

Lojkine, Jean. "Contributions to a Marxist Theory of Capitalist Urbanization." In *Urban Sociology: Critical Essays*, edited by C. G. Pickvance, 85–118. New York: St. Martin's Press, 1976.

Luis & Associates. "A Tale of Ten Cities: Attracting and Retaining Talent." Report prepared for the 2nd Annual Meeting of the International Regions Benchmarking Consortium, Barcelona, Spain, November 2009. www.estudislocals.cat/wp-content/uploads/2016/11/Talent_of_ten_cities.pdf.

Malone, Kenny. "An Idea to Mitigate Rising Seas: Lift the Entire City." Interview, WLRN TV, Miami, March 20, 2015.

Marti Garro, Lucila. "Del shopping a los negocios: Miami se perfila como la nueva meca para los empresarios argentinos." *La Nación*, December 21, 2015. www.lanacion.com.ar/1855553-sin-titulo.

Martin, Roger, and Richard Florida. "Insight—Rise Revisited: Creativity Index." Martin Prosperity Institute, Rotman School of Management, University of Toronto. www.martinprosperity.org/tag/creativity-index/.

Martinez, Ramiro, Jr., and Matthew T. Lee. "On Immigration and Crime." In *Immigration and Crime,* edited by R. J. Martinez and M. T. Lee, 485–524. New York: New York University Press, 2006.

Mato, Daniel. "La industria de la telenovela: Referencias territoriales, mercados y representaciones de identidades trasnacionales." *Cuadernos de Literatura* 8, no. 15 (2002): 138–60.

Merton, Robert K. "Social Structure and Anomie." *American Sociological Review* 3, no. 5 (1938): 672–82.

Mesch, Gustavo S., and Orit Manor. "Social Ties, Environmental Perception, and Local Attachment." *Environment and Behavior* 30, no. 4 (1998): 504–19.

Metropolitan Center, Florida International University. "Miami Soul of the Community Indicator Study." Florida International University, Miami, 2012. www.miamifoundation.org/wp-content/uploads/2016/10/The-Miami-Foundation-Soul-of-the-Community-Indicator-Study-Full-Report.pdf.

Miami Association of Realtors. "Brazil Is Top Foreign Country Searching for South Florida Real Estate." Occasional Report. December 17, 2015. www.miamirealtors.com/news/2015/12/18/brazil-is-top-foreign-country-searching-for-south-florida-real-estate.

Miami-Dade Chamber of Commerce. "Top Business Projects for 2015 and Beyond." Report, 2014.

———. "Transit Projects and Infrastructure to Support an Increasingly Global Population." Report, 2015.

Miami-Dade County. "Analysis of Current Economic Trends—First Quarter of 2015." Report, 2015. www.miamidade.gov.

———. "Housing." Report prepared by Green Print Project Team, 2015. www.miamidade.gov/greenprint/planning/library/milestone_one/housing.pdf.

———. "Miami-Dade County Profiles—American Community Survey, 2015." Annual Report, 2016. www.miamidade.gov.

———. Department of Regulatory and Economic Resources. "Economic and Demographic Profile, 2014." Report, 2015. www.miamidade.gov.

———. Department of Regulatory and Economic Resources: Planning Research and Economic Analysis. "Income and Poverty in Miami-Dade County: 2013." www.miamidade.gov/business/library/reports/2013-income-poverty.pdf.

Miami-Dade County. Metropolitan Planning Organization. "Miami-Dade County Compendium of Transportation: Facts and Trends Report," July 2014, 5–8. www.miamidade.gov.

Miami Diario. "Alcalde Tomás Regalado sobre Fidel Castro: Se celebra la muerte de un dictador." November 26, 2016. www.miamidiario.com/politica /cuba/miami/florida/fidel-castro/tomas-regalado/muerte-de-fidel-castro /fidel-castro-murio/murio-fidel-castro/368612.

Miami Foundation. "Miami and Civic Participation: A Look at Voting and Volunteerism." www.ourmiami.org/stories/civic-participation/.

Miami Herald. "Editorial: Affordable Housing for All," April 26, 2015. www .miamiherald.com/opinion/editorials/article19428933.html

———."Miami-Dade Approves $49 Million Bailout of Frost Science." April 5, 2016.

Miami New Times. "Best of Miami: 'Sweet Home Hialeah,' by Enrique Santos and Joe Ferrero Best Local Youtube Performance," 2009. www .miaminewtimes.com/best-of/2009/people-and-places/best-local-youtube-performance-6402123.

Miami Today. "Flying Goldmine." April 20, 2017.

———. "Port Asian Service, Volume Rise 11%." April 20, 2017.

———. "Transit Use Still Falling," June 6, 2016.

Mills, C. Wright, Clarence Senior, and Rose Kohn Goldsen. *The Puerto Rican Journey.* New York: Harper, 1951.

Minaya, Ezequiel. "Online School Has 100,000 Students, One Subject." *Wall Street Journal,* June 17, 2014. www.wsj.com/articles/online-school-has-100–000-students-one-subject-1403050947.

Morelix, Arnobio, Robert W. Fairlie, Joshua Russell, and E. J. Reddy. "The Kauffman Index: Startup Activity. Metropolitan Area and City Trends." Kansas City: Ewing Marion Kauffman Foundation, June 2015 and August 2016. www.kauffman.org/kauffman-index/reporting/~/media/7420f664c9a 049129e8f3047fce4069c.ashx; www.kauffman.org/kauffman-index /reporting/~/media/079d9a863fcb4cc1a5ea4837ef252924.ashx.

Morgan, Curtis. 1992. "At Long Last, Neighbors: The Storm That Tore South Dade Has Brought Many of Its People Together." *Miami Herald,* September 5, 1–2F.

Moulite, Jessica. "Color of Climate: How Black Activists are Preparing South Fla. Residents to Weather the Storm of Climate Gentrification." *The Root,* August 8, 2017. www.theroot.com/color-of-climate-how-black-activists-are-preparing-sou-1797877930.

Moynihan, Daniel P. "The Negro Family: The Case for National Action." In *The Moynihan Report.* Washington, DC: Office of Policy Planning and Research, United States Department of Labor. March 1965. www.blackpast.org /primary/moynihan-report-1965.

Muir, Helen. *Miami, U.S.A.* Miami, FL: Pickering Press, 1990.

Munzenrieder, Kyle. "Opa-Locka Hialeah Flea Market Raided: 22 Shop Owners Charged with Food Stamps-for-Cash Scheme." *Miami New Times,* May 11, 2016.

———. "The Six Phases of a Gentrifying Neighborhood in Miami." *Miami New Times,* October 8, 2015. www.miaminewtimes.com/news/the-six-phases-of-a-gentrifying-neighborhood-in-miami-7960349.

Nee, Victor, and Brett de Bary Nee. *Longtime Californ': A Documentary History of an American Chinatown.* New York: Pantheon, 1973.

Nehamaso, Nicholas. "La corrupción en América Latina alimentó el boom inversor de Miami." *La Nación,* April 4, 2016. www.lanacion.com.ar/1885865-la-corrupcion-en-america-latina-alimento-el-boom-inversor-de-miami.

Nehamaso, Nicholas, and Kyra Gurney. "Panama Papers: Argentina Probes Ties between Ex-Presidents, Miami Real Estate Empire." *Miami Herald,* July 16, 2016. www.miamiherald.com/news/business/real-estate-news/article90028812.html.

Nehamaso, Nicholas, and Leo Sisti. "Before He Went on Lam, Italian Fugitive Used Miami Firms to Set Up Offshore." *Miami Herald,* April 5, 2016. www.miamiherald.com/news/business/real-estate-news/article69251392.html.

New Times. "The Worst Wind." Special Issue, September 2–8, 1992.

Nijman, Jan. *Miami: Mistress of the Americas.* Philadelphia: University of Pennsylvania Press, 2010.

Oates, Greg. "Interview: Miami Tourism CEO Explains the Essence of Destination Branding." *Skift,* September 20, 2015. www.skift.com/2015/09/10/interview-miami-tourism-ceo-explains-the-essence-of-destination-branding/.

Odzer, Ari. "Venezuela's Exiles Have Been Good for South Florida's Economy." *NBC Latino,* March 8, 2013. www.nbclatino.com/2013/03/08/venezuelas-exiles-have-been-good-for-south-floridas-economy/.

Oppenheimer, Andrés. "Will Miami Disappear under the Rising Sea? Here's Why It Won't." *Miami Herald,* September 15, 2017.

Ovalle, David. "3 Miami-Dade Teens Formally Charged in Killing of 6-Year-Old King Carter." *Miami Herald,* March 16, 2016. www.miamiherald.com/news/local/crime/article66364077.html.

———. "22 Face Charges in Miami Drug Money Laundering Ring Involving 'El Chapo' Cartel." *Miami Herald,* April 7, 2017.

Ovalle, David, Joey Flechas, Vera Bergengruen, Carlos Frías, and Patricia Mazzei. "Cuban Exiles Pour onto Miami Streets to Celebrate Fidel Castro's Death." *Miami Herald,* November 26, 2016. www.miamiherald.com/news/nation-world/world/americas/cuba/article117201053.html.

Padilla, Herberto. "Miami: El mundo en blanco y negro." *El Miami Herald,* January 18, 1986.

Página/12. "K, antineoliberal." November 5, 2005. www.pagina12.com.ar
/diario/elpais/subnotas/58860-19435-2005-11-05.html.

Park, Robert E. "The City: Suggestions for Investigation of Human Behavior in
an Urban Environment." In *Human Communities: The City and Human
Ecology,* edited by R. E. Park, W. W. Burgess, and R. D. McKenzie, 1–46.
Chicago: University of Chicago Press, 1967.

———. *Human Communities: The City and Human Ecology.* New York: Free
Press, 1952.

Pedraza-Bailey, Silvia. "Cuba's Exiles: Portrait of a Refugee Migration." *International Migration Review* 19 (1985): 3–34.

Pérez, Lisandro. "Cuban Miami." In *Miami, Now!,* edited by Guillermo J.
Grenier and Alex Stepick, 83–108. Gainesville: University of Florida Press,
1992.

———. "Hurricane Has Severely Tilted Community Demographics." *Miami
Herald,* September 27, 1992, 4M.

Pew Research Center. "IV. Ranking Latino Population's in the Nation's Metropolitan Areas." www.pewhispanic.org/2013/08/29/iv-ranking-latino-
populations-in-the-nations-metropolitan-areas/.

Piñeiro, Claudia. "Miami." In *Sam no es mi tío,* edited by Diego Fonseca and
Aileen El-Kadi, 109. Doral, FL: Santillana, 2012.

Pirenne, Henri. *Medieval Cities: Their Origins and the Revival of Trade.*
Princeton, NJ: Princeton University Press, 1925.

Podoshen, Jeffrey, Lu Li, and Junfeng Zhang. "Materialism and Conspicuous
Consumption in China: A Cross-Cultural Examination." *International
Journal of Consumer Studies* 35, no. 1 (2011): 17–25.

Political Cortadito [Blog]. "Coral Gables: Raul Valdes-Fauli Plans Comeback as
Mayor." August 18, 2015. www.politicalcortadito.com/2015/08/17/raul-valdes-
fauli-comeback-mayor/.

Portell-Vila, Herminio. *Nueva historia de la República de Cuba.* Miami:
La Moderna Poesía, 1986.

Portes, Alejandro. "The Cuban-American Political Machine: Reflections on Its
Origins and Perpetuation." In *Debating Cuban Exceptionalism,* edited by
Burt Hoffman and Laurence Whitehead, 123–37. London: Palgrave Macmil-
lan, 2007.

———. *Economic Sociology: A Systematic Inquiry.* Princeton, NJ: Princeton
University Press, 2010.

———. "The Informal Economy in the Shadows of the State." In *Dialogues with
the Informal City: Latin America and the Caribbean,* edited by Ariel C.
Armony, Adib Cure, and Carie Penabad, 14–25. Miami, FL: University of
Miami Center for Latin American Studies, 2014.

———. "The Social Origins of the Cuban Enclave Economy of Miami." *Sociological Perspectives* 30, no. 4 (1987): 340–72.

Portes, Alejandro, Juan M. Clark, and Manuel M. López. "Six Years Later: The Process of Incorporation of Cuban Exiles in the United States: 1973–1979." *Cuban Studies* 11, no. 2 (1981): 1–24.

Portes, Alejandro, and Patricia Fernandez-Kelly. "No Margin for Error: Educational and Occupational Achievement among Disadvantaged Children of Immigrants." *Annals of the American Academy of Political and Social Science* 620, no. 1 (2008): 12–36.

———. *The State and the Grassroots: Immigrant Transnational Organizations in Four Continents.* New York: Berghahn Books, 2015.

Portes, Alejandro, Patricia Fernandez-Kelly, and William Haller. "Segmented Assimilation on the Ground: The New Second Generation in Early Adulthood." *Ethnic and Racial Studies* 28, no. 6 (2005): 1000–1040.

Portes, Alejandro, Patricia Fernandez-Kelly, and Donald Light. "Life on the Edge: Immigrants Confront the American Health System." *Ethnic and Racial Studies* 35, no. 1 (2011): 3–22.

Portes, Alejandro, Luis Eduardo Guarnizo, and William J. Haller. "Transnational Entrepreneurs: An Alternative Form of Immigrant Economic Adaptation." *American Sociological Review* 67, no. 2 (2002): 278–98.

Portes, Alejandro, and William Haller. "The Informal Economy." In *The Handbook of Economic Sociology,* 2nd ed., edited by N. Smelser and R. Swedberg, 403–25. New York: Russell Sage Foundation, 2005.

Portes, Alejandro, and Kelly Hoffman. "Latin American Class Structures." *Latin American Research Review* 25, no. 1 (2005): 351–76.

Portes, Alejandro, and Aaron Puhrmann. "A Bifurcated Enclave: The Economic Evolution of the Cuban and Cuban American Population of Metropolitan Miami." *Cuban Studies* 43 (March 2015): 40–63.

Portes, Alejandro, and Rubén G. Rumbaut. *Immigrant America: A Portrait.* 4th ed. Berkeley: University of California Press, 2014.

———. *Legacies: The Story of the Immigrant Second Generation.* Berkeley: University of California Press, 2001.

Portes, Alejandro, and Steven Shafer. "Revisiting the Enclave Hypothesis: Miami Twenty-Five Years Later." *Research in the Sociology of Organizations* 25 (2007): 157–90.

Portes, Alejandro, and Alex Stepick. *City on the Edge: The Transformation of Miami.* Berkeley: University of California Press, 1993.

Postrel, Virginia. "Inconspicuous Consumption: A New Theory of the Leisure Class." *Atlantic,* July–August 2008.

Rabin, Charles. "Father Loses 2nd Son in Ambush; All 4 of His Children Shot This Month." *Miami Herald,* June 28, 2016.

———. "Gunfire Shatters Months of Calm at Complex Where Young King Carter Was Killed." *Miami Herald,* May 10, 2016.

Raymond, Christopher, Gregory Brown, and Delene Weber. "The Measurement of Place Attachment: Personal, Community, and Environmental Connections." *Journal of Environmental Psychology* 30, no. 4 (2010): 422–34.

Redford, Polly. *Billion Dollar Sandbar: A Biography of Miami Beach*. New York: E. P. Dutton, 1970.

Regalado, Tomás, and James Cason. "In Miami-Dade, GOP Candidates Must Address Climate Change in Debate." *Miami Herald*, March 9, 2016, Op-Ed sec., 1.

Reid, Andy. "South Florida Climate Change Efforts Move toward Action Stage." *Huffington Post*, February 5, 2013.

Rieff, David. *Going to Miami: Exiles, Tourists, and Refugees in the New America*. Boston: Little, Brown, 1993.

———. "Multiculturalism's Silent Partner: It's the Newly Globalized Consumer Economy, Stupid," *Harper's Magazine*, August 7, 1993.

Robbins, John Charles. "City, County to Meet on Out-of-Sync U.S. 1 Signals." *Miami Today*, April 16, 2016.

———. "City Moves Fast to Slow U.S. 1 Traffic Entering Neighborhoods." *Miami Today*, August 13, 2016.

———. "Miami Kicks in More Money for Battling Sea Level Issues." *Miami Today*, May 4, 2017.

———. "New Trolley Routes Draw Big Numbers." *Miami Today*, August 11, 2016.

———. "South Dade Transit Plan Priority Aim." *Miami Today*, June 23, 2016.

———. "Three-Year-Old Miami Trolley's Users Rise 4% Year over Year." *Miami Today*, August 13, 2016.

———. "A Way to Unwind Marine Stadium, Seaport Deeds." *Miami Today*, May 5, 2016.

Robinson, Andrea. "Miami Zoning Law Allows Wiping Out of Neighborhoods, Gentrification." *Miami Times*, May 10, 2017. www.miamitimesonline.com /news/miami-zoning-law-allows-wiping-out-of-neighborhoods-gentrification /article_59c90350–358e-11e7-a8ac-cb49138557d8.html.

Rodríguez, Margarita. "Navigating Uneven Development: The Dynamics of Fractured Transnationalism." In *The State and the Grassroots: Immigrant Transnational Organization in Four Continents*, edited by Alejandro Portes and Patricia Fernandez-Kelly, 139–59. Oxford: Berghahn Books, 2015.

Rohter, Larry. "Miami, the Hollywood of Latin America." *New York Times*, August 18, 1996.

Roth, Daniel Shoer. "A Half-Century Serving Migrants." *Miami Herald*, November 12, 2012.

Rowe, Sean. "Hugo's Homeboys." *New Times*, September 2–8, 1992, 13–14.

Salah, Michael, and Jay Weaver. "Opa-Locka: State to Take over Troubled City's Finances." *Miami Herald*, March 11, 2016.

Sampaio, Lívia. "EUA a Granel." *Folha de São Paulo,* April 22, 2012. www1
.folha.uol.com.br/fsp/cotidiano/38633-eua-a-granel.shtml.

Sampson, Robert J. *Great American City: Chicago and the Enduring Neighborhood Effect.* Chicago: University of Chicago Press, 2013.

Sassen, Saskia. *The Global City: New York, London, and Tokyo.* Princeton, NJ:
Princeton University Press, 1991.

Satterfield, David. "We Will Rebuild Hits $11 Million." *Miami Herald,* Septem-
ber 19, 1992, 1A, 20A.

Saxenian, AnnaLee. "Brain Circulation: How High-Skilled Immigration Makes
Everyone Better Off." *Brookings Review* 20, no. 1 (2002): 28–31.

———. *Local and Global Networks of Immigrant Professionals in Silicon Valley.*
San Francisco: Public Policy Institute of California, 2002.

———. *The New Argonauts: Regional Advantage in a Global Economy.* Cambridge, MA: Harvard University Press, 2006.

———. *Silicon Valley's New Immigrant Entrepreneurs.* San Francisco: Public
Policy Institute of California, 1999.

Shahbazi, Rudabeh. "Focus on South Florida: The Digital Divide." CBS Miami,
June 12, 2016. www.miami.cbslocal.com/2016/06/12/focus-on-south-florida-
the-digital-divide/.

Shumow, Moses, and Juliet Pinto. "Spanish-language Immigrant Media in
Miami-Date County, Florida: Discursive Arenas for Transnational Civil
Societies." *Latin Americanist* 58, no. 4 (2014): 59–83.

Skocpol, Theda, and Morris Fiorina. *Civic Engagement in American Democracy.* New York: Russell Sage Foundation, 1999.

Smiley, David. "Police Investigate New Spate of Liberty Square Shootings."
Miami Herald, December 31, 2015.

———. "10,000-Foot Injection Well Could Change How Miami Flushes." *Miami
Herald,* April 8, 2016.

Smith-Spark, Laura. "Crowds Flood Streets of Miami's Little Havana to Cheer
Castro's Death." CNN, November 25, 2016. www.cnn.com/2016/11/26/us
/miami-fidel-castro-death-reaction.

Sofen, Edward. *The Miami Metropolitan Experiment.* Bloomington: Indiana
University Press, 1963.

Sohmer, Rebecca. "Growing the Middle Class: Connecting All Miami-Dade
Residents to Economic Opportunity." Report. Brookings Institution,
Washington, DC, 2004. www.brookings.edu/research/growing-
the-middle-class-connecting-all-miami-dade-county-residents-to-
economic-opportunity/.

Sokol, Brett. "When It Comes to Contemporary Art, Miami Wants More, More,
More." *New York Times,* November 30, 2017. www.nytimes.com/2017/11/30
/arts/design/institute-of-contemporary-art-miami-miami-contemporary-
art.html.

South Florida Regional Planning Council. *Comprehensive Economic Development Strategy, 2012–2017.* Miami-Dade County Government Report, 2012.

Stepick, Alex. "Miami's Two Informal Sectors." In *The Informal Economy: Studies in Advanced and Less Developed Countries,* edited by Alejandro Portes, Manuel Castells, and Lauren A. Benton, 111–31. Baltimore: Johns Hopkins University Press, 1989.

———. "The Refugees Nobody Wants: Haitians in Miami." In *Miami Now! Immigration, Ethnicity, and Social Change,* edited by Guillermo J. Grenier and Alex Stepick, 57–82. Gainesville: University of Florida Press, 1992.

Stepick, Alex, Guillermo J. Grenier, Max Castro, and Marvin Dunn. *This Land Is Our Land: Immigrants and Power in Miami.* Berkeley: University of California Press, 2003.

Stepick, Alex, and Alejandro Portes. "Flight into Despair: A Profile of Recent Haitian Refugees in South Florida." *International Migration Review* 20 (Summer 1986): 329–50.

Suarez, Andres. *Cuba: Castroism and Communism, 1959–1966.* Cambridge, MA: MIT Press, 1967.

Sung, Betty Lee. *The Story of the Chinese in America.* New York: Collier Books, 1971.

Supriya, Routh, and Vando Borghi, *Workers and the Global Informal Economy.* New York: Routledge, 2016.

Suttles, Gerald D. *The Social Order of the Slum.* Chicago: University of Chicago Press, 1968.

Tamayo, Juan O. "Politicians Call for Revision of Cuban Adjustment Act." *Miami Herald,* February 13, 2013.

Telles, Edward, and Vilma Ortiz. *Generations of Exclusion: Mexican-Americans, Assimilation and Race.* New York: Russell Sage Foundation, 2008.

Thomas, William I., and Florian Znaniecki. *The Polish Peasant in Europe and America: Monograph of an Immigrant Group.* Chicago: University of Chicago Press, 1918.

El Tiempo. "Consejos para comprar en el exterior en tiempos de dólar caro." September 19, 2015. www.eltiempo.com/archivo/documento/CMS-16379709.

Time. "Paradise Lost?" November 23, 1981, 22–32.

USA Hispanic Press. "América recibe con condolencias y festejos en Miami la muerte de Castro." November 27, 2016. www.usahispanicpress.com/america-recibe-condolencias-festejos-miami-la-muerte-fidel-castro/.

U.S. Bureau of Economic Analysis. "Miami-Dade County, 2014."

U.S. Bureau of Labor Statistics. "Occupational Employment Statistics, 2015." www.bls.gov/oes/current/oes_33124.htm.

U.S. Census Bureau. *American Community Survey, Miami-Dade County, 2014.* Washington, DC: U.S. Department of Commerce.

———. *American Community Survey, Miami-Dade County, 2015*. Washington, DC: U.S. Department of Commerce.

———. *American Community Survey, 3-Year Estimates, Miami-Dade County, 2011*. Washington, DC: U.S. Department of Commerce.

———. "Opa-Locka: Breakdown of Families in Poverty." *American Community Survey, 2015*. Washington, DC: U.S. Department of Commerce.

U.S. Department of Commerce, Office of Travel and Tourism Industries. "Survey of International Air Travelers: U.S Travel and Tourism Statistics." 2011, 2012, 2013, 2014, 2015.

Veblen, Thorstein. *The Theory of the Leisure Class*. Oxford: Oxford University Press, 2009.

Vetere, Alejo. "Negocio inmobiliario con acento argentino en Miami." *La Nación*, February 23, 2014. www.lanacion.com.ar/1666450-negocio-inmobiliario-con-acento-argentino-en-miami.

Viglucci, Andres. "He Kept the Netherlands Dry; Now He Aims to Defend Miami and the World from Rising Seas." *Miami Herald*, February 4, 2017.

Wagner, John, and Karen DeYoung. "Trump Announces Revisions to Parts of Obama's Cuba Policy." *Washington Post*, June 16, 2017. www.washingtonpost.com/politics/trump-announces-revisions-to-parts-of-obamas-cuba-policy/2017/06/16/dee8671c-52ab-11e7-91eb-9611861a988f_story.html?utm_term=.279ed76aa5a3.

Walker, Doug. "The Media's Role in Immigrant Adaptation: How First-Year Haitians in Miami Use the Media." *Journalism & Communication Monographs* 1, no. 3 (1999): 158–96.

Wanless, Harold. "The Coming Reality of Sea-Level Rise: Too Fast, Too Soon." Report, Institute on Science for Global Policy, 2015.

Weaver, Jay. "FBI Agents Bust Miami Medicare Ring While Some Suspects Flee to Cuba." *Miami Herald*, April 28, 2016.

———. "Medicare Fraud Rampant in South Florida." *Miami Herald*, August 3, 2008.

———. "Stierheim Bows Out: Says City May Be Beyond Saving." *Miami Herald*, March 28, 2016.

Weaver, Jay, Michael Sallah, and Katie Lepri. "FBI Agents Blow Lid Off Opa-Locka City Corruption Probe." *Miami Herald*, March 10, 2016.

Weiss, Jessica. "New Group Offers Young Cuban-Americans Free Trips to Cuba." *Miami New Times*, April 29, 2016.

Whitefield, Mimi. "Obama Ending 'Wet Foot, Dry Foot' Cuban Immigration Policy." *Miami Herald*, January 12, 2017.

Wilson, Frederica. "Staying Afloat amid Climate Change." *Miami Herald*, February 15, 2016.

Wilson, William J. *The Truly Disadvantaged: The Inner City, the Underclass, and Public Policy*. Chicago: University of Chicago Press, 1987.

Wimmer, Andreas, and Nina Glick Schiller. "Methodological Nationalism and Beyond: Nation-State Building, Migration, and the Social Sciences." *Global Networks* 2, no. 4 (2002): 301–34.

Wooldridge, Jane. "Manny Diaz: Life after Miami's Top Job." *Miami Herald,* September 23, 2012.

Wootson, Cleve R., Jr. "Marco Rubio: Fidel Castro's Death Changes Nothing in Cuba." *Washington Post,* November 27, 2016.

Yúdice, George. "Miami: Images of a Latinopolis." *NACLA* 39, no. 3 (2005): 35–39.

Yun, Lawrence, Daniel Hale, and Gay Cororaton. "2015 Profile of International Home Buyers in Miami." National Association of Realtors, January 2016. www.miamire.com/docs/default-source/international-research-and-resources/miami2015surveyppt_final_jan2016.pdf?sfvrsn=2.

Zhou, Min. *New York's Chinatown: The Socioeconomic Potential of an Urban Enclave.* Philadelphia: Temple University Press, 1992.

Zukin, Sharon. *Naked City: The Death and Life of Authentic Urban Places.* New York: Oxford University Press, 2010.

Zukin, Sharon, Philip Kasinitz, and Xiangming Chen. *Global Cities, Local Streets: Everyday Diversity from New York to Shanghai.* New York: Routledge, 2015.

Index

CPSIA information can be obtained
at www.ICGtesting.com
Printed in the USA
LVHW012147070120
642793LV00005B/696